UNIVERSITY OF NORTH CAROLINA
STUDIES IN THE ROMANCE LANGUAGES AND LITERATURES
Number 124

STUDIES IN HONOR OF
ALFRED G. ENGSTROM

STUDIES IN HONOR OF
ALFRED G. ENGSTROM

EDITED BY

ROBERT T. CARGO and EMANUEL J. MICKEL, JR.

CHAPEL HILL

THE UNIVERSITY OF NORTH CAROLINA PRESS

DEPÓSITO LEGAL: V. 3.997 - 1972

ARTES GRÁFICAS SOLER, S. A. - JÁVEA, 28 - VALENCIA (8) - 1972

TABLE OF CONTENTS

	Page
BIOGRAPHY Robert T. Cargo and Emanuel J. Mickel, Jr.	9
FRANCESCA REVISITED: DANTE'S MOST NOTABLE SUCCESSORS Sarah F. Bell	13
BAUDELAIRE'S *CHANT D'AUTOMNE* Robert T. Cargo	27
SOME ASPECTS OF AGE AND TIME IN *LE CID* George B. Daniel	45
THE MONSTER IN MEDIAEVAL LITERATURE Urban Tigner Holmes	53
ANATOLE FRANCE AND THE HERITAGE OF JEAN JACQUES ROUSSEAU H. R. Huse	63
WAS CALDERÓN'S *LA VIDA ES SUEÑO* WRITTEN IN A HURRY? Sturgis E. Leavitt	81
THE POETIC IMAGE OF THE "NOIRE IDOLE" Emanuel J. Mickel, Jr.	87
BYRON AND NERVAL: TWO SONS OF FIRE James S. Patty	99
GAUTIER'S USE OF COMPARISON IN *MADEMOISELLE DE MAUPIN* Albert B. Smith	117
THE *HOMO DUPLEX* IN NINETEENTH-CENTURY FRENCH LITERATURE James M. Smith	127

RAMÓN CARNICER Y BATLLE (1789-1855) — CONDUCTOR, DIRECTOR, COMPOSER   139
Sterling A. Stoudemire

A SKETCH BY CONSTANTIN GUYS, AND AN ACCOUNT OF HIS RELATIONSHIP WITH THE GONCOURT BROTHERS   155
Alison M. Turner

TABOUROT'S SIEUR GAULARD: THE GRATIFYING DUNCE   171
F. W. Vogler

PHILOGYNY AS AN ELEMENT IN MAUPASSANT'S WORK   177
A. H. Wallace

CHARLES FONTAINE'S IDEAS ON POETRY   197
W. L. Wiley

ELIPHAS LEVI AS POET   209
Thomas A. Williams

BIBLIOGRAPHY OF ALFRED G. ENGSTROM   227

TABULA GRATULATORIA   229

ALFRED GARVIN ENGSTROM

ROBERT T. CARGO AND EMANUEL J. MICKEL, JR.

Alfred Garvin Engstrom was born on October 11, 1907 in Rockford, Illinois to Alfred Adolph Engstrom (1870-1917) and Maria Garvin Foote Engstrom (1870-1959). The families of his father and mother were, in many ways, worlds apart, but each was remarkable and rich in its heritages. The Engstroms were Swedish, very gentle, affectionate, and poetic, almost other-worldly, and extremely sensitive to religious mysticism and to all the world of nature. The Footes had been notable in upper New York state as statesmen, judges, civic leaders, and highly successful businessmen and both the Garvin and Foote families were widely known for their integrity and dependability in all their affairs. All of them were omnivorous readers with splendid memories and most of them were interested beyond the ordinary in history and genealogy (Professor Engstrom's grandfather, John Crocker Foote, was national president of the Mayflower Society, an interest which Professor Engstrom continues).

Professor Engstrom was only ten years old when his father died in 1917, and his mother necessarily assumed the roles of both parents. She was an actively religious person, a very loving mother and a very understanding one. She permitted her son to buy almost unlimited quantities of books without direction or restriction of any kind. She encouraged his keen interest in music and art (the latter was her own special forte), read in many fields to keep pace with his own growing interests, and encouraged him to travel. In 1927, for example, he went on a lengthy cruise to the North Cape which took him to Iceland, Sweden, Norway, Finland, Estonia, Lapland, and finally England. Whatever he was interested in interested her in the most minute detail — shells, birds, poetry, violins, stars, folklore, magic — and yet she wisely left him entire freedom to follow his own inclinations. Few young men can ever have been so fortunate in a parent or so fortunate in their family heritages.

Professor Engstrom attended elementary schools in Rockford and Belvidere, Illinois. Because he had contracted polio, he attended Belvidere High School in broken periods from 1920-1927. It was during his convalescence that he became keenly interested in ornithology because he could sit in his wheel chair on his grandfather's sunporch and watch birds through field glasses. Some unusual Belvidere friends became his mentors in this area and helped him to keep formal records and to know the beautiful world of the wide Kishwaukee River, which flowed just behind the garden of his home. In these years some excellent teachers in the Belvidere High School encouraged his growing interest in languages, especially Latin and French, and in literature — and his mind was turned in the direction it was to go ever after. These years of illness were also years of wide reading at home in fields rarely touched by high school students. In 1927 he was graduated as President and Valedictorian of the Senior Class, and the long North Cape cruise followed immediately afterward.

In the autumn of 1928, Professor Engstrom enrolled at The University of North Carolina, chosen, in part, because the North Carolina climate allowed him to walk more easily, and studied Latin (Terence, Pliny, and Horace) under Van Courtlandt Elliott. He took Greek with the legendary "Bully" Bernard (Thomas Wolfe's Buck Benson) and heard, as he says, "the clang of Apollo's silver bow." In 1932 he was awarded the Eben Alexander Prize in Greek, an honor which he has always especially valued. He was a member and President of Sigma Delta Fraternity. In 1933 he was elected to Phi Beta Kappa. He was graduated from The University of North Carolina with an all-A record and Honors in French, his thesis being "The Symbolist Movement in French Literature." This degree with honors was the first such granted in the university.

Upon conclusion of his undergraduate education, Professor Engstrom continued his studies at The University of North Carolina toward the Master's degree, having been named a Teaching Fellow in 1934 in the Department of Romance Languages and Part-time Instructor in 1935. His Master's thesis, "Similarities and Differences in the Poetry of Gautier and Baudelaire and their Treatment of Similar Themes," earned him the M. A. degree in 1935. In 1936 Professor Engstrom was named Instructor in French and continued his studies toward the doctorate. The summer of 1937 was spent travelling and studying in France. On June 10, 1939 he was married to Mary Claire Randolph of Kansas City, Missouri, a brilliant student of English literature who became widely known in the region as one of the English Department's most gifted teachers. What Mrs. Engstrom has meant to Professor Engstrom over the years can scarcely be expressed. It has been a beautiful relationship of mutual love and devotion. In 1941 Professor Engstrom completed his much admired thesis, "The French Artistic Short Story Before Maupassant," and was awarded the Ph. D. with a major in French and minor in Spanish. He continued in the department as an Assistant Professor in 1942, was promoted to the rank of Associate Professor in 1946, followed by promotion to the rank of Professor in 1951. The years were marked by growing fame as a teacher, a fame which has become legendary throughout the state of North Carolina and wherever his students have gone. In 1960 he won the Tanner Award, the university award given to the year's outstanding undergraduate teacher. This was followed in 1961 by an even greater recognition of his brilliance in the classroom, appointment as Alumni Distinguished Professor of French, a position especially created to honor professors at The University of North Carolina who are especially successful as teachers and scholars. Since 1961 Professor Engstrom has occupied this position in the Department of Romance Languages.

In addition to his success as a teacher, Professor Engstrom has had a distinguished career of administrative service to the university, serving on many important university committees, including the Faculty Council, the Administrative Board of the School of Library Science, the Graduate Executive Council, the Administrative Board of the Library and the Council on Honors, to name but a few. Especially noteworthy was his tenure as Chairman of the Joint Book Committee Representing the Graduate School, the Humanities, the Sciences and the Social Sciences, culminating in a detailed report which greatly aided the needs of the University Library. As reflected by a number of these committees, Professor Engstrom has given much of his time to the important task of building the library and the development of the Honors Program.

Within the department he has exerted much influence on teaching in the undergraduate and graduate programs, remaining active as a teacher at both levels. His graduate teaching includes courses in nineteenth century literature, French literary criticism, and seminars on Baudelaire and Flaubert. His courses have always been characterized by broad interests in Classical and English literature, folklore, psychology, and language. With his colleague, the late Urban T. Holmes, Jr., he founded the journal, *Romance Notes,* and has been serving on the editorial boards of the *University of North Carolina Studies in the Romance Languages and Literatures,* the *University of North Carolina Studies in Comparative Literature,* and the *Southern Humanities Review.*

Since 1963 Professor Engstrom has lectured widely throughout the Southeastern United States. Among the colleges and universities visited were the University of Alabama, the University of Richmond, Mary Washington College, Randolph-Macon, Washington and Lee University, Lynchburg College, Elon College, Vanderbilt University and Wake Forest University. From 1964 to 1969 he delivered a series of nine lectures at Elon College for the Liberal Arts Forum. The Forum subsequently named its annual spring Humanities Lecture for him and invited William Carlos Williams as the first speaker in 1970.

To have studied with Professor Engstrom is to know the signal importance of the teacher and the warm relationship which can exist between professor and student. In his classes one is introduced to the rich and exciting experience offered by the various forms of artistic expression, a world of new vistas, correspondences and insights to inspire the young scholar. Yet instruction has never stopped at the classroom door for the interested student, in that Professor Engstrom willingly gives hours of his office time for further exploration of ideas developed in class and in one's reading. Warm encouragement and careful guidance characterize his instruction. Moreover, under his careful tutelage the student learns not to neglect the slightest detail of form or style.

It would be impossible to know Professor Engstrom and not recognize the value of the humanities to man and society. He has long been admired for his sensitivity and insight into literature and for his inspirational qualities as a teacher, but he is even more cherished as a person by all of us who have had our lives transformed and enriched by his radiant spirit. Too often the teacher's devotion to his students and profession is not given sufficient praise and certainly this *Festschrift* represents meager recognition for his contribution and generosity to us all. It can only serve as a symbol of our gratitude.

FRANCESCA REVISITED: DANTE'S MOST NOTABLE SUCCESSORS

SARAH F. BELL

University of North Carolina at Greensboro

Dante's evocation of Francesca da Rimini is the oldest in literature. Without it Francesca and Paolo would probably never have been known to us. They are, however, among the most familiar personages in the *Divine Comedy*. In the more than six hundred and fifty years since Dante wrote the immortal lines of the episode, their story has become an integral part of our culture and one of the most widely used themes in literature and the arts.

An examination of Wilhelm von Locella's thorough cataloguing [1] of the use of the Francesca theme shows that the western world has been interested in the story of Paolo and Francesca ever since Dante first told it in Canto V of the *Inferno*. However, it was not until the beginning of the nineteenth century that any major original literary works using this theme appeared. At that time the sudden blossoming of such productions, and their proliferation throughout the century, amounted to what might, perhaps, be called a literary explosion. With the possible exception of Leigh Hunt's *The Story of Rimini* (1816), a long, stilted, and today all but unreadable poem, the notable works are dramatic in form, which seems entirely appropriate and not too surprising in view of the fact that Dante's own treatment of the subject is highly dramatic.

---

[1] *Dante's Francesca da Rimini in der Literatur, bildenden Kunst und Musik*, nach den Plänen und Entwürfen des Professors Baron Guglielmo Locella Bearb. und Hrsg. von Baronin Marie Locella; mit 19 Kunstbeilagen und 75 Abbildungen im Text (Eszlingen a. N., 1913). See also the more recent work by Nevio Matteini, *Francesca da Rimini; storia, mito, arte* (Rocca San Casciano, 1965).

There are in western literatures some three dozen plays, excluding librettos and parodies, on the subject. Many of these are obscure and inaccessible, but four of them are well worth considering: Silvio Pellico's *Francesca da Rimini* (1814), George Henry Boker's *Francesca da Rimini* (1853), Stephen Phillips' *Paolo and Francesca* (1899), and Gabriele d'Annunzio's *Francesca da Rimini* (1901). One other play, *Francesca da Rimini* (1902) by Francis Marion Crawford, though intrinsically unimportant, is of some interest because of the momentary success given it by Sarah Bernhardt and because of its faithfulness to historical facts. In addition, two other well-known playwrights have written plays which utilize this general theme: José Echegaray in *El gran Galeoto* (1881), and Maurice Maeterlinck in *Pelléas et Mélisande* (1892). These seven are the plays to be considered here.

A glance at their dates shows that the plays were composed within a period of less than one hundred years, five being written in the nineteenth century and the other two in the first years of the twentieth, confirming that Romantic and post-Romantic dramatists found the Paolo and Francesca theme particularly suitable for their purposes. The literature on the subject reflects its popularity. Much of the critical comment comes within the first few years of this century when the renown of the Phillips and d'Annunzio plays, the revival of Boker's play by Otis Skinner, and the success of Sarah Bernhardt in Crawford's play caused a flurry of attention, especially in the literary magazines. Since that time apparently no fictional work of major significance based wholly on the subject has appeared. But criticism, though sometimes repetitious, shows that interest in the Francesca theme is still alive.

Dante's story is the simplest version coming down to us. He hardly more than intimates the details, showing only the great love that survived even Hell. The known facts of the episode are few,[2] and may be summarized as follows: Francesca was the daughter of Guido da Polenta, lord of Ravenna. Her father married her around 1275 to Giovanni (known also as Lianciotto, Sciancato, and Gianciotto), son of the old Malatesta di Verucchio, tyrant of Rimini, as a reward for his aid in subduing the Ravenna Ghibellines. Giovanni was estimable

---

[2] Charles Yriarte in *Françoise de Rimini dans la légende et dans l'histoire* (Paris, 1883) examines the various manuscripts, documents, chronicles, and historical accounts to determine what is fact and what legend. Matteini also devotes a portion of his book to such an examination.

but misshapen. Francesca soon deceived her husband with his younger brother, Paolo. Surprised together, they were both killed by Giovanni, around 1285. Francesca had one child, Concordia, by her husband. Paolo had married Orabile for political reasons about six years before Giovanni's marriage and had several children by her. Numerous details were added to this story by Dante commentators such as Boccaccio, who, for example, says that Francesca was the victim of the deception that she was marrying Paolo rather than Giovanni.

Each author under consideration here makes independent use of the various sources, adapting them to his own dramatic vision, and adding necessary details of situation of his own creation. It is not the aim of this study to compare the details of the various plots, which has been done elsewhere,[3] nor to make a more general comparative study, which has also been done,[4] but rather to examine the plays to see, as far as possible, whether or how they show (beyond basic situation) the direct influence of Dante,[5] especially with reference to the main female character; for it is Francesca who receives the emphasis in Dante's poem.

Before looking at the dramatic Francescas, perhaps Dante's should be briefly reviewed in order to establish a basis of comparison. There is no intention here of entering the continuing discussion as to the interpretation of Canto V.[6] It suffices to say that the present writer

---

[3] Gusta Barfield Nance in her unpublished dissertation, "The Paolo and Francesca Story in Modern Drama" (The University of Wisconsin, 1953), makes detailed summaries of twenty-two plays on the subject. A number of other writers also do this to a much lesser extent: among them Gertrude Urban in «Paolo and Francesca in History and Literature," *The Critic*, 40 (1902), 425-438; Ugo de Maria in " 'Francesca da Rimini' nel teatro, da E. Fabbri a G. A. Cesareo," *La Romagna*, 3 (1906), 64-87, [147]-167, [193]-224; Archibald Henderson in "The Story of Rimini," *The Arena*, 39 (1908), 20-26, 142-148; and Matteini in op. cit., who gives résumés of several of the minor plays.

[4] Especially in Nance; in Montrose J. Moses, ed., *Representative Plays by American Dramatists. With an Introduction to Each Play*, III (New York, 1921), [73]-94; and in Edward Sculley Bradley, *George Henry Boker, Poet and Patriot* (Philadelphia, 1927), pp. 123-160.

[5] Nance has made a few observations in this connection, but only in passing and with no consistent effort to explore such a line of inquiry. Rather, her purpose, as stated in the Preface to her dissertation, is "the exposition of twenty-two modern dramatic treatments of the tragic love story of Paolo Malatesta and Francesca di Guido da Polenta." (p. iv.)

[6] Baldo Curato's *Il canto di Francesca e i suoi interpreti* (Cremona, 1962) is of help in pursuing this line of inquiry.

prefers the majority conception of the canto, which is in general idealistic, and that the remarks in this study are based on that preference.

It has been amply pointed out already that Canto V belongs to Francesca. The attention is focused almost entirely on her. She is the first soul in the *Divine Comedy* to tell her story, in what is recognized as one of the most beautiful and touching passages of the entire work. She and Paolo are situated against a background of personages famous because of their love: Semiramis, Dido, Cleopatra, Helen, Paris, Achilles, and Tristan. The two lovers draw Dante's especial attention because they are borne so lightly on the wind. It is at Dante's friendly request that Francesca relates the story of the awakening of their love. By the omission of all irrelevant details the emphasis is on this love, in which the part of Fate can be felt, and Francesca's complete commitment to it. Dante does not exonerate the lovers, but the story is such an appealing and pathetic one that at the end of the relation he faints with pity for their situation. Francesca, as usually interpreted, is so open, so modest and courteous, so gentle and dignified, yet so aware of her guilt, that the reader immediately feels the pathos and powerful impact of her story. The love of Francesca and Paolo is known historically to be a mature passion between a married man and woman; but Dante emphasizes the youth, and in spite of the guilt allows a certain noble quality to their sentiment. When love took them by surprise as they were reading the story of Lancelot together, it was not for a fleeting moment but for eternity. Dante's story, then, is a condensed and intense one, the essence of a fatal and fated passion which led to the downfall of the two involved.

Paolo's role in Canto V is an almost completely effaced one. Very little can be said positively of him. Perhaps the words "cor gentil" can apply to Paolo; for as Francesca says, it is in the gentle heart that love is kindled. Other than that we have only his movements in unison with Francesca and his silent weeping at the end of the canto. For this reason dramatists writing on the subject have found little guidance from Dante in creating the character of Paolo, and have had to rely on their own inspiration or on what little is known of him through other sources.

The part played in Canto V by Giovanni is limited to the line, "Caïna attende chi a vita ci spense," (Line 107.), which means that no comparison can be drawn with the various dramatic Giovannis.

Silvio Pellico was one of the first Italian authors to dramatize the story. *Francesca da Rimini* (1814) belongs to the Romantic period. Perhaps partly for this reason his Francesca differs considerably from Dante's. She is overly emotional, melancholy, and lacking in the restraint and dignity of Dante's heroine. Also she shows strong religious belief and awareness of her conjugal duty, both lacking in Canto V. After her marriage she remains resolutely virtuous and at the end dies innocent of adultery. Basically, she resembles her prototype in only two respects: her gentleness and her tenderness toward Paolo.

Pellico's Paolo is unprepossessing. Like Francesca's sentiments his are effusive, reducing the dramatic intensity of the original episode. No real comparison can be made with the undefined Paolo of Dante. But neither his traditionally handsome person nor his soldierly qualities are brought out in this play as in some of the others.

This treatment of the theme departs, as indicated by Francesca's innocence, more drastically from the original situation than do the four other plays directly on the subject. Pellico takes from Dante one specific episode, the reading of the Lancelot romance, but greatly lessens its effectiveness by making it the instrument of the awakening of an innocent, but undeclared, love before Francesca's marriage to Lanciotto. So, while the play draws from Dante in some respects other than the basic situation, there is much that is not in the *Divine Comedy* or even other sources.

Boker's *Francesca da Rimini* (1853) belongs to the Romantic period also. In this play Lanciotto receives the emphasis. Dante devoted only one verse to him, but here he is "a great soul, prisoned in a misshapen body, intense in every feeling, tinctured with bitterness, isolated by deformity, tender and magnanimous, but capable of frantic excess and terrible ferocity; a being marked out for wreck and ruin and bearing within himself the elements of tragedy and desolation." [7]

However, it is Francesca and Paolo who are the main concern in this study. Boker's Francesca resembles Dante's heroine in that she is honest, refusing to tell her husband-to-be that she loves him when

---

[7] As quoted from William Winter (who helped revise Boker's play for the 1882 performance) in Arthur Hobson Quinn, *A History of the American Drama from the Beginning to the Civil War*, 2nd ed. (New York, 1943), p. 350.

she does not. She is also modest, delights in Paolo, and feels the happiness of her love once it is admitted. But Francesca has several characteristics not found in the original version. She is shown as a dutiful daughter, though unable to forgive her father completely for his deceit in causing her to believe Paolo was to be her husband. Early in the play she disclaims gentleness, one of the major traits of Dante's Francesca, in words addressed to Paolo:

> I am not gentle, or I missed my aim.
> I am no hawk to fly at every lure.
> You courtly gentlemen draw one broad rule—
> All girls are fools. It may be so, in truth,
> Yet so I'll not be treated. [8]

She quickly becomes skilled in concealing her surprise, on seeing the deformed man who is to be her husband:

> Thus I begin the practice of deceit,
> Taught by deceivers at a fearful cost.
> The bankrupt gambler has become the cheat,
> And lives by arts that erewhile ruined me.
> Where it will end, Heaven knows. [9]

But this dissembling is simply her way of enduring in an unhappy situation, and not a basic flaw.

Boker had to fill out by his own imagination the picture of Paolo as primarily a handsome courtier with a gift for flattering words, though one who is fond of his brother and aware of Lanciotto's trust in him. He is perhaps indebted to Dante, however, for the conception of Paolo's remorse, for it is Paolo who is weeping in the *Divine Comedy*. Certainly, as in Dante, there is enough attractiveness in both Paolo and Francesca to arouse a feeling of sympathy for them in spite of their guilt.

With regard to plot Boker seems to have drawn from Dante in a few respects. Just as Fate is implied in the Dante episode, here again the lovers are drawn together against their wills. In the first act an old nurse predicts the mingling of Polenta and Malatesta blood.

---

[8] II.iii. In Moses, p. 135.
[9] III.ii. In Moses, p. 155.

Again as in Dante, the reading of the Lancelot romance is the downfall of the lovers. Finally, Boker shows awareness of his indebtedness to Dante by mentioning him as a member of the court of the Polenta family at Ravenna.

The details of plot and the setting of *El gran Galeoto* (1881) by José Echegaray are entirely different from those of the Dante episode, but it is essentially a modern play on the same ageless theme. Echegaray came after the Romantic movement proper in Spain. Nevertheless, his theatre is fundamentally Romantic, with the contemporary theatre of ideas incorporated into it.

The basic situation in *El gran Galeoto* is the same as in the *Inferno*. Here Teodora, the young wife, represents Francesca; and Ernesto, the youthful protégé of her husband, is Paolo. The characters otherwise have little to do with Dante's, however. Teodora is an attractive but ordinary human being, bourgeois, respectable, highly moral, content with her role as the wife of an older man whom she loves. Ernesto, the romantic, somewhat dreamy, but also virtuous poet is likewise hightly sympathetic, but with no origins of character in the *Divine Comedy*.

If Echegaray's characters are not drawn after Dante's, other elements come from him. The title itself shows that Echegaray is aware of his debt. Francesca in Canto V of the *Inferno* says of the romance of Lancelot, in which Gallehaut was the go-between: "Galeotto fu il libro e chi lo scrisse!" (Line 137) In Echegaray's play society has the role of Gallehaut. With its spirit of malicious gossip it is the go-between for the two who love against their wills. It also fills the role which Fate is felt to play in Dante.

But more important is the fact that the emphasis is placed on the development of the unconscious love between Ernesto and Teodora, as it is in Dante. Echegaray treats their love with restraint, playing down its physical aspects, as does Dante, but it is always in the background at least. The reader is conscious of it or its effects, if Ernesto and Teodora are not.

Other factors [10] than the title and the situation alert the reader to Echegaray's awareness of his indebtedness to Dante. In Scene IV of

---

[10] Gertrude G. Brainerd has also noted some of these factors in "The Paolo and Francesca Theme in Modern Drama: D'Annunzio, Phillips, Maeterlinck, Echegaray," *Poet Lore*, 27 (1916), 402.

the dialogue Ernesto says: "Brote mi drama, que hasta título tiene, porque allá, bajo la luz del quinqué, veo la obra inmortal del inmortal poeta florentino, y dióme en italiano lo que en buen español fuera buena imprudencia y mala osadía escribir en un libro ó pronunciar en la escena. Francesca y Paolo, válganme vuestros amores." [11] Later we see that Ernesto keeps on his work table a copy of the *Divine Comedy,* open at the Francesca episode. At another point a minor character repeats in his own words the circumstances of Francesca and Paolo's reading of Lancelot and Guinevere and asks Ernesto to explain what they have to do with his play. Thus Echegaray is directly obligated to Dante in several ways if not in characterization or details of plot.

Maeterlinck's *Pelléas et Mélisande* (1892) is one of the best-known Symbolist plays. Again, this is a work not directly concerning the Paolo and Francesca story but having the same theme, and in a number of respects resembling Dante.

Character is not Maeterlinck's main concern. His aim is to represent man's condition through symbols rather than through the portrayal of human types. For this reason Pelléas and Mélisande are not sharply drawn. They are moved by Fate or Destiny, which may also be seen in Dante, though not explicitly stated as here, rather than through any will of their own. However, a few traits of character can be discerned. Mélisande is a childlike figure, and one of great innocence in contrast to the more womanly Francesca. Also unlike Francesca, who felt no compunction at consigning her husband to Caïna, she feels pity for her husband Golaud. But she resembles Francesca in her commitment to her love once it is realized.

Pelléas, like Dante's Paolo, is a shadowy figure, with little but his youthfulness to characterize him. But his and Mélisande's love, shown by Maeterlinck as the destined union of two souls, has some of the beauty of the love described between Francesca and Paolo by Dante.

Finally, Maeterlinck follows the plot in its simplest and oldest form, giving the details of the story as little emphasis as possible. His single motif is the development of passion between Pelléas and Mélisande and jealousy in Golaud. The treatment suggests rather than depicts. In these respects Maeterlinck is much like Dante.

---

[11] *El gran Galeoto, drama en tres actos y en verso, precedido de un diálogo en prosa* (Madrid, 1881), p. 16.

Stephen Phillips, writing in the idealistic and romantic vein, apparently had the Dante episode well in mind, for the plot of his *Paolo and Francesca* (1899) also follows the simplest lines. Gertrude Brainerd [12] has suggested that the play also has something of Dante's mood. But Phillips' Francesca has little in common with Dante's except her tenderness toward Paolo. She is childlike, simple, innocent (just out of the convent), and somewhat vaguely drawn. Paolo, like his Dante prototype, is even more indefinite as the melancholy Romantic lover. Phillips has been critized for making the temperaments of his characters English, and for endowing them with touches of modern altruism. [13] It may be said in his defense, however, that Dante, in giving his episode the universal quality that it undeniably has, made it a situation applicable to any country and any era.

The destiny of the two lovers is sealed in the first act when Giovanni says: "Any that came between us I would kill." [14] And it is Fate, implied in Dante also, that moves them. The blind old servant Angela says at the end of Act I:

> Unwillingly he comes a wooing: she
> Unwillingly is wooed: yet shall they woo.
> His kiss was on her lips ere she was born.. [15]

In their fatal love the emphasis is on youth, as it is also, implicitly, in Dante. And as in Dante, the avowal of their love comes while reading of Lancelot and Guinevere.

Sections of the last act seem to be inspired by the lot of Paolo and Francesca in the *Divine Comedy*. Paolo asks of God:

> Even by such attraction we two rush
> Together through the everlasting years.
> Us, then, whose only pain can be to part,
> How wilt Thou punish? For what ecstasy
> Together to be blown about the globe!

---

[12] Op. cit., p. 395.
[13] Moses in his introduction to Boker's *Francesca da Rimini* (in *Representative Plays by American Dramatists*), p. 92; and Edith Wharton in "The Three Francescas," *The North American Review*, 175 (1902), 19-20, best state this objection.
[14] I.i. *Paolo & Francesca: A Tragedy in Four Acts* (London and New York, 1900), p. 18.
[15] I.i. *Ibid.*, p. 30.

> What rapture in perpetual fire to burn
> Together! — where we are is endless fire.
> There centuries shall in a moment pass,
> And all the cycles in one hour elapse!
> Still, still together, even when faints Thy sun,
> And past our souls Thy stars like ashes fall,
> How wilt Thou punish us who cannot part? [16]

Even Giovanni echoes the *Divine Comedy* when he cries after killing Paolo and Francesca:

> The curse, the curse of Cain!
> A restlessness has come into my blood,
> And I begin to wander from this hour
> Alone for evermore. [17]

Phillips, then, has drawn more on Dante than some of his predecessors.

Gabriele d'Annunzio suffuses his *Francesca da Rimini* (1901) not only with the local color of thirteenth-century Italy but with the psychology of that epoch. Arthur Symons speaks of this play as "a study of an age of blood." [18] Certainly, with its combination of Symbolism, Realism, and Romanticism, it reflects in a manner that none of the other plays does, the Italy in which the tragedy took place, and rounds out the characters more fully as human beings. Perhaps for this reason it is the most vital of the plays on the theme, but also less like Dante's episode than some of the others.

The characters in the story are robustly drawn in keeping with their vivid background. Francesca is unafraid to play with Greek Fire, to look on blood, or to engage in "qualunque mortale gioco." [19] Dante's Francesca does not have the opportunity to show such high-spirited qualities. But in the great welter of detail a few similarities between the d'Annunzio and the Dante characters may be seen. D'Annunzio's

---

[16] IV.i. *Ibid.*, p. 112.

[17] IV.i. *Ibid.*, p. 118.

[18] "Francesca da Rimini," *The Fortnightly Review*, NS 71 (1902), 239; or in the similar introduction to his translation of d'Annunzio's *Francesca da Rimini* (New York, 1902), p. xi.

[19] II.iii. In Gabriele d'Annunzio, *Tutte le opere* [*a cura di E. Bianchetti*], Vol. III: *Tragèdie, sogni, e mistèri, con un avvertimento di Renato Simoni,* I Classici Contemporanei Italiani (Verona, 1949), 563.

heroine is, in addition to her spirit, womanly. As John C. Metcalf has suggested,[20] she is graceful in speech and manner, as is Dante's heroine; and she shows sensitiveness to music and to beauty, a quality which one could guess of Dante's Francesca. Her own attractiveness and the deceit of her father make her a sympathetic character in spite of the fact that in this play the reader is partially aware of some of the more unpleasant aspects of the adultery.

Paolo is by far the best Paolo of any of the seven. He is an accomplished archer, horseman, and warrior, as well as an impassioned lover. But, of course, this characterization does not come from Dante.

Three incidents at least, all in Act III, recall more directly Dante's episode. First, Francesca evokes the wind in the circle of lust in the *Inferno*, and also the evident longing of Dante's heroine for peace, when she asks of Paolo:

> Paolo,
> datemi pace!
> È dolce cose vivere obliando,
> almeno un'ora fuor della tempesta
> che ci affatica.[21]

Later Paolo mentions having met Dante and being greatly affected by the sweetness of his poetry. Then at the end of the act comes the scene of the reading of the Lancelot romance, as in Dante. In fact, Metcalf,[22] among others, points out that d'Annunzio here was so true to his source that he employed the old French romance used by Dante, quoting it, translated into Italian, in his play.

Finally, d'Annunzio acknowledges a more general debt to Dante by prefacing his play with the first sonnet from *La vita nuova* and an answering sonnet, "Paolo Malatesta a Dante Alighieri."

Francis Marion Crawford's *Francesca da Rimini* (1902) is perhaps the least important, intrinsically, of the plays considered, but is of interest as the most nearly historical treatment in the seven. It is perhaps odd that Crawford, whose expressed literary purpose was entertainment, and who was distrustful of Realism as a means of attaining this purpose, should be the only author to write a serious play

---

[20] "An Old Romantic Triangle," *The Sewanee Review*, 29 (1921), 54.
[21] III.v. Op. cit., p. 632.
[22] "An Old Romantic Triangle," pp. 53-54.

in the Realistic current on the usually idealized subject of Francesca and Paolo. In founding his play on the fact that the liaison between Francesca and Paolo had been in progress several years and that they were no longer in the bloom of youth when discovered and murdered by Giovanni, Crawford removes his Francesca from the idealistic vein largely followed by those, beginning with Dante, who preceded him, and creates a Francesca who has little to do with Dante's or later ones. Here the reader is fully aware of the adulterous aspect of the affair, which is played down by Dante. Unlike Dante's characters, these are middle-aged. In the *Inferno* any bitterness or hate may be seen only in the brief "Caïna attende chi a vita ci spense." (Line 107.) Here both are freely shown. Dante's Francesca is modest and restrained; Crawford's brazen, immodest, and defiant.

In a few respects, however, Crawford does draw from the *Inferno*. In Dante the presence of Fate is felt. Here Fate is freely talked about, although one cannot really believe in it. Crawford uses the reading of the Lancelot romance, but only as a means of trying to relive the original episode after a liaison of fourteen years. Francesca's description of the reading is very similar to Dante's: "All alone we were — thinking no evil — yet now and then the reading made us lift our eyes to one another, and your cheek grew very pale." [23] And again, "We read how the mighty lover kissed Guinevere's softly smiling lips." [24] Then Francesca uses the line: "We read no more that day," [25] in direct translation of Dante's verse: "Quel giorno più non vi leggemmo avante." (Line 138) At a few other points in the play Crawford makes less immediate use of Dante. In Act I Francesca, after Giovanni's abortive attempt to stab her, speaks in tones that vaguely recall Dante's Hell: "One thrust — it could scarcely have hurt me — then darkness and then down, down, down to lowest hell, forever, to be racked and tortured to the end of ages." [26] And at the end of the play she echoes Dante's relegation of Giovanni to Caïna when she says to her husband: "The curse of Cain upon you." [27]

---

[23] I.iii. *Francesca da Rimini: A Play in Four Acts* (New York, 1902), p. 21.
[24] I.iii. *Ibid.*
[25] I.iii. *Ibid.*
[26] I.iii. *Ibid.*, p. 16.
[27] IV.i. *Ibid.*, p. 72.

Thus, several of the western world's dramatists have found a source for some of their best plays in Dante's immortal fifth canto. All of the seven plays considered here have not only taken their subject from Dante, but have in a number of other respects drawn their inspiration directly from him. One critic has aptly said: "Le poète toscan nous a laissé de ces amours une image qui reste à jamais si vivante dans nos coeurs, que toute autre image qu'on essaie de nous en montrer risque de nous paraître incomplète et médiocre, en regard de celle-là." [28] Yet each version is in some measure the love story Dante told more than six hundred and fifty years ago, attesting to the continuing vitality of the master.

---

[28] T. de Wyzewa, "Deux Nouvelles *Francesca da Rimini*," *Revue des Deux Mondes*, 5ᵉ Période, 8 (1902), 936-937.

BAUDELAIRE'S CHANT D'AUTOMNE

Robert T. Cargo
University of Alabama

I

Bientôt nous plongerons dans les froides ténèbres;
Adieu, vive clarté de nos étés trop courts!
J'entends déjà tomber avec des chocs funèbres
4 Le bois retentissant sur le pavé des cours.

Tout l'hiver va rentrer dans mon être: colère,
Haine, frissons, horreur, labeur dur et forcé,
Et, comme le soleil dans son enfer polaire,
8 Mon coeur ne sera plus qu'un bloc rouge et glacé.

J'écoute en frémissant chaque bûche qui tombe;
L'échafaud qu'on bâtit n'a pas d'écho plus sourd.
Mon esprit est pareil à la tour qui succombe
12 Sous les coups du bélier infatigable et lourd.

Il me semble, bercé par ce choc monotone,
Qu'on cloue en grande hâte un cercueil quelque part.
Pour qui? —C'était hier l'été; voici l'automne!
16 Ce bruit mystérieux sonne comme un départ.

II

J'aime de vos longs yeux la lumière verdâtre,
Douce beauté, mais tout aujourd'hui m'est amer,
Et rien, ni votre amour, ni le boudoir, ni l'âtre,
20 Ne me vaut le soleil rayonnant sur la mer.

Et pourtant aimez-moi, tendre coeur! soyez mère,
Même pour un ingrat, même pour un méchant;
Amante ou soeur, soyez la douceur éphémère
24   D'un glorieux automne ou d'un soleil couchant.

Courte tâche! La tombe attend; elle est avide!
Ah! laissez-moi, mon front posé sur vos genoux,
Goûter, en regrettant l'été blanc et torride,
28   De l'arrière-saison le rayon jaune et doux!

> "Il n'est pas rare qu'en automne les anciennes amours renaissent et que les souvenirs deviennent suppliant."
>
> —Louise de Vilmorin, *Le Retour d'Erica*

Of the poems in *Les Fleurs du Mal* comprising the Marie Daubrun cycle, only two were not already present in the edition of 1857 — *Chant d'Automne* and the following poem, Baudelaire's farewell to Marie, *A une Madone*. The two additions to the cycle represent works first published in 1859 and 1860 respectively, then included in the second edition of the volume in 1861. The first of these, *Chant d'Automne*, while displaying some curious linguistic and structural features, is of even more interest through content rather than form. It is our belief that a close examination of the text may reveal certain elements which have not yet, seemingly, been observed.

Chant d'Automne is one of only two poems in the three love cycles that is structured into numbered sections.[1] It is the only poem of the cycle inspired by the Green-Eyed Venus in which Baudelaire addresses Marie exclusively with the formal pronoun *vous*. It is one of the very few poems in the volume for which the immediate inspiration is an auditory stimulus.[2] In the course of the following *explication de texte* we want to elucidate these aspects of the poem and to

---

[1] The other poem, *Le Chat* (LI), inspired likewise by Marie, is divided into two numbered parts that are closely related. *Un Fantôme*, written to Jeanne, is merely a four-part sonnet sequence.

[2] Probably the only other sounds in *Les Fleurs du Mal* that alone serve to induce a mood of revery and reflection that results in poetic creation are those of the carillons "qui chantent dans la brume" (*La Cloche fêlée*) and the

point toward a more satisfactory interpretation, one we believe, that will permit a reading of the poem without having the analysis break down on the improbable excuse that *Chant d'Automne* refers in part to biographical details unknown to the reader.

It is rather obvious upon initial contact with the poem that at least one important critical question to resolve pertains to the two separate divisions. These two parts which may at first appear unrelated are joined by subtle but clearly defined links as our analysis will show. The first section of the poem describes preparations that are being made for the coming winter which the poet looks toward with dread. The part concludes with Baudelaire's associating winter with his emotional life and with death, hence preparing us for the symbolism which is emerging gradually but which reaches maturity only in Part II. Baudelaire's frequent device for directing the reader's attention to symbolic usage by means of the capitalized form of the noun is absent from this poem, yet the three seasons, each dominated by its sun, form a closely knit symbolic pattern. The second part, beginning with the very personal declaration of love, "J'aime de vos yeux la lumière verdâtre," marks a decided change of tone and development. An event that the poet had experienced has been described, but the incident is one fraught with profound implications that transcend the real event. The interval separating the two sections marks the period of reflection when raw experience is transformed into poetry. The poem thus offers perhaps the most striking example in *Les Fleurs du Mal* of that Baudelairian aesthetic of which any number of texts speak.[3]

* * *

> Bientôt nous plongerons dans les froides ténèbres;
> Adieu, vive clarté de nos étés trop courts!
> J'entends déjà tomber avec des chocs funèbres
> 4 Le bois retentissant sur le pavé des cours.

The seasonal metaphor that unifies the poem structurally and thematically makes its appearance in the opening lines. The time is

---

clock "sonnant minuit" (*L'Examen de Minuit*). *L'Horloge* seems to be almost as much visual as auditory in inspiration.

[3] "...Tout pour moi devient allégorie," Baudelaire wrote in *Le Cygne*, to cite a well-known example.

autumn; the poet bids farewell to summer which has passed and thinks of approaching winter with its "froides ténèbres." The temporal adverb, *Bientôt*, which begins the poem suggests the imminence of winter and in conjunction with the future tense, *nous plongerons*, has omnious connotations. Winter, here associated with ideas of physical discomfort primarily, assumes a moral significance, but gradually it will mature into a symbol of sexual impotence and finally will become merged with the notion of death.

Although Baudelaire does not present them chronologically, the three seasons that are mentioned in the poem are clearly ordered through verbs. We may reconstruct the logical, sequential element of time in the following manner: "C'était hier l'été;" "voici l'automne;" "Tout l'hiver va rentrer...." The past summer that is called "nos étés trop courts" (1. 2) will appear again as "l'été blanc et torride" (1. 27). The poet's attitude toward this summer, irrevocably gone ("Adieu," 1. 2), is expressed in the adjectival phrase, "trop courts" (1. 2). It is with nostalgia that he thinks back upon its "vive clarté," which by the end of the poem has intensified in the poet's memory to "blanc et torride." Summer, with its unforgettable sun, white hot and torrid in intensity, has been linked to life, "vive" (1. 2), and this will stand in sharp contrast to the cold, polar sun of winter, "le soleil dans son enfer polaire" (1. 7).

Because of the particular order of ideas opening the poem, one cannot say definitively that Baudelaire, having heard the sound of firewood being unloaded in courtyards, "Le bois retentissant sur le pavé des cours," thinks of the awesome approach of winter, although this would seemingly make for the best reading, given the role of the auditory sense in the poem.[4] The stimulus having been undergone, one might expect the resultant observation to follow. The poet's reversal of the usual sequence by having result precede cause, however, is an effective means of dramatizing the significance of the symbol rather than the reality of the incident.

---

[4] In other words, it might be possible to read the first stanza as an expression of the poet's realization somehow that winter is approaching. So real is this impression that he seems to hear "déjà" the sound of preparations for its arrival. Such an interpretation necessarily requires line 3 to be read with something like "en esprit" understood after "J'entends." We reject this approach.

The verb, *J'entends* (l. 3), while emphasizing the auditory pattern of the imagery that prevails in the poem, is linked to *J'écoute* of line 9, which must be read as a counterpart of line 3. The first verb indicates the passive aspect of the event: the sound imposes itself upon the person. The second verb marks a willful action on the part of the poet. The full symbolic meaning is not yet clear to him in lines 3-4, however, where the general term, *le bois,* falling with "chocs funèbres" inspires in Baudelaire at first only a vague dread and a reminder of winter. "J'écoute en frémissant chaque bûche qui tombe." Given a moment for reflection "chaque bûche" now fills the poet with anxiety and fear, "en frémissant." Attention should also be given to the alliterative, if not onomatopoeic, *retentissant* of line 4, in which the dental *t*'s echo the sound *tomber* of the preceding line.

> Tout l'hiver va rentrer dans mon être: colère,
> Haine, frissons, horreur, labeur dur et forcé,
> Et, comme le soleil dans son enfer polaire,
> 8 Mon coeur ne sera plus qu'un bloc rouge et glacé.

Since Marie does not figure except indirectly in the first division of the poem, we propose reading *nous plongerons* and *nos étés* of stanza 1 as a statement pertaining to the human condition. It is not limited to Baudelaire, nor to Baudelaire and Marie, but refers to man in general. In the second stanza, however, the poem takes a decidedly more personal turn: "Tout l'hiver va rentrer dans *mon* être." Winter will arrive in all its fury and rage: "*Tout* l'hiver." The symbolic usage of winter is indicated, and hence the intended symbolism of the other seasons since they are parallel, by the series of abstract nouns that follow and that spell out the moral and physical qualities that are represented by *hiver*: "colère, / Haine, frissons, horreur, labeur dur et forcé." Of the five nouns, only *frissons* could represent a non-figurative usage, although here it is probably intended to function on both a literal and a figurative level. It is important to note that the symbolic *hiver* that Baudelaire speaks of is not the winter of old age, not yet at any rate. In 1859, Baudelaire, of course, at thirty-eight was hardly an old man,[5] but the winter of his life, especially his emotional life, is represented by moral qualities for the most part:

---

[5] But Baudelaire did write in *Fusées* (XIV): "—On dit que j'ai trente ans; mais si j'ai vécu trois minutes en une ... n'ai-je pas quatre-vingt-dix ans?"

anger and hatred, shudders and horror, and uninspired work. The effectiveness of the passage (ll. 5-6) is due in no small measure to the repetitive *r* sounds which suggest the shivers and shudders that the cold of winter will bring on. We see that the poet is concerned initially that the sound he has heard suggests the imminent demise of love, of which the heart is the seat, as the last two lines of this stanza indicate. The personal application continues in these final lines with Baudelaire predicting that his heart, as a result of winter, will soon be like a polar sun, "un bloc rouge et glacé" (l. 8). The adjective *rouge* is fittingly applicable both to sun and to heart, while the second of the pair, *glacé,* represents, in terms of the heart at any rate, a different level of meaning. Literally it is a proper description only for the coldness of the polar sun. Baudelaire has thus skillfully juxtaposed *rouge* that operates on the literal level with the figurative use of *glacé* in a manner that recalls the handling of the series of nouns above. Both *bloc* and *glacé* serve to stress the similarity of the heart devoid of love and the coldness of the polar sun. We have seen, however, that the entire second stanza is given over to hypothesis, as the future tenses indicate: "va rentrer" (l. 5) and "ne sera plus" (l. 8).

> J'écoute en frémissant chaque bûche qui tombe;
> L'échafaud qu'on bâtit n'a pas d'écho plus sourd.
> Mon esprit est pareil à la tour qui succombe
> 12   Sous les coups du bélier infatigable et lourd.

With the third stanza, Baudelaire begins linking the sound of fire logs falling on courtyard paving stones with death, already prefigured in the word "funèbres" of line 3. The process is a gradual one. The "échafaud" that one might hear being built is the clearest indication in this stanza of the effort to associate winter with death. The poet finds himself almost overcome by the realization of the meaning of what he hears and the mind under the repeated and persistent symbolic sounds almost gives way. In lines 11-12, Baudelaire has introduced not the image of the "tour foudroyée" from the tarot, although there may be parallels, but rather the image of the medieval tower that is gradually destroyed and reduced to rubble by the relentless action of the battering ram. If we take *esprit* as an example of synecdoche standing for man, then two possible meanings seem to emerge. The "coups du bélier infatigable et lourd" (l. 12) represents, on the one hand, a metaphorical expression for the adversities that plagued the poet's life, which have gradually taken their toll, and which increasingly make this relatively young man think of himself by the concluding lines of the poem as being on the brink of the tomb. Any number of events from the poet's past life could be offered as explanatory: the *conseil judiciaire,* the trial, his mother's marriage to Aupick, his syphilis, his failure to gain the recognition that he felt he deserved, financial worries, the list seems endless. But to this point, the poem concerns not physical death but the death of love, and by extension, impotency. This being the case, it seems necessary to look at the "tour" and the "bélier" both as having erotic overtones, the tower especially, since it is a phallic symbol representing masculine power and sexual prowess. This interpretation of the tower recalls the "tour abolie" of Nerval in *El Desdichado* and although Baudelaire's poem does not have the intensity and conciseness of Gérard's sonnet, the two pieces are not unrelated. Both express extremes of loneliness, solitude, and despair.

> Il me semble, bercé par ce choc monotone,
> Qu'on cloue en grande hâte un cercueil quelque part.
> Pour qui? — C'était hier l'été; voici l'automne!
> 16 Ce bruit mystérieux sonne comme un départ.

Stanza 4 represents the culmination of Baudelaire's efforts to link winter with the notion of death. The sound which the poet likened to "l'échafaud qu'on bâtit" (l. 10) has become "Qu'on cloue en grande hâte un cercueil quelque part" (l. 14). The verb *bâtit* has become the more resounding and forceful *cloue* and the hard, alliterative sounds of the line hammer out a frightful, ominous note: "*Qu*'on *c*loue en grande hâte un cer*c*ueil *qu*el*qu*e part." *Echafaud,* that produces death, has become *cercueil,* receptacle of the dead. But the poet's uncertainty, his reluctance to accept the inevitable are contained in the phrase "Il me semble" (l. 13), in the very progression itself, in the anxious question "Pour qui?" (l. 15), and in the vague and mysterious *quelque part* (l. 14), which also serves to emphasize the auditory nature of the first section of *Chant d'Automne.* The poet, having heard but not seen, cannot be more specific. It is a "bruit mystérieux" (l. 16). It is probable that Baudelaire intended the phrase "en grande hâte" (l. 14) to mean "prematurely" and not "hastily," since the sounds, described as "chocs funèbres," "coups du bélier infatigable et lourd," and "choc monotone," all suggest a slow but relentless quality. The idea of prematurity of the preparations that signify the arrival of winter is supported above in line 3 in the adverb *déjà,* which serves to indicate the unexpectedly early arrival of events that have been heretofore experienced annually. The action would only appear to be premature, however, since the poet, like a latter-day Villon, is not yet accustomed to thinking in these new terms. The anguished voice we hear in the poem comes from a man who has realized that he will not see another summer.

Bercé (l. 13), like the "trop courts" above, is significant for what it reveals about Baudelaire's attitude. With connotations of comfort and sleep and pleasure we must see Baudelaire as accepting the arrival of winter that brings sexual impotence and physical death, welcoming it, if not enthusiastically then certainly stoically, and looking upon it as release from the rigors imposed on a body now fatigued by the torrid summer of passion and everyday life itself. Undeniably, he regrets the past ("en regrettant l'été blanc et torride," l. 27), but the future holds relief in store. "For whom is the coffin being prepared?" the poet asks. The remainder of the line, it would appear, constitutes the answer. We must not think that the "cercueil" is for the poet himself, although ultimately (l. 25), Baudelaire does arrive at a consideration of his own death, but it would be premature to try to ascribe that to line 15. "C'était hier l'été." Summer has died. The preparations are for its being laid to rest. [6] It is now autumn ("voici l'automne!"). [7] The rapidity of the transition from summer to autumn, already prepared in the *déjà* earlier, is admirably conveyed in the short independent clauses of line 15.

To summarize Part I, we might say that summer has gone, it is autumn, winter approaches. Of the sixteen lines that comprise the first division, only two are couched in reality:

> J'entends déjà tomber avec des chocs funèbres
> Le bois retentissant sur le pavé des cours.

---

[6] The personification of the season and the particular turn of phrase with a certain allegorical quality may bring to mind the bright, optimistic *rondeau* of Charles d'Orléans on the disappearance of winter and the arrival of summer: "Yver, vous ne demourrés plus, / Les fourriers d'Esté sont venus!"

[7] The movement here is remarkably close to that in *Recueillement,* a poem that appeared in 1861, where Douleur, like a fretful, nagging child calling for "le soir," causes the poet to exclaim: "Tu réclamais le soir; il descend, le voici."

The remainder of Part I, indeed the remainder of the entire poem, constitutes Baudelaire's reflection on the meaning that this sound has for him. Had the poet stopped at line 16, aesthetically the poem would be complete; it would not, of course, be a love poem, for up to now there has been no allusion even to Marie Daubrun. [7a]

* * *

It is necessary before entering into a discussion of the second part of *Chant d'Automne* to recall briefly the poet's relationship with Marie. Baudelaire's liaison with the actress spanned the years from 1854-1856, although the really close affair may not have lasted more than a few months of that time. Since our poem and the "poème d'adieu" represent works composed in 1859, just prior to their publication, together they reflect a desperate effort to regain the favors of Marie and the ensuing disappointment at failure to do so, replaced as Baudelaire was in Marie's affection by Théodore de Banville. We know that Baudelaire spent a considerable part of the first six months of 1859 in Honfleur with his mother and he returned to the capital in June of that year:

> Another preoccupation [his return had been precipitated by business and financial matters] also kept Baudelaire in Paris during the summer and autumn of 1859. Marie Daubrun, who had been absent from the capital between 1857 and 1859, returned there to play in *Les Pirates de la Savane* at the Théâtre de la Gaîté, and he renewed his relationship with her. Perhaps it was she herself who sought him out this time, for she was in need of help. Banville was in hospital, very seriously ill, and she therefore required support in her career from another quarter. [8]

The final rupture which Baudelaire prophetically saw approaching, came within days after the appearance of *Chant d'Automne*:

> A few days after [*Chant d'Automne*] appeared, on the last day of November 1859, in *La Revue Contemporaine,* when Banville came out of the nursing-home where he had been having treatment, [Marie] left with him for the south of

---

[7a] The first section of *Chant d'Automne* is presented as a complete poem for an exercise in *explication* by Katz and Hall, *Explicating French Texts* (New York, 1970), p. 78, with no indication that it is a mere fragment.

[8] Enid Starkie, *Baudelaire* (New York, 1958), p. 363.

France where he was to recuperate. They seemed to have lived openly and happily together in Nice [...].[9]

* * *

Part II marks a conspicuous turn in the development of the poem. Marie is introduced into the fabric of the composition and the symbolism of the autumn season is resolved. Baudelaire pleads for Marie's love: he will accept her on any terms she may wish; she would be "la douceur éphémère/D'un glorieux automne."

> J'aime de vos longs yeux la lumière verdâtre,
> Douce beauté, mais tout aujourd'hui m'est amer,
> Et rien, ni votre amour, ni le boudoir, ni l'âtre,
> 20 Ne me vaut le soleil rayonnant sur la mer.

The poet addresses Marie directly ("J'aime la lumière de vos longs yeux," to reconstruct the normal syntax), using the formal *vos*, which is echoed later by the possessive adjectives of "votre amour" (l. 19) and "vos genoux" (l. 26) and the series of imperative verbs: "aimez-moi" (l. 21), "soyez mère" (*ibid*.), "soyez..." (l. 23), "laissez-moi" (l. 26), all of which underline the urgency of the poet's plea, the strained relations that the poet felt, and the distance that separates him from Marie. The "lumière verdâtre" (l. 17) is, of course, a reference to the peculiarly colored eyes of Marie, the Green-Eyed Venus, and as such the phrase stands as a kind of identification stamp that marks the recipient of the poem. The bizarre but beautiful qualification of her eyes as "longs," exuding a greenish glow, is affective rather than merely an ordinary flat statement of fact. Images of ephemeral, fragile tenderness prevail in the lines addressed directly to Marie, "Douce beauté" (l. 18) and "douceur éphémère" (l. 23), along with images that stress a non-sexual, familial relationship, "mère" (l. 21) and "soeur" (l. 23). Lines 18-20 in the above stanza show Baudelaire's bitterness over the reflection that has already transpired. He is inconsolable ("tout aujourd'hui m'est amer") and the coordinating conjunction *Et* (l. 19) stands as a powerful indication of the futility that he acknowledges while making his urgent plea. He admits that the present cannot eradicate memories of the past: "Et rien, ni votre

---

[9] *Ibid.*, p. 364.

amour, ni le boudoir, ni l'âtre,/Ne me vaut le soleil rayonnant sur la mer." *Amour,* Marie's love in an abstract, general, composite sense, is seen as being twofold. There is the physical side, represented by "le boudoir" and the domestic side, represented by "l'âtre." [10] *Boudoir,* however, was not what Baudelaire had first written, and a variant to line 19 offers a significant indication of the poet's original thinking. In place of "ni le boudoir," the first edition read "la chambre étroite." The change probably came from a desire to eliminate the discordant and overtly erotic reference to Marie. But these gentle, autumnal pleasures with which he associates Marie, and which appear in several of the poems inspired by her, cannot replace memories of the radiant summer sun, "le soleil rayonnant sur la mer" (l. 20). Of the three suns in the poem, Baudelaire seems most hesitant to identify the one of summer and his reticence probably stems from the feeling of guilt that seizes him at coupling such a bold, daring confession with so pathetic a request. As another variant indicates, however, the summer sun, originally "ardent soleil," was more conspicuous than it appears in the final version.

We believe that the nature of this "soleil" is fundamental to a comprehension of the poem itself. Marc Eigeldinger, in a penetrating analysis of the solar image in Baudelaire's poetry, has made the following observation concerning the meaning that the brilliant summer sun generally has in *Les Fleurs du Mal*:

> La clarté brutale du soleil signifie l'anéantissement de toute vie, tandis que la lumière, enveloppée de brume et d'opacité, crée un climat idéalisé, propice au surgissement du souvenir et à l'essor de l'imagination. [11]

The sun that appears in line 20 of *Chant d'Automne* would not, obviously, fit into the pattern perceived by Professor Eigeldinger in the totality of Baudelaire's poetry. The critic does mention our specific sun image, however, but in terms that stress the archetypal or mythical significance of the image for Baudelaire:

---

[10] Baudelaire's sensitivity, albeit restrained, to the joys of the home has perhaps not been sufficiently emphasized. See, for example, *Le Crépuscule du Soir* ("Encore la plupart n'ont-ils jamais connu / La douceur du foyer et n'ont jamais vécu.") and also the prose poem that bears the same title.

[11] Marc Eigeldinger, "La Symbolique Solaire dans la Poésie de Baudelaire," *Revue d'Histoire Littéraire de la France*, LXVII, 2 (1967), 138.

> L'image du "soleil rayonnant sur la mer" et celle des "soleils marins" dans "La Vie antérieure" expriment admirablement les noces cosmiques de l'eau et du feu. Baudelaire imagine le soleil surgissant des abîmes de la mer, renaissant du baptême des eaux qui raniment sa vigueur. [12]

While we do not quarrel with such an opinion, we do feel that there remain certain questions pertaining to detail unanswered. To impose this level of interpretation upon the poem without first laying a foundation for it through *explication* may not satisfy most readers. It is, therefore, desirable at this point to attempt to resolve more completely the central metaphor of suns and seasons before proceeding further. The word *soleil* appears only three times in the poem and each time is intended to be linked to one of the three seasons mentioned. The radiant and resplendant sun upon the sea is, as we have seen, the sun linked to summer: "le soleil rayonnant sur la mer" (l. 20). [13] The autumn sun appears in lines 23-24: "soyez la douceur éphémère /D'un glorieux automne ou d'un soleil couchant." The winter sun: "le soleil dans son enfer polaire" (l. 7). It is clear that Baudelaire, in the second stanza of Part II (ll. 23-24) and in the final stanza (ll. 26-28), draws the parallel between Marie and autumn, thus inviting, even requiring a resolution of the entire pattern of allied images in a manner that is logically dictated. It would seem plausible, therefore, that Baudelaire meant to indicate Jeanne Duval by the summer and its torrid sun. The sense of the first stanza of Part II then becomes obvious. The poet expresses his love for Marie, but confesses that he cannot forget Jeanne and the passion that marked that liaison. The poem at this point becomes a curious love lyric indeed. The poet

---

[12] *Ibid.*, p. 143.

[13] The phrase inspired a lovely passage in Proust's *A l'ombre des Jeunes filles en fleurs*:

> Me persuadant que j'étais "assis sur le môle" ou au fond du "boudoir" dont parle Baudelaire, je me demandais si son "soleil rayonnant sur la mer" ce n'était pas — bien différent du rayon du soir, simple et superficiel comme un trait doré et tremblant — celui qui en ce moment brûlait la mer comme une topaze, la faisait fermenter, devenir blonde et laiteuse comme de la bière écumante, comme du lait, tandis que par moments s'y promenaient, çà et là, de grandes ombres bleues, que quelque dieu s'amusait à déplacer, en bougeant un miroir dans le ciel....

Cited in Charles Baudelaire, *Les Fleurs du Mal,* édition critique établie par Jacques Crépet et Georges Blin (Paris, 1942), p. 395.

writes to his beloved to plead that she not abandon him but also to declare candidly that the present cannot remove the deeply rooted memories of the past and another love. This reading justifies completely, therefore, the opening line of the succeeding stanza.

>   Et pourtant aimez-moi, tendre coeur! soyez mère,
>   Même pour un ingrat, même pour un méchant;
>   Amante ou soeur, soyez la douceur éphémère
> 24 D'un glorieux automne ou d'un soleil couchant.

Evidence in the poem itself, if it is properly read, if our interpretation up to here is correct, clarifies these lines then. We might paraphrase the first two lines as follows: "In spite of my nostalgia for the past, in spite of this insulting frankness, I ask for your indulgence. Love one who can be so mean and such an ingrate." It is not necessary nor even justifiable to write as does Professor Adam: "Quand on sait à quel point Baudelaire bannit de ses vers le moindre hasard, on est certain que Marie avait reproché à son ami d'être un ingrat et un méchant." [14] Obviously Baudelaire's candor has brought on the reproach from Marie, but the reasons are quite clear. One might say that the self-accusation contained in line 22 reflects clearly Baudelaire's deep-seated feelings of guilt for finding himself in a position to have to make such a humiliating plea for Marie's love. At the same time the dilemma serves as yet another indication of the profound and abiding devotion he held always for Jeanne. In his anguish and not unlike Hugo's Don Ruy Gomez, he suggests a maternal relation ("mère"), a physical attachment ("amante"), or a sororal one ("soeur"). The decision will be Marie's; he asks only for the "douceur éphémère /D'un glorieux automne ou d'un soleil couchant." As I read the line, "automne" and "soleil couchant" are aspects of the same relationship, the latter merely stressing the ephemeral character of the anticipated and longed-for liaison. We believe, as earlier stated, that Marie and her love are clearly represented by "automne" and "soleil couchant." We could do no better than cite Lloyd James Austin for a clarification of this seasonal reference to Marie and its special pertinence:

---

[14] Baudelaire, *Les Fleurs du Mal*, ed. Antoine Adam (Paris, 1961), p. 347, note 5.

> Baudelaire ne voulait certes pas l'insulter en lui faisant sentir qu'elle vieillissait. Si l'automne et le soleil couchant étaient pour lui la saison et l'heure qui *correspondaient* à Marie, dans l'esprit du poète, c'est à cause de leur douceur, de leur éclat voilé.[15]

Jean Prévost, on the other hand, read the line in question as applicable more to Baudelaire himself than to Marie:

> The *soleil couchant* dont il est question ne désigne pas la jeune actrice, mais bien le poète, qui éprouve pour la dernière fois les douceurs de la chaleur et de la lumière, qui veut avant sa mort goûter une fois encore les plaisirs de l'arrière-saison.[16]

We feel that Prévost's view focuses too narrowly on the poet and tends to disregard Marie's role in the symbol and to insist without justification, within the limits of *Chant d'Automne* at any rate, on prior loves associated with autumn. Our own view, that the setting sun-autumn image forms a unit in which both members of the couple share, coincides with that of Professor Austin, who has, quite accurately we feel, made the following observation:

> Mais Baudelaire était persuadé, et non sans raison, qu'il était lui-même parvenu à l'automne de sa propre vie [...].
>
> Donc double correspondance ici: entre l'automne et le poète, entre l'automne et Marie. Correspondance abstraite en ce qui concerne lui-même: il ressemble à l'automne parce qu'il a atteint l'avant-dernière saison de sa vie. Correspondance concrète quant à Marie: car elle avait pour lui la "douce beauté" de cette saison d'où la "vive clarté" de l'été est absente [...].[17]

> Courte tâche! La tombe attend; elle est avide!
> Ah! laissez-moi, mon front posé sur vos genoux,
> Goûter, en regrettant l'été blanc et torride,
> 28   De l'arrière-saison le rayon jaune et doux!

---

[15] Lloyd James Austin, *L'Univers poétique de Baudelaire* (Paris, 1956), p. 290.
[16] Jean Prévost, *Baudelaire* (Paris, 1964), pp. 190-191.
[17] Austin, p. 290.

"Courte tâche!" Baudelaire attempts to undergird and strengthen his supplication. If Marie agrees to fulfill the role of mistress, "amante," to enter into a mature and calm physical relationship, then the death of which Baudelaire speaks, "La tombe attend" (l. 25), must be considered as a figurative expression for sexual impotence, bringing complete release from physical desire. If the relationship is a more paternal one, if Marie agrees to stay with him to dispell his loneliness, to shower kindness and gentle affection like an Electra upon an Orestes, or a mother upon a son, then we must accept the line at its literal meaning. Death, in this latter instance, would release Marie from her responsibilities of nurse-maid to an "old" man. I fail to see that Baudelaire in the final lines of the poem indicates beyond perhaps the slightest degree any optimism as to a felicitous resolution of his dilemma. It is possible, however, that line 26 points either to a preference or to a mild expectation of the poet as to which of the suggested roles Marie may accept: "Mon front posé sur vos genoux." In addition to the attitude of supplication, the line represents a projection of the maternal image foreshadowed earlier in "bercé" (l. 13) and stated overtly in "soyez mère" (l. 21).[18] The concluding stanza contains the second occurrence of transposed syntax in *Chant d'Automne*. We may read the last three lines as Baudelaire's final, almost hysterical plea: "Laissez-moi goûter le rayon jaune et doux de l'arrière-saison," with my head resting on your knees and longing for the past white-hot summer.

As we have seen from our discussion, Baudelaire has built the poem around a tightly woven pattern of seasonal imagery that not only serves to give unity to the composition but serves more importantly as a vehicle for the principal theme. The following outline represents the basic symbolic structure of the poem:

---

[18] The image here is quite close to one that occurs in *Le Voyage* where the mother and mistress appear to be unified in a sort of feminine ideal: ".../Dit celle dont jadis nous baisions les genoux" (l. 136).

Women	Emotions	Seasons	Suns	Verbs	
Jeanne	passion	"nos étés trop courts" "l'été blanc et torride" "C'était hier l'été"	"le soleil rayonnant sur la mer"	past:	"C'était"
Marie	mature love	Chant d'Automne "voici l'automne" "glorieux automne" "l'arrière - saison"	"un soleil couchant" ("le rayon jaune et doux")	present:	"voici"
***	sexual impotence	"Tout l'hiver" ("froides ténèbres")	"le soleil dans son enfer polaire"	future:	"nous plongerons" "va rentrer" "ne sera plus"

* * *

In the foregoing analysis we have attempted to clarify those details in the poem which heretofore have appeared obscure, to demonstrate the basic unity of *Chant d'Automne,* and to suggest the richness and complexity of a poem which must surely be considered one of Baudelaire's finest compositions. The intricate pattern of metaphors is resolved only in the final two stanzas with the establishing of the Marie-autumn parallel and thus it is really only in retrospect that the poem can be effectively interpreted. Standing as it does in the penultimate position in the Marie Daubrun cycle, *Chant d'Automne* offers yet another indication of the enduring power that the Black Venus continued through the years to exert over Baudelaire. In conclusion, one is inevitably drawn to the prose poem, *Un Cheval de Race,* which we believe was inspired by Jeanne Duval, and a passage where the poet seems to imagine his beloved having arrived at a time of amorous bliss, in which he shares, when the ardor of summer with its fierce passion and the constancy of autumn with its warm, deep affection are joined in an ideal love:

> Et puis elle est si douce et si fervente! Elle aime comme on aime en automne; on dirait que les approches de l'hiver allument dans son coeur un feu nouveau, et la servilité de sa tendresse n'a jamais rien de fatigant.

SOME ASPECTS OF AGE AND TIME IN *LE CID*

George B. Daniel
University of North Carolina

The year of *Le Cid* was deeply significant in the progress of the Thirty Years' War. The single, the only, event of 1636 was the Corbie Compaign.[1] The spirit of defeat, which loomed ineluctably, was dramatically conveyed in a letter by the Duc de La Vallette to Père Joseph.

> Nos troupes sont affaiblies; nous n'avons ni argent ni équipement; nous n'avons pas de chevaux pour tirer nos chars d'artillerie qu'il faut absolument si nous comptons continuer.[2]

The army was decimated. Richelieu's appeals to the French went unheeded. Simply, the French were tired of war. During the month of August, General Werth entered Corbie. A few weeks later he occupied Compiègne, only forty miles from Paris, the next victim. Panic seized the citizens of the capital city. All remnants of civilization seemed to have disappeared. Torture and cannibalism were accepted procedures. Pestilence and famine were rampant. Louis XIII was present to lead his troops. Richelieu provided the sickly lot of soldiers, most of whom deserted when possible, as best he could. Then a miracle occurred. The threat to Paris gave rise to a pulsating wave of patriotism.

---

[1] C. V. Wedgwood's *The Thirty Years' War* (London, 1938) is of particular interest.
[2] In Geoffrey Treasure, *Seventeenth Century France* (New York, 1966), p. 177.

Corneille had completed his *Illusion comique* and continued to write *Le Cid*, which was to become a manifiesto of chauvinism, exemplifying the concept of the absolute monarch.[3] Its victory was to be signaled by the play's extraordinary success.[4]

Time plays a prime role in the realization of this concept. In *Etudes sur le temps humain* Georges Poulet depicts the Cornelian hero as inevitably the plaything of time.

> Il est le produit du passé; il est poussé vers le futur et le présent est pour lui un lieu de conflits où s'affrontent des tendances opposées, une balance fragile dont l'équilibre est sans cesse rompu par les impulsions successives de la vie du coeur... Le temps de l'amour est un temps de contrainte et de débats.[5]

In the consideration of the role of time in the plays of Corneille, it is appropriate to remember that with it is coupled love, the wellspring of any and every action.[6] It is through this medium that communication, if ever, is obtained.[7] Unsegmented, time in the plays of Corneille is represented by specific types. The Past is best defined through Old Age, the Present through Middle Age, and the Future through Youth. Each age is described by a quality. Aligning itself with Old Age is Reconciliation.[8] Middle Age is best understood

---

[3] For a contemporary treatment of this concept, Guez de Balzac's *Le Prince* has been indispensable; in *Oeuvres*, by L. Moreau (Paris, 1854). See also J. Declareuil, "Les idées politiques de Guez de Balzac," *Revue du droit public et de la science politique en France et à l'étranger*, XXIV (1907), 633-74.

[4] A detailed account is given in Henry Lyonnet, *Le Cid de Corneille* (Paris, 1929), p. 53-66.

[5] Edinburgh, 1949, p. 126.

[6] See Octave Nadal, *Le sentiment de l'amour dans l'oeuvre de Pierre Corneille* (Paris, 1948), p. 164, and Serge Doubrovsky, *Corneille et la dialectique du héros* (Paris, 1963), pp. 87-132.

[7] I find Martin Esslin's statement in his analysis of Ionesco's *La Leçon* particularly relevant concerning the question of power. "The political implication of domination is certainly present in *The Lesson*, but it is only one, and perhaps a minor, aspect of its main proposition, which hinges on the sexual nature of all power and the relationship between language and power as the basis of all human ties." *The Theatre of the Absurd* (New York, 1969), p. 119.

[8] In *Le Cid de Corneille* (Paris, 1929), Gustave Reynier finds this quality essential to an understanding of Don Diègue's character. See especially p. 116.

through Pride,[9] and Youth through Hope. Don Diègue, Don Gomès, and Rodrigue fill these roles admirably in *Le Cid*.

Each age is driven by specific attitudes toward love. Don Diègue is sustained by the love of tradition and strives to reconcile man with Nature, thereby achieving a final tranquility.[10] Don Gomès, on the other hand, impatient man that he is, is identified in the realm of love by paternal love, and Rodrigue by the thirst for physical love.[11] God, country, family and self are represented in these types of love.

As I have said, Reconciliation, Pride, and Hope are qualities which confront each other in *Le Cid*. The three types of love nourish the play and imbue it with an astounding vibrancy.

Action in *Le Cid* is framed by the Present.[12] It will be recalled that in the first scene of the original version, Don Gomès reveals to Elvire his great pleasure at the prospects of Rodrigue being his son-in-law. As the play unfurls, and Don Gomès is destroyed, Don Fernand assumes the role of the Present, and it is he who speaks the last lines.

In addition to being impatient and filled with pride, the Present has other facets, the most important being movement. This movement is demonstrated by overweening intolerance, insufferable authoritarianism, and a remarkable interest in material gains.

Although Don Gomès is satisfied with Rodrigue as the possible father of his grandchildren, he cannot be bothered. He is preoccupied with the meeting of the Council, and sees already a scepter passed to him. The word *scepter* (bras) is a leitmotif of the play. The scepter of Gomès's dreams is certainly that which maintains stability in the state. This scepter is what it is because of Gomès (vs. 196-207).

An essential trait of Pride is confidence, which, in turn, leans dangerously toward introvertive, inflexible, disdainful action.[13] In the famous scene of the *Soufflet* (I, 3), Gomès reveals all the traits of the Present, with disdain being by far the most noteworthy. Gomès is insensitive to the relativity of things and deeds. His fate is sealed. By

---

[9] F. Tanquerey underlines this aspect in "Le héros cornélien," *Revue des cours et conférences*, XXXV (1934), 577-94.
[10] Doubrovsky, p. 91.
[11] *Ibid.*, p. 106 and Nadal, p. 164.
[12] *Théâtre choisi*, ed. Maurice Rat (Paris, 1961). All verse references are from this edition.
[13] See Ernest Merien-Genast, "Corneille als Dichter des Stolzes," *Romanische Forschungen*, LI (1937), 83-109 and especially, 90-93.

insulting Don Diègue, he has defied the State, thereby becoming its enemy. The Present sees existence only through the microscope of the absolute. This entire scene informs the audience of the irony of the duel scene later. What has seemed a reality to Gomès is only an illusion.[14] He, too, is fallible and human.

Corneille has shown the Present, thus far, in a most adverse light. Nevertheless, Gomès the authoritarian, divested of human emotion, is also a great knight. He must be. He is the father of Chimène, who, to be worthy of Rodrigue, must be the daughter of a fearless and generous man. Thus, the self-praise that Gomès indulges in, is, at the same time in some aspects, praise of Rodrigue; for Gomès is what Rodrigue will become — "le bras de l'état." Gomès acts as though in a hypnotic trance in which he is metamorphosed into the king. The cry, "Tout l'état périra, s'il faut que je périsse," (v. 378), demonstrates his total egocentricity.

Gomès becomes, as it were, a half-God. Now the scepter that Gomès thinks he sustains on his own is sustained by a Christian God. In creating his illusion, Gomès insults this God. The *Soufflet*, which Gomès gives to Don Diègue, is, by inference, given to God. Gomès has fractured the structure of the State. He will pay with his life.

Don Fernand, the real, the true half-God, appears for the first time in Act II, scene 6. His appearance is significant in that the anger of God is slow in making its presence felt, but it is irrevocable. It is here that Corneille states unequivocally an aspect of the role of the absolute monarch — that of judge. "Il [Gomès] verra ce que c'est que n'obéir pas," (v. 568), is a reminder to all that the subject's primary function is to obey.

Gomès, the great, the powerful, has, in one single act, become a traitor. Rodrigue will be the executioner for the State and God. This explains why Rodrigue, young and without experience, can kill the champion. God has inspired Rodrigue, and gives him the strength to sever the arm raised in defiance. Thus, the verse, "Ton bras est invaincu, mais non pas invincible," (v. 418), is fraught with deeper meaning and fills the spectator with pity for Gomès, because he has refused to admit to human weakness. Gomès's whole being is infused with the desire to live, the supreme trait of the Present, and yet, metaphorically, it commits suicide.

---

[14] Doubrovsky (p. 125) touches on this idea.

As has been suggested, the cycle of time shifts in *Le Cid*. After the death of Gomès, the Present passes to Don Fernand. He will not remain the Present. After Rodrigue's return, it is he who will become the Present (another Gomès in the best sense of the term). Don Fernand will replace Don Diègue as the Past and someone else, evidently the heir apparent, will become the Future.

As we move from a consideration of the Present to the Past in *Le Cid*, we find Don Diègue indulgent, concerned that justice be accomplished, laws obeyed, and past deeds not forgotten.

Don Diègue's task of seeking reconciliation should not, from any point of view, be difficult to effect. For him, the solution to all problems lies in the happy union between two young people in love. "Joignons d'un sacré noeud ma maison à la vôtre," (v. 166), he says to Gomès. This simple and dignified suggestion dissipates into thin air when the blow is struck. Attacked physically, stripped of his sword, Don Diègue's famous "Ô rage, Ô désespoir, Ô vieillesse ennemie," (v. 237), is assuredly the State, robbed of its virility, crying out in pain. [15]

It is not the Past but the Future that comes to the rescue of the fallen State. In the celebrated first meeting between father and son (I, 5), Don Diègue's question: "Rodrigue, as-tu du coeur?" (v. 261), is, symbolically, addressed to all the youth of France. Is youth ready to accept the concept of the absolute monarch? Rodrigue's answer, "Tout autre que mon père / L'éprouverait sur l'heure," (v. 262), is truly admirable. "Why do you speak to us in that fashion?" "Why doesn't the State have confidence in us?" "Doesn't the State understand that youth is perfectly aware of conditions created by the absolute monarch?" In the absolute monarchy everyone is happy.

Another function of the Past is to remind others that Duty is basic to a society governed by an absolute monarch. Passionate love, which is always prompt to bring free will into play, tends toward being a destructive force in such a society.

The fires of passion (*amour-plaisir-liberté*) are staunched by obedience (*devoir-honneur*). The ideal of justice created by Don Diègue

---

[15] P. Bénichou analyzes the problem in his chapter "Le drame politique dans Corneille," pp. 52-76, *Morales du Grand Siècle* (Paris, 1948). See also Bernard Dort, *Pierre Corneille dramaturge* (Paris, 1957), p. 45.

is a justice which crushes any being opposed to the State. The passion shared by Rodrigue and Chimène will divert itself, at least for him, into campaigns, battles and victories.

Don Diègue's admonition to his son, "Ton prince et ton pays ont besoin de ton bras," (v. 1072), becomes the motto of any absolute monarchy. Rodrigue weakens before his father's structured illusion. Rodrigue can, while transferring his physical desire to that of conquering the Moors, regain his individuality.

The role of Chimène before the Past is signally important. She symbolizes freedom for Rodrigue. Her presence is necessary, according to this viewpoint, from the moment of her father's death, who, in fact, is the only free person in the entire play. Gomès exercised his freedom in insulting the State. Chimène is the incarnation of that same spirit. The problem of protecting the rights of an individual in an absolute monarchy is ever present in *Le Cid*. If the monarch is a half-God and answerable to no one, how is justice accorded?

The king is the constant guardian of Free Will, which posits objective justice.[16] Chimène's fainting spells herald not only her love of Rodrigue, but also remind the audience of the very human tendency to doubt the king's true objectivity.

In part, then, Chimène's role is to prove the king's humanity. It is his humanity which assures proper expression to Free Will. That quality makes Don Fernand capable of judging and deciding. That is a reason why he assumes the role of Chimène's father. Don Diègue's function, in the scenes with Chimène, is to demonstrate the role of the Past as being that of reconciling freedom and judgment.

The Future, our third time, is nourished by Hope. The Hope that Rodrigue symbolizes is that of the reaffirmation of the absolute monarch. Hope chooses youth as its perch. Youth is characterized first and foremost by a remarkable concern with *Gloire* (Reputation).[17] What do I think of myself? What do others think of me? Rodrigue encounters *Gloire* from the beginning scenes. Chimène loves Rodrigue and is impatient to respond to her desires. The Infante is also consumed with desire. Her love serves to remind the State that Rodrigue is

---

[16] *Ibid.*, p. 51.

[17] For a recent and lucid survey of this problem, see J.-J. Gabas, "Remarques sur la notion de gloire dans le théâtre de Corneille," in *Essays presented to J. Heywood Thomas* (Cardiff, 1969), pp. 89-102.

worthy of any lady. Therefore, he is worthy of becoming the State's major warrior.[18]

Rodrigue is a man of unparalleled valor in Cupid's domain. What do men think of him? Don Gomès finds him brash; Don Diègue adores him; Don Sanche respects him, and Don Fernand esteems him capable of leading his armies. Adored, admired, honored, Rodrigue has been accepted. To exist in this happy state is a quality dear to youth and to the Future.

As Corneille depicts Rodrigue, he is somewhat proud in the presence of Don Gomès and his father, and humble with Chimène. Exaggeration is a further characteristic of youth sketched by Corneille. Rodrigue becomes a matamore and succeeds in virtually hypnotizing the court with the account of his conquest of the Moors (IV, 3). The tendency to exaggerate in matters concerning military exploits is balanced by those in love. Rodrigue pushes the test of his love of Chimène to extremes evidenced by visits to his fiancée's apartments.

The interplay and tensions created by the confrontation of the Present, the Past and the Future in *Le Cid* and their final peaceful co-existence form a veritable symphony enhanced by *sententiae*, the basic component of the Cornelian theater.

Corneille the theoretician speaks and writes about Time marked by the clock, but he turns his true genius to Man and Time, an obsession in his century.

---

[18] See Donald Sellstrom, "The Role of Corneille's Infanta," *The French Review*, XXXIX (1965), 234-240, for a similar opinion.

THE MONSTER IN MEDIAEVAL LITERATURE

URBAN TIGNER HOLMES
University of North Carolina

If any one of us feels superior over the credulity of mediaeval man who could believe in the existence of such things as monsters he should be reminded that early in October, 1970, at Achnahannet, Scotland, the Loch Ness Investigation Bureau closed its tenth season. During last summer a twenty-four hour watch was maintained. The Bureau received financial aid from the entrance fees of tourists who came to view photographs, records, equipment, and, if possible, the Loch Ness Monster himself. Additional funds were provided by the World Book Publishers in Chicago. At the same time another expedition was at Drumnarochit and Urquhart on the same lake, where other efforts of a similar kind also were in progress during those months. This second group of scientists was a bit more pugnacious. They used recordings of love sounds and mating lures from genuine, extant sea animals, large in size; these records were played as come-ons. The backer of this second venture is an American firm that imports Black and White whiskey. (It might be added in jest that this sponsor could have helped his research by keeping the observers well supplied with the product that has already brought him fame and fortune.)

I will now come quickly to our main point. This present paper could be titled "St. Augustine; understanding of what is meant by the concept of a monster, and how this concept has been used in mediaeval fictional writing." It may be asked why I am concerned with this subject which is quite far removed from my usual interests. It is because I have been for several years preparing a book on the mediaeval man's concept of human nature. In the summer of 1969

I was reading in Rabanus Maurus' *De Universo* (composed c. 846) and I came upon this passage: [1]

> Portents seem to be contrary to Nature, but the Divine Will is in operation within everything established in Nature. A Portent, therefore, is not against Nature but against what is *considered Nature*. Portents, *ostenta*, *monstra*, or *prodigia* are so called because they show what is due to come to pass. *Monstrum* is derived from the verb *monstrare* "to show" hence it shows the significance of what will presently appear.... Such Portents exist, some with a size of body far beyond that of ordinary Man, others because of the crookedness of the whole body, are like dwarfs which the Greeks called Pigmies because they are only a cubit high. [2] Some monsters have an excess of one part, others a lack of the same. We must believe that whatever truly exists, and is described as a mutation of Nature, can exist only through the will and command of God, who disposes everything justly and rightly — for God is just in all his ways and holy in all his works. [3]

The principal matter in this statement by Rabanus it that a *monstrum* or monster is sent by God who alone can alter Nature to make such creatures. These are sent as omens, or portents, leading up to some important event that is to follow. Wilful change of the regularity of Nature can be made as God wills, but only by God. Giants and dwarfs are the commonest of such prodigies. The word *monstrum* derives from *monstrare* "to show." (Linguists today accept this as the correct etymology, deriving *monstrare*, in turn, from *monere*, "to warn"). [4]

St. Augustine, the greatest theologian of the Middle Ages, stressed this interpretation and Rabanus Maurus has used him as his source. We will quote directly from *The City of God*: [5]

> Just as it is possible for God to create any kind of Nature that he chooses, even so it is no less plausible for him to alter any qualities in his creations that he may wish to change.

---

[1] Migne, P. L. CXI, Ch. 7: De Portentis.

[2] *Ibid.*, cols. 195-6.

[3] *Ibid.*, col. 199.

[4] C. T. Onions, *The Oxford Dictionary of English Etymology* (Oxford, 1966).

[5] *City of God*, trans. Marcus Dods, Modern Library (New York, 1950), 243-79; 530-32.

It is from this basis that there has grown a whole forest of Portents or Monsters which the Pagans call *monstra, ostenta, portentia,* and *prodigia*. There have been so many different kinds of these that merely to recall them would make it impossible for me ever to finish this work.... It is also asked whether we are to believe that certain monstrous races of mankind, spoken of in secular history, had sprung from Noah's sons, or father, I should say, from that one man Adam from whom we are all descended. It is reported that some such races have only one eye in the middle of the forehead; some have their feet turned backwards from the heel; some are double sexed: the right breast that of a man, the left that of a woman — thus they alternately beget and give birth; still other races are said to be but a cubit high and are therefore called by the Greeks Pigmies.... There is a race also where the individuals have two feet but only one leg. These are marvellously swift though they do not bend the knee. They are called Skiapods, because in the hot weather they lie on their backs and shade themselves with their feet... What shall I say of the Cynophali, whose dog-like heads and barking proclaim them to be beasts and not men?.... But whosoever is born a man, that is, a rational mortal animal, no matter what unusual appearance he presents in color, movement, sound, no matter how peculiar he is in some part, power, or quality of his nature, no Christian man doubts that this being springs from the one protoplasm. We can distinguish common human nature from that which is peculiar and therefore wonderful. This applies also to entire races. However, we must examine this matter cautiously and guardedly, admitting that sometimes such things have been told about races that have never had any existence; in addition, some of these peoples when they do exist are not really humans but beasts; but when they are human they are necessarily all descended from Adam.

Many such details given by St. Augustine are mentioned elsewhere, but we are giving him credit for being the chief authority in the eleventh and twelfth centuries. The ancient Latin Grammarians were already aware that the word *monstrum* was derived from *monstrare* "to show." The grammarian Festus who wrote on the history of words at the beginning of the Christian Era says:

Monstrum comes from *monendo*, because a *monstrum* shows what is to be in the future, and advises on the will of the gods. *Monstra* is the name of creatures who depart from the mode of Nature, such as a snake with feet, a bird which has four wings, a man with two heads, a liver which disintegrates when it is cooked.[6]

The mediaeval philosophers followed this and taught that Nature reflects the divine Forms in a progressive and orderly way. John of Salisbury has this opinion when he states, "Natural laws are a sequence of causes... in all perceptible things... nothing happens except as a result of natural causation. One cannot always see... but the will of God is the First Cause of all."[7] Adelard of Bath, Bernard Sylvester, William of Conches, and Yvo of Chartres define Nature in this way. Violations of Nature's norms come only from a wilful act of God. Of course, the Devil has the power to create illusions. God has given the Devil some latitude in the deception and temptation of Man, but these illusions are just that — they are not real. They can disappear before the Sign of the Cross.

One kind of Monster is where a human is transferred into a bird or beast. St. Augustine says of this: "Such things as these may be false, so extraordinary as to be with good reason disbelieved... but it is to be firmly trusted that Almighty God *can* do whatsoever he pleases whether in punishing or in favoring... the demons, on the other hand, can accomplish nothing by their own natural power (but only what God wills them to do).... I cannot believe that even the body, much less the mind, can really be changed into bestial form and lineaments by any reason, art, power of the demons. In that case it would be only a phantasm of a man; but juggleries of this sort would not be difficult for demons if they were only allowed to do so by the judgment of God."[8]

In his "On the god of Socrates" Apuleius had said two hundred years before St. Augustine, when deploring the evils of magic:

> I do not refer to these extraordinary accidents which occur from time to time and which result from the unknown powers of Nature arranged and ordered by Divine Providence, such as the birth of abnormal animals and freakish phenomena of earth and air which are always terrifying and sometimes in-

---

[6] In *Glossaria Latina*, ed. J. W. Pirie and W. M. Lindsay (Hildesheim, 1965), pp. 200, 274, 349.

[7] John of Salisbury, *Metalogicon*, tr. D. D. McGarry (Berkeley, 1952), 28-30.

[8] *City of God*, 623-625.

jurious, and which crafty demons falsely claim can be produced and mitigated by magical rites.[9]

It is customary for scholars to refer to all the strange animals found in mediaeval writings as Bestiary lore. We know that some of the Bestiary animals, in many instances, had no real existence, but most of them were commonplace types in mediaeval art and literature; they were not shocking. We are referring to such creatures as the unicorn, the griffin, and the phoenix.[10] Gerald the Welshman, in the twelfth century, answered the criticisms levelled at him that he sometimes distorted Nature and God's creations in his descriptive book on Ireland. He replied that we are not always sure what God's norm was in many cases.[11] I add that this was particularly the case with serpentine and crawly creatures. Some of the strange Bestiary animal forms were "monstrous" — combinations of two or more animal or bird forms, but with the exception of those I have just listed by name (unicorn, griffin, and phoenix) they are not often mentioned outside of Bestiaries, and no evil is attached to them. The idea that certain animals and monstrous figures are associated with evil is probably very ancient. Perhaps such an association began in the *Phaedrus,* or its possible predecessors, when evil nature was first assigned to many of the creatures. Fables continued which were used to satirize certain evil types of men. Lucretius, St. Basil, and St. Ambrose all had their part in attributing the illustration of moral truths to animal forms. The concept that a thing is abhorrent which does not conform to the common patterns of nature is deeply bred in us since the "age of the Fauns and the Satyrs," so we need not pause too long over this matter. Our contention is that this is not owed primarily to the mediaeval Bestiaries.

A distinguished art critic, V. H. Debidor, has something to say on this:[12]

---

[9] *Ibid.,* 260.

[10] Florence McCulloch, *Mediaeval Latin and French Bestiaries* (Chapel, Hill, N. C., 1960). Most of the monsters with which we are presently concerned are modified human beings and not animals.

[11] *Opera Omnia* (Rolls Series), VI, 163.

[12] *Le Bestiaire sculpté du moyen âge en France* (B. Arthaud, 1961), pp. 348-9. I owe this reference to my associate J. R. Danos.

> ...dans la perspective chrétienne du Moyen Age, ces monstres ne sont que des contours d'ombre que trace l'absence ou le refus de la lumière de Dieu: parce qu'ils sont du règne des ténèbres, ils attestent le royaume de lumière; parce que Dieu est vivant, ils sont contre-vivants, d'une vitalité à la mesure de Celle qu'ils contre-balancent, perpétuellement invaincus dans le temps, mais à jamais vaincus dans l'éternité. En déchaînant ce bestiaire maléfique dont il semble hanté, halluciné, possédé, le Moyen Age remporte sur le mal la victoire-clef qu'appelle la phrase baudelairienne: "la plus belle des ruses du diable est de nous persuader qu'il n'existe pas."
>
> Mais les bêtes médiévales sont aussi filles et servantes de la lumière: elles obéissent à Dieu depuis le premier chapitre de la Genèse jusqu'au dernier de l'Apocalypse.... Ils racontent ils chantent la Geste de Dieu....

It must be remembered too that strictly speaking all animals were closer to God because, unlike us, they did not have original sin, or Free Will which could be turned towards evil.

In studying the mediaeval use of Bestiary and monstrous figures in the graphic arts we are also face to face with the schools of thought represented by Emile Mâle and Henri Focillon — the Anecdote versus the Arabesque. Were these strange animals found in mediaeval sculptures related to anecdotal meaning, or were they merely designs of line and form? Both viewpoints must be true; but it *is* important that in some instances common Bestiary and monstrous forms expressed design only.

We return to St. Augustine on the subject of animals. Again we quote from him: [13]

> There is a question about all those kinds of beasts which are not domesticated, which are not produced like frogs out of the earth but are propagated by male and female parents, such as wolves and other animals of that kind; it is asked how they could be found in widely separated islands after the Deluge, in which all the animals not in the Ark perished. The breeds had to be restored from those that were preserved in pairs, in the Ark. It might indeed be said of those very near the mainland that they crossed to the islands by swimming after the Flood; but there are some islands so far that we do not fancy any animals could swim to them...

---

[13] *loc. cit.*, p. 530.

it cannot be denied that by the intervention of angels they could have been transferred by God's order or permission. If, however, they were produced from the earth as of their first creation, when God said, "Let the whole earth bring forth the living creatures," this makes it more evident that all kinds of animals were preserved in the Ark not so much for the sake of restoring their stock, as for prefiguring the various nations that were to be saved in the church....

It is clear from this that St. Augustine thought all animals were descended from the pairs preserved in the Ark, just as all genuine humans were descended from Adam and thereby from the sons of Noah. Such normal, natural things could be altered in individual cases only to suit God's will — for a purpose.

But all human beings have a soul, and the beasts do not. This is a great difference and we do not believe that mediaeval men were confused on this point. A creature that had a soul was baptizable. In the Old Portuguese *Livro dos Linhagems* (13th century) a seawoman is captured and is immediately baptized with the name Marinha. She gives birth to normal children. Her mate is in despair because she cannot talk; he tricks her into shrieking and at that point a piece of meat (a polyp?) falls out of her mouth and she can speak thereafter. Her mate now finds her worthy of marriage. [14]

In Chrétien's *Yvain* there is the giant herdsman whom Calogrenant sees. [15] He is ugly and hideous and Calogrenant refers to him as a Moor. He is seated on the stump of a tree with a great club in his hand. Calogrenant says, "I approached the peasant, and saw that he had a head larger than that of a horse or any other beast; his hair was bushy and his forehard was without hair, more than a span (nine inches) in width. He had large hairy ears like an elephant, great bushy eyebrows and a flattish face, with the eyes of an owl and the nose of a cat; his mouth opened wide like that of a wolf and he had the teeth of a wild boar, sharp and yellow — a black beard, twisted mustaches, a chin that touched on his chest, and a spine that was long and humped." This creature might well have been a beast; so Calogrenant said, "I thought he could not speak and had no power of

---

[14] In K. S. Roberts, *Anthology of Old Portuguese* (Lisbon, n.d.), 59-60.
[15] Chrétien de Troyes (ed. Foerster), *Yvain*, vv. 288-407.
[16] The pertinent words here are in vv. 328-32.

reason." Reason, of course, comes from the soul. When asked what he was the figure replied, "I am a man." This reassured Calogrenant that he was from God — a portent. He asked further, "What kind of man are you?" "None other than what you now see." There were different kinds of human beings, sent as portents from God. This strange figure was, therefore, no devilish phantasy. There is something similar in the *Aucassin et Nicolette*. [17] The vital turning point in that story comes just after Aucassin also has encountered a monstrous peasant. "Big he was and marvellously ugly and hideous; he had a great bushy head of hair more black than charcoal, and there was more than a full span between his eyes. He had huge cheeks, wide nostrils, a huge flat nose, coarse lips more red than a hot coal, and big yellow teeth." Aucassin was afraid but he spoke to him, "God help you fair brother!" "May God bless you," said the other.... This exchange of salutations established the fact that the creature was no mere illusion from the demons. We have thought that this scene was a parody of the one portrayed in the *Yvain*, but we are not sure.

It would be best for us to keep away from Chrétien's Grail romance, a narrative which it has been so difficult to interpret, but it will be recalled just the same that Perceval's adventures take a decisive new turn only after the coming of the Hideous Damsel on the scene. [18] Surely she also was a portent. In the *Erec* it was surely the dwarf accompanying Yder who turned Erec into his series of adventures. [19] There is the dwarf and the cart in the *Lancelot*. [20] Is that not a portent rather than a Celtic inspiration? St. Augustine very definitely defined dwarfs as portents. In Marie de France's *Lais* there are portents at the right places. In the *Guigemar* it is an albino hind, with the antlers of a stag, who speaks and sends Guigemar on into his adventures of suffering for the sake of love. [21] She has other kinds of portents which appear at the crucial moments. In *Lanval* there are fairy women. [22] In the *Yonec* there is a hawk which is really a man, with soul and other human attributes. [23] Other elements in this story

---

[17] Ed. R. W. Linker, XXIV.
[18] *Perceval* (ed. W. Roach), vv. 4613-44.
[19] *Erec* (ed. Foerster), 145-233.
[20] *Lancelot* (ed. Foerster), vv. 347-67, 4501-07.
[21] Marie de France (ed. Ewert), *Guigemar*, vv. 89-122.
[22] *Lanval*, vv. 44-194.
[23] *Yonec*, vv. 105 ff.

attest that he was sent by God. He takes the Sacrament before he touches the lady. We must not labor this point too hard, but remember that in *Eliduc* the appearance of the marvellous stoat who resusscitates its mate portends a change in relationship between Eliduc and his loving wife. His wife is moved to such magnificent generosity that she gives up her husband, without a murmur, to his new love — an act of supreme generosity beyond the ordinary.

We are not making a great claim. We are merely suggesting that in these monster episodes, which we moderns ordinarily label as miscellaneous marvels, often with an overtone of Evil, there are meaningful warnings in the sense established by St. Augustine and others.

In Graubünden, Switzerland, there is a wonderful ceiling of painted wooden panels in the Church of St. Martin at Zillis.[25] This succession of 153 paintings, made in the twelfth century, portrays the life of Christ, followed by seven others giving scenes from the life of the patron, St. Martin. There is a border of forty-eight squares which runs entirely around the outer edge of these ceiling pictures. In these, we are told, are: "Fabelwesen mit Fischschwänzen und Nereiden mit Instrumenten als Sinnbilder des Bösen, Dämonischen unverführerischen." Why should such devilish forms be surrounding the life of Christ? It is my belief that these monsters, which are *not* Bestiary animals, were placed there to call attention to the Worldshaking Coming of our Lord, and also to St. Martin the patron of that Church.

Perhaps there is some continuation of this in Folklore when an individual believes his good luck is altered to bad when, in the morning, he meets a deformed person — a monster — who thus ruins his day. But change of luck, of course, could be for the Good more often than for the Evil. In mediaeval stories and sculpture the writer and artist could certainly have been aware that a change of direction in the career of the protagonist could be well punctuated by the intervention of a monstrous portent.

We are not prepared to say much about Dante at this point, but it is notable that the divisions of Dante's Hell — upper Hell, City of Dis, Punishment of Violence, Fraud, and Treason, are emphasized by

---

[24] *Eliduc*, vv. 1031-33.
[25] Erwin Poeschel, *Die romanischen deckengemälde von Zillis* (Erlenbach, E. Rentsch, 1941).

monsters. At the beginning of the upper region there is Minos (not the judge of *Aeneid* VI, 432, but a monster who girds himself with his tail). Cerberus is at the entrance to the Third Circle (gluttony), Pluto (like Minos, transformed into a monster) is at the entrance to the Fourth Circle. At the gates of the city of Dis are the Furies. The Minotaur, the Centaurs, and Harpies are in the desert of Violence. At the edge of the great barrier with its waterfall, Virgil and Dante find Geryon, who conveys them to the Fraudulent. Standing at the edge of the lowest reach of Hell are the Giants.

ANATOLE FRANCE AND THE HERITAGE OF JEAN JACQUES ROUSSEAU

H. R. HUSE
University of North Carolina

The Noble Citizen

When Jean Jacques Rousseau was developing his paradoxical philosophy, he chose as his starting point the assumption that man is fundamentally good. In America, we have generally accepted this flattering dictum. We are not unaware that the Devil, through his wiles, sometimes gets into us, but we are convinced that man was created in the divine image, that he knows right from wrong, and that he is at least wise enough to understand his own interest. This is the rock or sand on which we have erected our democratic institutions and the framework of our beliefs. Nearly all we do or think politically implies faith in man's honesty, justice, and good sense, in freewill and moral responsibility, and in the sacred rights of the sovereign majority.

Anatole France attempted to destroy the structure of beliefs which Rousseau and his followers built on the most gratuitous, arbitrary, and vain of assumptions. France's philosophic system, if it can be called a system, is Rousseauism upside down.

Imitating the precedent of Rousseau, France proclaims as loudly as he can the very opposite fundamental assumption, that is, that man is essentially bad. In so arbitrary a matter, he realizes that no argument or apology is necessary. Epithets can only be matched. Whether man is "good" or "bad" depends at best upon a viewpoint, an assumed relationship. We can take as representatives of our kind the heroes, geniuses, and martyrs of the past or present, or, on the other hand, we can look down on those beneath us. Our attitude must vary accordingly. Even a clown doubtless appears godlike to his dog.

In any case, Anatole France chooses the superior viewpoint, and throughout his work is content to match the Rousseauistic affirmations of man's goodness with equally emphatic denials. He is never weary of asserting that man is selfish, cowardly, perfidious, gluttonous, and lecherous. "Why else would redemption have been necessary?" "Do we not all descend from this venerable Eve in whom all our ignoble instincts have their august source?" That there may be in some unknown world beings still more vicious than men seems to him possible although almost inconceivable. In a dozen places he affirms calmly that men are monkeys or ferocious beasts.

The best he can say is that some individuals do have talents and rise above the mass. And yet this talent is precisely what human nature usually pardons least. "In talent there is an insolence that is expiated amid dull hatred and profound calumny." Talent, moreover, is exclusive to a very small number. "What is called the genius of a people reaches consciousness only in imperceptible minorities, in a few individuals who think with greater force and precision than the others."

A late, and apparently serious remark, is as follows: "I believe men generally worse than they appear to be. I have rarely opened a door inadvertently without discovering a spectacle which made me look at humanity with disgust, pity, or horror."

To many, these assertions will appear at best ill-tempered and ungenerous. Our natural inclination is to look up at man. We are all born humble and insignificant. To reach a superior viewpoint we must grow above the level of most of our fellows, which is statistically impossible for the majority. So we tend toward a haughty conception of man. The village housewife finds nothing more natural than the dignity of local celebrities, and no politician ever hints even to the crudest of crowds that men are monkeys. Rousseau's viewpoint was destined to be popular, and it will remain popular for many a year.

Still, it is one thing for a servant girl to believe in her angelic descent and in man's greatness, and another for a philosopher to assume this view, — that is, for a leader of thought, a man who, by profession, places himself on an eminence. In the latter case we suspect either presumption or lack of candor. In a moment of irritation, Anatole France called Rousseau a *plat coquin*, (a platitudinous rascal) and certainly no superior mind nowadays can share the Rousseaustic notions of the virtuous savage or his sentimental illusions about Nature. We have learned something of our origin and our atavism. We admit our relationship to our humble ancestors.

But even if the superior viewpoint were not more candid it would be preferable. A curious paradox is involved. An exalted conception of man, strangely, is not only a source of childish illusions, but of cruelties, suffering, and injustice. The political and other beliefs which have caused most blood to flow are precisely those which assume that we are rational beings, that we can distinguish clearly between right and wrong, and that our purpose on this earth is to regain our angelic stature. On this point Anatole France is insistent:

> Yes, I have a poor opinion of man, and it is to be hoped that no one should have any other. Otherwise, beware for the human race! Reformers will exact too much. Have you not noticed that the greatest cruelties, the most horrible massacres have been inspired by the idea that man is fundamentally good and virtuous? The little lawyers and quack doctors who led the French Revolution and who drowned France in blood wished precisely to restore primal goodness. They lacked the benevolence and indulgence which a sense of human infirmities gives...

> Pride and hatred in the fierce heart of man wish to settle domestic and other difficulties by murder and carnage. The true science of life is a benevolent scorn for men. Let us be humble... Let us not believe ourselves excellent... When you wish to make men good, wise, free, moderate, and generous, you are brought fatally to wishing to kill them all.

The Lands of the Free

We have all learned in school the slogans, psalms, and sacred formulas of democratic idealism. A sentimental republicanism, faith in the common man, certain egalitarian notions have become a part of ourselves: they determine our viewpoints, the climate and complexion of our minds. We sing hymns to Freedom, listen gravely to such phrases as "Give me Liberty or give me Death!" and we think of the French and our own revolutions as their leaders conceived them, namely, as the institution of equality and of virtue upon the earth. Yet, it has become more and more painfully obvious that our society has not become classless, that privileged groups remain, and that the reign of equality and justice is still a dream.

Just what was accomplished by the revolution to which we are taught from the cradle to sing our praise? According to Anatole France, it displaced one class from the seat of power in favor of another. And, in elevating the bourgeois, it instituted the reign of money and the rise of the acquisitive.

Anatole France, like many others, dismissed lightly the high-sounding virtues of the new era, the sonorous abstractions and pious moralizing which served as a smoke-screen for the tyranny of wealth. Words did not deceive him. He sought out the crude realities hidden within verbal thickets. And the more he contemplated the acquisitive in their triumph — the pigs at the trough — the less he liked them. The best he could say of the new rulers was that "they had guillotined the frivolous virtues," that they had proscribed the "facile smile."

Certainly in an absolute sense Liberty cannot exist in society since it is not in nature. Not an animal is free. Many of the poor beasts have only the freedom to flee as best they can from their enemies whose food they ultimately become. Thus have the gods decided. We are free to work out our destiny with the sweat of our brows and to serve our masters, whether these masters are ideas or tangible tyrants such as kings, employers, spellbinders, the "power élites," or the Pentagon.

Nevertheless, some might object that democratic liberty does imply certain concrete privileges for everyone. The *lettres de cachet* have disappeared, and other subtler forms of compulsion have taken their place. Viewed from a distance, the change appears as a transference of power from the government to other hands. The freedom of the press, for instance, is quite real in the sense that editors can now thumb their noses at the government and even mock their public, but their subservience to their sources of income hardly stops this side of prostitution.

"It is a question whether the poor are not oppressed when the government is weak." The freedom from interference that big business demands of government so insistently is often its own freedom to exploit the weak, the innocent, and gullible. Often the difference between liberty and licence depends upon whose actions and interests are involved.

... ...

A more important matter is the cornerstone of democracy, the right of the majority to decide all questions. Here was a fine plan to insure the greatest happiness for the greatest number. It assumed that the common man knows his own interest. But the public seldom knows what it wants: it must be told. It has no strength; it is unintelligent and inert. Crowds have at all times showed a superior aptitude for servitude.

"Soverignty should reside in science, not in the people." "A stupidity repeated by thirty-six million tongues is still a stupidity." We laugh at the fiction of the divine right of kings, blind to the fictions on which governments supposedly by the people, for the people, and of the people, are based.

The system of representation, by means of which the majority exerts its power, is an expedient compromise with necessity. This device usually elevates to power not the learned, scientific, and philosophical, but demagogues and spellbinders who understand instinctively the art of manipulating the gullible masses. The business of representing others becomes primarily a means for feathering one's own nest. All clamor for the sacrifice.

The abbé Coignard, one of France's spokesmen, foresees the effect of legislative control of government:

> Demos will have neither the obstinate prudence of a Henri IV nor the propitious inertia of a Louis XIII. Ministers will be called upon to execute vague desires that the legislatures themselves will not fully understand. They will be resigned to talking instead of acting. Statesmen will become rhetoricians. Talent would ruin them. They will have to make an effort to speak without saying anything, and the least stupid will be obliged to lie more than the others. Executives will grow pale and impotent in the sad attempt to read orders for acting on the five hundred faces of a legislature.

... ...

But representative government is not without its influence. One effect is "to discourage the good and to make the incompetent ambitious." "On all sides ambitious incompetence will rise from the depths of rural obscurity to the highest positions in the state, and, since probity is not natural to man, but must be cultivated with great care, swarms of grafters will descend upon the public treasury." Republics, moreover, are costly, since there are always so many poor relatives of the men in power to provide for.

The Age of the Plutocrats

The ultimate justification for what we call democracies is the equality of opportunity they are supposed to afford. But, although the revolution removed one set of artificial barriers, others have developed. Opportunities for swindling are abundant, and the acquisitive can pursue their talents almost unrestrained, but there is less chance for the successful pursuit of other abilities. And even in trade and industry the inheritance of a few millions and the opportunity to develop the manners and mental habits of the ruling class are advantages the poor boy cannot always and everywhere overcome.

Equality of opportunity is an article of faith which reacts favorably on the character of believers. It gives pride to the individual, a power of self-assertion, and prevents others from trampling on his susceptibilities with impunity. He must be treated with deference and swindled with flattery. There is perhaps an advantage in this; — and yet what appalling misery this faith has entailed! Since everyone is as good as everyone else, no artificial restrictions of class or birth impose a check upon desires and energies. The peasant of the *ancien régime* probably tortured himself little with thoughts of what the nobles enjoyed: his hopes, ambitions, and consequently his desires were limited. Now the great business is keeping up with the Joneses. The cruel, wearing, incessant, pushing, inexorable competition goes on. Our advertisers understand the obsession: years ago they ceased talking about quality and price. Instead they show the humiliation of non-buyers, and fan the envy of the noble citizen. Anatole France noticed this characteristic of modern democratic life:

> Democratic life leaves a great margin for desire. It permits Jeanne Avril and Catherine Duval [average girls] to entertain vast hopes: it offers them a new 'perhaps'. It excites ambitions by multiplying chances. In that way it enervates and depraves. It creates neurotics, morphino-maniacs, psychopathic cases. As a climax to the misery, the conditions of the struggle have become more painful than formerly. By authorizing all hopes, the new society excites all energies. The combat for existence is more bitter than ever, victory more insolent, defeat more inexorable.

Everywhere, with the illusion of equality of opportunity, one finds frustration, restlessness and instability. Where a hundred per cent of the population is clamoring to enter the charmed circle of the two or five per cent at the top, the triumph of the few is insolent, the failure of the many, certain.

... ...

The complaint, in any case, is hardly against democracy, since that condition has not yet been realized. Our modern industrial republics cannot be conceived as true democracies. The nobles were dispossessed for the sake of profiteers and business men, and the exalted principles have served mainly as a smoke-screen.

Moreover, while abuses occur in all forms of government, this plutocracy has some peculiarly dismal features. The principal iniquity is the separation of power from responsibility which the abstractions and formulas of democracy permit. The result is hypocrisy and a pervasive fraudulence. An American observer, Edgar Lee Masters, complained:

> Our whole national life is one of falsehood, dishonesty, and hypocrisy. Monopolies control the means of life and are specially armed by law to do so; and this bears doubly hard upon the thinkers whose minds are preoccupied with thinking for the race instead of getting something for themselves. Business is a form of larceny.... All this life of lying, swindling, and pretending is coupled with the loudest psalm-singing in the world.

Anatole France's criticism is no less pointed:

> Seeing clearly I perceive that beings who have no moral or intellectual superiority oppress the others. If societies wish to be founded on the suffering of the weak, the strong should produce, excel, sacrifice themselves in order to merit their privileges. But we persist in living under inequality while our mediocrity is equal, and while there reigns everywhere the same avidity to enjoy grossly and with exaggeration.

Inequalities would be easier to bear if accompanied by real distinction. But there is none. It is difficult to perceive the dignity of certain of our bankers and tycoons, or of the *Mafiosi*.

Anatole France contrasts the present age with the past:

> Capitalists have come after the Knights of the Holy Sepulchre, after the paladins, the great doctors, the warriors, the saints, the heroes. Having no foundation, no true moral capital, society revolts. How to restrain the crowd henceforth? Everyone demands happiness and believes that it consists in eating well, in having private vehicles, — not in hoping, in being resigned, in feeling oneself a part of the family of the universe. We preserve some vague words which correspond to no reality, such as Love and Fraternity, but we have lost the sense of them, or we give them a stupid or expedient meaning.
>
> Together with Faith and Hope we have lost Charity, the three virtues which, like three ships with the image of the Holy Virgin at their prows, carried poor souls over the ocean of life. They have all gone down in the same tempest. Who will bring us a new faith, a new hope, and a new charity?
>
> Sick physically, denatured by dint of civilization, perishing from cancers and tuberculosis, infirm morally, society seems to me in danger. And since it shows itself without virtue, without genius, without great men, without enthusiasm, and abounds in misery and suffering, it is worthy of perishing.

Before the first world war, when all seemed relatively rosy, Anatole France wrote as follows:

> People do not perceive that the world is crumbling. This however, is quite visible. The world, every world, lives on ideals. But the sum of idealism seems exhausted, spent. Nothing sustains us any more, and our hypocritical civilization is a mass of iniquities in ruins. Formerly people lived on beliefs, heroism, intelligence. They lived savagely, but with ardor.... In the Middle Ages, the slogans were to compose songs, to crusade, to withdraw from the world. Today our horrible ideals are to succeed, to bluff, to combine. Nothing resists them. People no longer know how to think, how to write, and, apart from political eloquence which is the art of deceiving with words, of promising without keeping the promise, of throwing dust in others' eyes, nothing exists.

Ahead of Spengler, and before the present disorder, Anatole France developed the pessimism which is now so generally shared:

I see ignorant frivolity, noisy vanity extinguish the light of European civilization as they extinguished the light of ancient civilization.... We are in the condition in which the Roman world found itself on the eve of the barbarian invasions. A world is ending and a new world begins.... The fruitless strength of capitalistic Europe cannot last for very long.

The Majesty of the Law

Anatole France, who plays with many abstractions, could hardly neglect the law by means of which the rights of persons and of classes are sanctioned, and which give force, often a cruel force, to the dictates of a conventional morality or of economic advantage.

Anatole France believed that laws, like moral beliefs, are not universal, fixed, and absolute, or based upon reason, but relative, expedient, and contingent. As a product of social life, law depends upon the changing conditions of that life. Constitutions and codes vary according to time and place. In some societes even infanticide and the killing of the old have been permitted. After revolutions, whole series of laws are annulled and others are substituted in their place. "When men have put you outside the law, they are the law, as you became the law when you overthrew the tyrant who was the law before you." The sanction of law is really the power of the group that proclaims it.

> Legal justice is the sanction of established injustices. Was it ever seen opposed to conquerors and contrary to usurpers? When an illegitimate power arises, the law has only to recognize it to make it legitimate. Everything is a matter of form, and often between guilt and innocence, there is only the thickness of a sheet of legal paper.

Children are sometimes beaten by their playmates because they are weak. That, says Anatole France, is an excellent reason: "childhood has an implacable logic." When the peddler, Crainquebille, was arrested for crying out *"Mort aux vaches,"* ("Death to the police!"), his fault was in not being stronger. "If he had had himself declared emperor, dictator, president of the Republic, or even a municipal counselor, he would not have been condemned to fifteen days in prison and a fine of fifty francs." But Crainquebille was not a Mussolini. Vagrants and vagabonds are imprisoned for being in the very situation in which St. Francis, "the best of saints," placed all his followers. "Mendicancy is forbidden only to the poor."

A Tooth for a Tooth

The story of M. Aristide, a gentleman fond of hunting, illustrates the subjectivity of our ideas of justice. One day this kindly man saw a cat killing a song-bird. His keen sense of justice is outraged at this brutal act, and, full of horror and indignation, he avenges the wrong by shooting the cat.

Anatole France agrees that, at first sight, it is pleasant to see warblers saved and their brutal enemies punished. But the justice of this execution is not so clear if you look closely at the matter. In this case the cat, a hunter like M. Aristide, might also have believed in the doctrine of first causes and have supposed that all song-birds were hatched purposely for him.

In France's opinion, there are really no good and bad men. Nor is there any justice among men. "The laws are made by the rich and powerful for the conservation of power and riches." "What men decorate with the name of justice is, in reality, only a minister of base prudence and cruel vengeance." "Human laws are the daughters of anger and fear."

> Justice in the philosophical sense of the word is nothing: in the vulgar sense it is the saddest of virtues. No one wants it. Faith offers Mercy in place of it, and Nature, Love. It is enough for a man to call himself 'just' to inspire a veritable aversion. Retributive justice is a horror to persons and things. In human society it is only a mechanism, indispensible certainly, and therefore respectable, but cruel, surely, since it has no other function than to punish, and since it puts jailors and hangmen to work.
>
> As for abstract justice, one wearies of the struggle, resigned never to seize this fugitive swifter than the light, announced everywhere, found nowhere, not even in the heavens which are also an eternal theater of carnage and death, where astronomy shows us the pitiless action of the same laws of life by means of which evil is perpetuated on earth.

Anatole France prefers simple "theophages" who do not know what they are saying or doing to fanatical scribblers of laws "who use the guillotine to make us virtuous and wise and to incline us to admire the Supreme Being who has made these legislators in his image."

Poverty and Crime

"The poor believe that there is one law for the rich and another for them. This is not strictly correct. Burglary is forbidden to the rich and poor alike. Still, the law weighs lightly on the rich, and the connection between poverty and crime is so intimate as to make the two almost inseparable."

France knew nothing of the higher reaches of crime, of the contemporary gangsters who have learned that the main duty in American life is to cease to be an underdog, to get on, to make money, and who have risen from overalls to be "big men." Instead, he considered mainly, besides political crimes, the usual run of felonies and misdemeanors. "The indelicacy of many of these acts, the grossness they reveal, rob the perpetrators of sympathy." But France observes that "probity and delicacy are infinitely easier to attain when you lack nothing than when you are despoiled of everything."

France believed that there is little guilt but only misfortune, and that laws and customs have always been harsh toward the poor. And, like M. Bergeret, he believed "that men are less ferocious when they are less poor...."

Moral Responsibility

Men have never believed whole-heartedly in freedom of the will. Philosophers have differed on this point. We have seen sons, victims of their heredity or environment, follow in their fathers' footsteps too often to believe that actions always represent a deliberate and unconditioned choice. "Christianity has endeavored to reconcile free-will with divine predestination without any notable success." And now the doctrine of determinism has at least lightly influenced us all. "The doctrine of moral responsibility is shaken in the firmest minds."

> Our sentiments are formed of a thousand things which escape us through their smallness, and the destiny of our immortal soul depends sometimes upon a breath too light to bend a blade of grass. We are the playthings of the winds.
>
> A mysterious step-mother determines at our birth all our acts, all the thoughts of our life, and we will be happy and good only in so far as she has wished it.... All is mystery in man, and we can know nothing that is not man. The doctrine of the irresponsibility of criminals is not a dangerous

novelty. Even if it should prevail, our laws would not be noticeably modified. Why? Because codes are based on necessity, and not on justice... There are in man obscure forces anterior to him, acting independently of his will, and that he cannot always master.

War and Peace

The First World War revealed to Anatole France more closely than all his previous experience how precarious human intelligence is. "This fragile flower which we have possessed for so short a time, bends and withers under the blast of great emotions." "We no longer listen to logic, we hear only our hatreds and our hopes."

... ...

Having no illusions about men, Anatole France perceives that the masses wage war willingly and with pleasure. "War takes men away from their wives, from the boredom of domestic life. It assures them wine, regular pay, a chance to see a bit of the country, and puts them in the path of adventures."

> Compare war and peace. The labors of peace are long, monotonous, often painful, and without glory for most of those who indulge in them; the actions of war are prompt, facile, within the grasp of the most obtuse intellect.

"Military service impresses men as the simplest, crudest, and most forceful expression of duty. It imposes on their imagination by the glamor and brilliance of the equipment used, by the amount of metal consumed; and it exalts finally by furnishing the only images of power, grandeur, and glory that most men are capable of imagining." Consequently they rush into war singing — or else are put in by force.

> Whether white or yellow, every race thinks itself the first in the world. Every people is belligerent and takes pleasure in carnage. When carnage is organized, it is called war, and passes for the most beautiful, most noble, and most advantageous occupation in the world.

Even the mild M. Bergeret recongnizes that he, too, is the issue of a long line of rough and barbarous ancestors, the heir of innumerable generations of men, primates and wild beasts, and that he has acquired with the germs of life the destructive instincts of ancient humanity.

... ...

France deplores both war and romanticism. They are frightful curses. What a pity it is to see grown men nourish a childish and furious love for guns and drums! The very rewards of victory are illusory. "War brings to the conqueror himself only ruin and misery, and it is a horrible and stupid crime now that peoples are united by common arts, science, and commerce." "You have to be rotten with literature and poetry to demand victory from war. The idea of waging war can no longer enter the heads of any except besotted bourgeois and delayed romantics."

... ...

"Methods of waging war change from age to age. In the eighteenth century an important business of the soldier was stealing pigs and chickens from the peasants." In other ages warfare had still other forms.

> In the ages called barbarous, princes and cities confided their defence to mercenaries who waged war as sensible and prudent men: sometimes there were only five or six casualties in a great battle. And when the knights went to war, at least they were not driven to it, they advanced to their death for their own pleasure. Doubtless that was all they were good for.

> But war has changed appearance. Formerly it had something of nobility, agility, and sportsmanship about it. It was as much a game as a slaughter, and it put to a test all individual gifts, all the animal dexterity of man. Few were killed, and its ravages were negligible compared with those caused by cholera and the pest. Now civilization and the progress of science have made it a kind of wholesale massacre, without the display of individual skill or personal qualities, a massacre among moles who kill their antagonists without knowing or seeing them. Heroism, the fine flower of the wars of yesterday, has been cut down. It is atrocious. May it have an end, and may we awaken from the nightmare.

... ...

At all times military leaders have been the object of a cult. "From Homer on, it has been a strange mania of poets to celebrate generals." Many of these "thunderbolts" have "bird-like brains in an ox's cranium." "And chance alone decides the fate of many battles. When two equally stupid generals confront each other, one of them is almost sure to gain the glory of a victory."

Napoleon is the type of the perfect military hero:

> His genius was vast and light. He thought what every grenadier in his army thought, but he thought it with unheard-of force.... In his touching and terrible puerility, he believed that a man might be great, and this childishness never left him even amid misfortune. [...] He was violent and frivolous, and in that way profoundly human. He maintained a simple, childish gravity which delights in games of sabres and guns. He never had a thought that was not an action, and all his actions were grand and commonplace. His mind was never bigger than his hand, this small and shapely hand which made mincemeat of the world.

The lives, thoughts, and actions of all popular heroes must necessarily be a secret flattery for the vulgar. If our American military leaders had been as intelligent as Einstein or as one of our obscure philosophers, "we would never have erected so many monuments to them and to their horses."

... ...

Concerning the end of war, the thought of Anatole France is hesitant. He hopes and yet doubts. "How to establish peace, since man issues from his mother's womb, so to speak, with a lance and helmet. He comes into the world to grab something that belongs to someone. We see this in ourselves and we see it in the beasts, from the bull down to the ant, which is more belligerent than a Prussian." He considers the cessation of war as unlikely, but asks us to predict, proclaim, and demand peace.

He ventures the hope that science, new economic needs, and a new organization of society will lead to peace. We can hardly believe that men's natures will change, but something can be expected of a new determinism. A new social order may impose a pacific life as formerly the very necessities of existence kept men in a state of war. "Meanwhile, let us call for peace in all our vows. Let us desire it because desire is a creative force, the only creative force in the universe."

But a late remark expresses his reservations: "Still, once again, let us not forget, alas! that the watchword of the universe is to kill. God, our God, is not only the God of Hosts; he is above all, — he is and will be — the God of extermination. He reflects our image."

The Coming Change

Constantly at the bottom of the mind of Anatole France is an attitude toward man which tempers his faith in utopias. He regards progress as necessarily slow. He is convinced that humanity has at all times the same fund of folly and stupidity to expend, and wonders if the insanities consecrated by time do not constitute the wisest investment man can make of his imbecility. Instead of rejoicing when an old error disappears, he dreams with anxiety about the new error, and wonders if it will not be more inconvenient and dangerous than the old.

He believes that changes in *régime* alter only slightly the condition of persons. We do not depend upon constitutions and charters, but on our instincts and our customs.

> There will always be revolts on earth followed by slaveries, short periods of repose after great massacres, and an immense, powerless pity. [...] Let us have zeal in our hearts and the necessary illusions. Let us labor for what we believe useful and good, but not in the hope of a sudden and marvelous success, not with the illusion of a social apocalypse: all apocalypses dazzle and deceive.

Nevertheless, for all these reservations, he is able to accept the inevitable change that is coming. He never hides his dislike for the present order, for the reign of equalitarian mediocrity which stupefies and stultifies. He looks toward the future: the idea of going backward even in a bodily sense gives him "a headache." He is interested in finding a new idea, even a new religion, and he faces the discomforts of revolutionary change with courage.

> Suffering, cruelty, and injustice are the necessary ferments for the establishment of any ideal, of any religion. Even if I were told that revolution would bring about suffering, I should still accept it, although I hate suffering, injustice, anarchy, extinction of enlightenment, the end of our civilization. But more than that I hate mediocrity, sterility. To suffer is still to live and to live intensely.

As for the means for accomplishing the new order, he professes occasionally a faith in liberal, idealistic determinism.

> Dreams of philosophers, have at all times inspired men of action who have started to work to realize them. Our thoughts create the future. Statesmen work on plans that thinkers bequeath to them. They are not the architects of the future, but the masons and helpers.

He admires the liberal rationalists of the eighteenth century:

> How many things begin in them and through them, things, infinitely precious! — I mean the spirit of tolerance, the deep sense of the rights of the individual, the instinct of human liberty. They were able to free themselves from vain terrors: they had free minds, and that is a great virtue.... They knew that life is a dream and they wished it to be a pleasant dream. They replaced faith with tenderness, hope with kindness. They were benevolent.

Concerning economic determinism, Anatole France is less explicit. He joins many others in railing against present irrationalities, but does not emphasize, as later thinkers have, to what an extent falsifications and mental deformities are products of economic interests. He does not stress the point that a cure for the distortions is to be found in a society that will be classless and that will have therefore no need for intellectual fraud and forgery.

As a sceptic, he could hardly be without some reservations. Is a classless society really possible? Except in a state of anarchy could we dispense with officials, judges and commissions to run our social and economic life? And would not these men constitute a new group holding power, and like other groups favor their friends and selves, and find reasons to justify their tenure and privileges? It would be something certainly to take the wind out of the sails of those who are motivated only by money, but, nevertheless, new tyrannies might again arise and become oppressive.

The Philosopher's Ethic

France, the gentlest of philosophers, is most eloquent concerning tolerance, the need for a humble opinion of ourselves, our motives, and the creations of our thought, and a consequent charity toward others.

> Nature, my only mistress and my only teacher, warns me that in no way is the life of man considered as having any

value. It teaches on the contrary, in all kinds of ways, that it has none. The sole purpose of being seems to be to become the food of other beings destined to the same end. Murder is a part of natural law.... Still, I must have perverse instincts, since I am repugnant to seeing blood flow. This is a depravity that all my philosophy has not yet succeeded in correcting.

France does not believe that men are naturally good. He sees that they "issue painfully from original barbarism and that they organize with great effort an uncertain justice and precarious kindness. The time is still far off when they will no longer wage war and when pictures of battles will be hidden from the eyes as immoral, and as offering a shameful spectacle...."

> The more I think of human life, the more I believe that it should have Irony and Pity as witnesses and judges.... Irony and Pity are two good counselors: One, smiling, makes life amiable; the other, weeping, makes it sacred. The irony I invoke is not cruel. It mocks neither love nor beauty. It is kind and benevolent. Its smile calms anger, and it teaches us to make fun of the wicked and the fools whom we might, without it, have the weakness to hate.
>
> If we understood the characteristics of souls as we do the figures of geometry, we would have no more animosity against a mind too narrow than a mathematician has for an angle which lacks by five or six degrees the qualities of a right angle.

A Note on the Continuing Battle

An attack on Rousseau's influence is being made at present by Robert Ardrey, the author of *African Genesis, The Territorial Imperative,* and *The Social Contract,* who bases his ideas on the findings of Konrad Lorenz and other ethologists. These scientists maintain convincingly that man is descended from predatory killer-apes, and that his instinct to fight for and to defend territory (property) is like other of our inherited instincts.

Ardrey in *The Social Contract* (page 95), quotes from the Durants a list of the items in the legacy of Rousseau, which sounds like the catechism of those Americans who, guided by the mass media and the thought-stylists, never manage to grow up, but remain immature and silly to the end of their lives.

WAS CALDERÓN'S *LA VIDA ES SUEÑO* WRITTEN IN A HURRY?

STURGIS E. LEAVITT
University of North Carolina

Juan de Vera Tassis, who published the plays of Calderón after the dramatist's death, makes a statement about *La vida es sueño* that is not to be found in the *Primera Parte* (1636) of the works of Calderón, where the play first appeared, nor does it appear in the *Primera Parte* of 1640. Vera Tassis asserts that the play was a "Fiesta que se representó a sus Magestades en el Salón de su Real Palacio."

In spite of Vera Tassis' reputation for not being altogether trustworthy, it would seem that he was right in this case. The language of *La vida es sueño*, for example, supports his assertion. Indeed, the very first word of the play, *hipogrifo*, would so indicate. What person in the theater down town would have the slightest idea what a *hipogrifo* was? And could he make any sense of the second line?

que corriste parejas con el viento.

Later in the play the highly figurative and sometimes exaggerated language tends to show that the play could only be appreciated by the cultured members of the Court, and not at all by the standees in the commercial theater.

If the play was written on command, and it seems to this writer that it was, there are passages in it that appear to be downright padding, a quite possible indication that the play was written in haste. For example, the extended discourse of Basilio in Act I runs on and on, beginning with elaborate praise of himself and concluding with a long account of Segismundo's imprisonment. What, we may ask, is most of this but padding?

Incidentally, there are unintentional touches of humor in this long speech, which, if taken seriously, emphasize the excessive length of the discourse. Basilio starts out by asking his audience to keep quiet and pay attention. Later on, after he has exhausted the subject of his own vast knowledge, the possession of which must surely have been known to his listeners, he evidently finds them inattentive. Thereupon, he is moved to call for some semblance of order:

> otra vez silencio os pido.

The admonition is effective, or seems to be. If Basilio's hearers did start whispering or muttering under their breath, Basilio is by then so engrossed in his favorite subject, horoscopes, that he does not notice.

Another example. Incongruously enough, who should show up in the midst of the battle in Act III but Rosaura, dressed as a cowboy (*vaquero*), no less. There is evidently a ceasefire somehow, while Rosaura tells her story, and a long one it is — more padding — at a critical moment in the play. With regard to the plot, one may well ask what help she would be, fighting on the side of Segismundo?

There was evidently not enough material in the Segismundo story to make a full three-act play. A secondary plot must be devised, and here Calderón does not distinguish himself. He does not have time. It is by one chance in a million that Rosaura's horse would run away near where Segismundo is imprisoned. How could it have strayed so far from the highway? And while we are asking questions, here are some more. What are Clotaldo and the guards doing, neglecting their duty by leaving Segismundo alone and unprotected? And why are the guards masked? Do they think they are playing some kind of game?

In his haste to work up the details of his plot, Calderon is forced to sacrifice his characters. There is not one that measures up to a high standard. The first of these is Clotaldo. He is supposed to be a man of high moral character, a worthy tutor to no less a person than Segismundo. Perhaps we should not inquire too closely into Clotaldo's affair with Violante, but at least we must admit that it was not a very good guarantee of integrity. We learn that he left this lady in the lurch when he found out that she was in "an interesting condition," to use a quaint phrase. Evidently, he had been reading *libros de caballería,* for he leaves behind a sword as a means of identification, *por si acaso.*

Apparently, Rosaura's mother never told her daughter much about the facts of life. If she had, perhaps Astolfo could never have done her wrong. At any rate, Rosaura has found a way to avoid an "interesting condition," and is free to go chasing off after her seducer. But what chance does she think she has of getting him to do the right thing? She is rather naïve, if she has any such hopes. As for Astolfo, when we see him making love to Estrella, what a dumb bunny he is to wear a picture of one girl while he is courting another!

We have already mentioned the longwindedness of Basilio, but the substance of what he had to say to the Court was that he was very much interested in the fate of his son. It is, therefore, most disconcerting to have him say that it is "necia curiosidad" that induced him to come to the cave to which Segismundo is returned after his appearance at Court. When Segismundo awakes from his sleep, the King withdraws,

> Desde allí a escucharle voy.

Where this "allí" is, is not certain, but it is clear that Basilio does not listen very long, as we would expect a devoted father to do, and hear Segismundo out. If he had, the play would end there. Another act must come along, of course, even if it means sacrificing Basilio as a logical character.

No mention has been made so far of Clarín, and little does he deserve mention. If he ever says anything funny except in the place where he is led to believe that it is his turn to be king, it has escaped the notice of the writer of this article.

The most serious shortcoming, which involves both plot and character, comes at the end of the play and is profoundly disappointing. We note with regret that Segismundo's offer to marry Estrella negates the most moving passage in the play, to wit, where Segismundo, back in the cave, tells about his "dream":

> sólo a una mujer amaba...
> Que fue verdad, creo yo,
> en que todo se acabó,
> y esto sólo se acaba.

The woman who made such an impression upon him, though he was not unmoved by another (Estrella), was Rosaura. But Rosaura must be "made an honest woman," to use another quaint phrase, and Astolfo is the man for that. To make things come out even, as is standard practice in Golden Age drama, there is no recourse but for Segismundo to take the second prize.

When Astolfo objects to marrying Rosaura:

> Aunque es verdad que la debo
> obligaciones, repara
> que ella no sabe quién es;
> y es bajeza y es infamia
> casarme yo con mujer....

Clotaldo attempts to silence him by saying:

> No prosigas, tente, aguarda:
> porque Rosaura es tan noble
> como tú, Astolfo, y mi espada
> lo defenderá en el campo;
> que es mi hija, y esto basta.

One might well expect Astolfo to say "How come?" and this is really what he means when he asks: "¿Qué dices?" Strangely enough, he seems satisfied at Clotaldo's rejoinder:

> Que yo hasta verla
> casada, noble y honrada,
> no la quise descubrir;
> la historia desto es muy larga;
> pero, en fin, es hija mía.

As a matter of fact, this statement would hardly be satisfactory to anyone. Neither would be the *historia,* if Clotaldo were to tell it.

Other instances of padding and other inconsistencies could be adduced to show that Calderón did not have time to tie things together properly. He was pressed to deliver the goods. They were to be delivered to the King on a certain date, and this was, in effect, a mandate. Anyway, when the play was put on, the Court audience did not have to pay admission. Everyone would be inclined to overlook any evidence of haste on the part of the composer, and when the play was over, to call it a day.

Notwithstanding all this, *La vida es sueño* has captivated the imagination of innumerable listeners and readers. It still does. Nonetheless, one cannot but wish that Calderón had had more time to compose it. With all his talent, he could have written a more notable play.

THE POETIC IMAGE OF THE "NOIRE IDOLE"

EMANUEL J. MICKEL, JR.
Indiana University

Although opium was well known for its medicinal value long before the nineteenth century, it was only in the 1830's that the drug's potential stirred the imaginations of various French writers and artists. Since the turn of the century, a number of important occurrences had brought the real and imaginary hallucinatory powers of this and other *excitants* to the attention of the French intellectual community. Considering the notions then current concerning the nature of creative writing and the preoccupation with themes related to escape from reality in both time and space, it is not strange that many writers of the period were fascinated by the artistic possibilities seemingly offered to them by these drugs.

Throughout the nineteenth and twentieth centuries the fascination with mind altering drugs has continued to grow in all levels of society, but an especially constant interest has been maintained in intellectual and artistic circles. Although interest has not centered around one particular drug or even one means of ingestion of the same drug, there is a remarkable similarity in the mythology which has grown up concerning the effects produced and the nature of the drug experience. Study of the literature influenced by drugs seems to indicate clearly that the lore concerning the drug experience and the literary tradition surrounding it have played a major role in determining the way a given author may employ it in his text. Indeed, it is often impossible to separate the myth from personal experience. Fascination with the myth or the theme itself is at least as significant as personal experience in the continuous development of literature concerning and influenced by drugs.

Since their introduction to the French literary world, many writers have employed various aspects of the drug experience in their works. As might be expected, the experience itself represents something different to each writer. For Gautier the fascination seemed to lie in the possibility of a released imagination, a myriad of strange, poetic forms otherwise unavailable to the poet.[1] In his planned novel, *La Spirale*, Flaubert intended the drug as a beneficent panacea for his beleaguered hero, a means of creating an alternate reality to replace what had become an insufferable existence. In the late nineteenth century some form of drug taking became one of the necessary ingredients of *snobisme* and one of the ultra refinements often present in the numerous works exploiting the fashionable theme of decadence. Another view of the drug experience can be seen in the literature from the colonies (especially Indo-China) and also that literature inspired by writers who saw in Oriental philosophy a conception of life superior to that of the materialistically oriented West. For these authors opium often represents the means by which man can attain the *sagesse* of the Orient, an opportunity to become immersed in the spiritual mysteries of a higher existence.[2] Throughout the period the drugs in fashion have had their supporters and detractors. Although medical opinion had become largely unfavorable by the turn of the century, the attractive qualities of the experience caused many to reject medical warnings as inaccurate or motivated by other interests.[3] Thus it is that the role played by the several drugs varies with the poet's opinion concerning the drug experience and the effect of this experience on the poet's intellectual and spiritual existence.

One of the more interesting and consistent poetic treatments of the drug, prevalent from the earliest writers to those of our own time, is the personification of the drug as the poet's mistress or muse. As a poetic figure the personification of the drug offers rich possibilities for expressing the drug relationship and the experience: the drug-

---

[1] For Gautier's treatment of opium and hashish, see his three essays, "La pipe d'opium," "Le hachich," and "Le club des hachichins."

[2] The present writer is currently preparing a study of the influence of drugs on French literature in the nineteenth and twentieth centuries.

[3] Aspects of this debate can be seen in the writings of Claude Farrère, who believed that the official campaign against opium was the result of pressure from alcohol interests rather than from any genuine concern about the dangers of the drug.

user's total devotion to the drug, the pain he experiences when apart from it, the ecstasy when near, the inspiration he believes to receive, and the debilitating nature of such an all-consuming worship — these and many nuances and ramifications thereof can all be expressed by means of this poetic device.

The convention began where much of the drug mythology had its source, in Thomas De Quincey's *Confessions of an English Opium-Eater* and its sequel, *Suspiria de Profundis*. De Quincey wrote in the introduction to the second volume that the purpose of the *Confessions* had been "...to reveal something of the grandeur which belongs *potentially* to human dreams." [4] In the sequel, written to illustrate the inevitable servitude and degradation which the author did not see earlier, De Quincey refers to his third and final "...prostration before the dark idol...." [5] The phrase and its implications struck a responsive chord among French writers in the nineteenth century for whom the "noire idole" became synonymous with opium. The adjective "dark" originally referred to opium's brownish-blackish color and was used by De Quincey as an additional suggestion of the infernal, abismal regions into which the worship of this idol had led him. The two words could scarcely epitomize more perfectly the role which many later writers attributed to the drug. Implicit in the noun is the concept of misdirected worship, the quest of the artificial paradise, emblematic of the satanic element in man's nature which attracts him toward what is self destructive and illusory. In this connection the coloring of the drug served perfectly as a symbolic indicator of the drug's real nature and confirmed its identification with perversity, debauchery, the black arts, the intense sensual pleasures of a decadent society and as a kind of demonic muse. In addition the phrase "noire idole" suggested precisely the image of opium as a treacherous mistress or muse, the specific image which I wish to analyze here in a select group of writers: Charles Baudelaire, Stanislas de Guaita, Guy-Charles Cros, Jean Ricquebourg, and Jean Cocteau.

The relationship between Baudelaire and the "noire idole" is complicated, involved as it is with the poet's own personal experience as well as his notion of what the experience symbolizes in man's nature

---

[4] Thomas De Quincey, *The Collected Writings of Thomas De Quincey*, edited by David Masson, Vol. XIII (London, 1890), 334.
[5] *Ibid.*, p. 337.

and in the human condition. In following the development of Baudelaire's thoughts concerning the drug experience from his early essay, *Du vin et du hachish* (1851) to his study, "Le poème du haschisch," published as the first part of *Les paradis artificiels* in 1860, it is apparent that the poet had become increasingly convinced of the pernicious aspects of drug use. In the 1860 study Baudelaire totally rejects the drug as an aid to the creative effort and sees in it rather a perfect symbol of the illusions man follows, driven by his "soif de l'infini." The drug represents the perfect instrument of Satan in his quest to ensnare and destroy man. In this respect, then, the drug relates to all the instruments of Satan and seems to have been especially associated with the Eve-role or demonic aspect of woman. In *Les Fleurs du Mal* one finds that many poems ostensibly treating the hypnotic and hallucinatory quality of feminine allurement and the poet's adoration could easily represent the drug-user's experience and attitude toward the drug.[7] This relationship is seen clearly in the prose poem, "La chambre double," where the "fiiole de laudanum" is personified as the poet's mistress. Baudelaire's poetic presentation of the drug in this prose poem will be echoed by a number of poets in the decades to follow.

In the first half of the poem the poet relates with astonishment how he suddenly is treated to a delectable vision, his room transformed into a kind of paradise. It is as if the poet suddenly awakens to find himself in the dream-like surroundings, since he begins the poem in full description of the transformed room, pausing only later to ask, "A quel démon bienveillant dois-je d'être ainsi entouré de mystère, de silence, de paix et de parfums?"[8] One does not realize until later the answer to this question, but indications of the drug induced nature of the vision are clearly present in the poet's description. The atmosphere of the room is described as "stagnante," heavy with scent; the soul enjoys a "bain de paresse," "un rêve de volupté." Both the

---

[6] Although Baudelaire made certain minor distinctions between the effects of opium and hashish, he essentially considered the effects and the relationship of these drugs to man to be the same.

[7] For further development of this thesis, see the present writer's study, *The Artificial Paradises in French Literature* (Chapel Hill, 1969).

[8] Charles Baudelaire, *Oeuvres complètes*, éd. Y. G. Le Dantec, révisée par Claude Pichois (Paris, 1961), p. 234. All references to "La chambre double" are drawn from this edition and will be cited henceforth in the text.

atmosphere and the pleasures described are the very ones common in most descriptions of the drug experience. Even more indicative is the visual description of the room. Objects change dimensions ("Les meubles ont des formes allongées, prostrées, alanguies" p. 233), seem themselves to be endowed with life, and speak a mute language ("Les étoffes parlent une langue muette" p. 234). The author is careful what designs are on the wall [9] ("Sur les murs nulle abomination artistique" p. 234) insuring that "...tout a la suffisante clarté et la délicieuse obscurité de l'harmonie" (p. 234). [10] Present in the dream is his "Idole, souveraine des rêves" (p. 234). The ecstasy of the moment, a life expanded into continuous pleasure, is increased by the suspension of time. The concluding lines prior to the interruption of the vision parallel Baudelaire's comments on the drug vision in "Le poème du haschisch":

> O béatitude! ce que nous nommons généralement la vie, même dans son expansion la plus heureuse, n'a rien de commun avec cette vie suprême dont j'ai maintenant connaissance et que je savoure minute par minute, seconde par seconde! (p. 234)

At the height of the ecstasy a knock on the door completely destroys the vision. [11] He now sees the room as it really is, horribly filthy,

---

[9] Baudelaire and Gautier both warn the drug-taker concerning the decorations on the walls, since these forms can contribute to the nature of the visions experienced.

[10] The individual's love of harmony and balance while under the influence of the drug is stressed by Baudelaire in the "Poème du haschisch":

> L'harmonie, le balancement des lignes, l'eurythmie dans les mouvements, apparaissent au rêveur comme des nécessités, comme des *devoirs*, non-seulement pour tous les êtres de la création, mais pour lui-même, le rêveur, qui se trouve, à cette période de la crise, doué d'une merveilleuse aptitude pour comprendre le rythme immortel et universel. (p. 377)

[11] Baudelaire stresses that the drug-taker should be free from interruption and from any pressing obligations:

> Je présume que vous avez eu la précaution de bien choisir votre moment pour cette aventureuse expédition. Toute débauche parfaite a besoin d'un parfait loisir... vous n'avez pas de devoirs à accomplir exigeant de la ponctualité, de l'exactitude... cette inquiétude, ce souvenir d'un devoir qui réclame votre volonté et votre attention à une minute déterminée, viendraient sonner comme un glas à travers votre ivresse et empoisonneraient votre plaisir. (p. 356)

confining and stifling. The beautiful fragrance becomes stench, the furniture disgustingly dirty, and worst of all, where time had formerly ceased, the poet is now painfully aware of each passing second.[12] In the midst of the desolation the poet sees a single "friendly" object, the ironic friend responsible for his momentary pleasure and intense misery:

> Dans ce monde étroit, mais si plein de dégoût, un seul objet connu me sourit: la fiole de laudanum; une vieille et terrible amie; comme toutes les amies, hélas! féconde en caresses et en traîtrises. (p. 235)

Considering its relationship to the poem, the entire passage is ironic, the epitome of the antithetical structure of the rest of the piece. In the current "monde étroit" the poet sees the object which had caused the expansiveness of the preceding moments. The "simile" of the "fiole" undoubtedly mocks the author, who recognizes that this "old" friend is nonetheless "terrible." He is painfully aware that this "amie," which had created the "Idole" and the ecstatic, voluptuous moments, while being "féconde en caresses," is yet responsible for his intense disgust with reality. The poignancy of the relationship is summed up in the words "vieille" and "traîtrises," for in them is present the long attachment of the poet to his "maîtresse," thus emphasizing the length and constant repetition of his misery, and the hopelessness of finding meaningful fulfillment in one so treacherous.

Later in the century the well known Rosicrucian poet, Stanislas de Guaita, the close friend of Maurice Barrès who was to devote most of his life to a study of the occult, treated his drug experience in similar terms. In his collection of poetry, *La Muse noire,* published in 1883, de Guaita devotes a number of poems to the drug experience. The title of the collection is also the title of the first poem. The "Muse noire" personifies the muse which guides the poet when he becomes tired of writing hymns to the muse of light. Described as a "négresse superbe," she is the mistress of orgy, violent pleasure, melancholy and grief. She describes herself as "orgueilleuse et jalouse" and comments that many poets deliberately flee her "baiser sinistre, enivrant, infernal." A mistress of ambiguous qualities, she is both "amoureuse et farouche."

---

[12] Again this contrast and the emphasis on the acute horror of reality are found in "Poème du haschisch."

In "Les Spectres," dedicated to Maurice Rollinat, the poet praises the hallucinatory imagination of this "poète maudit," known for his macabre poetry considered to have been inspired by Baudelaire. He notes that the poet rarely fills his poetry with the fragrance of flowers like the rose, but rather writes poetry under the influence of "La Jusquiame — sombre fleur..." gathered "Sur quelque fantastique rive." [13] In the last seven stanzas of the poem, de Guaita associates himself with the "poète maudit," suggesting that they both walk among spirits not without danger:

> Peut-être marchons-nous sans crainte
> Parmi de dangereux Esprits,
> Sans entendre leurs méchants cris,
> Sans frissonner à leur étreinte... (p. 43)

De Guaita concludes the poem by asking whether their experience is not really with a dangerous vampire whose kiss gradually saps their substance:

> Peut-être un fantôme vainqueur
> A-t-il sur nous collé sa bouche,
> Et, se vautrant sur notre couche,
> Sucé le sang de notre coeur? (p. 43)

In a poem seemingly written in a lighter tone, "La Morphine," with a subtitle, "Rondel Libertin," de Guaita presents the drug in a way which reminds one of both Baudelaire and Eugène Sue. [14] "Morphine" addresses the reader as the man's mistress and describes the ecstasy which she brings:

> Finalement l'homme s'endort
> Pour cuver l'extatique ivresse
> Qui l'enveloppe de paresse
> Et l'éblouit de songes d'or
>
> Sevré du chagrin, du remord,
> Sous le charme de ma caresse,
> Finalement l'homme s'endort
> Pour cuver l'extatique ivresse. (p. 89)

---

[13] Stanislas de Guaita, *La Muse noire* (Paris, 1883), p. 42. All citations of de Guaita's poetry are taken from this edition and will be cited hereafter in the text.

[14] The reader is referred to Sue's maritime novel, *Atar-Gull,* where the mistress of Brulart's dream-vision is presented in just these terms.

In her embrace the man enjoys an "extatique ivresse," shelter from the "chagrin" of reality, and a peaceful slumber filled with "songes d'or." In the final stanza the voice of the mistress is still one of kindness and love. Just as Baudelaire's "fiole" she is willingly "féconde en caresses."

> L'homme ravi murmure: encor!
> Et moi, complaisante maîtresse,
> En mes tendres bras je le presse
> Je l'étreins de plus en plus fort... (p. 90)

Much of the drug experience is included in the first four lines of this last stanza: the man's ecstasy, his adoration and his return for more pleasure. Even the attitude of the mistress (the adjectives "complaisante" and "tendres") discloses her nature as seen through the lover's eyes. In keeping with the poem and the lover's blindness, de Guaita carefully conceals the ominous outcome of the relationship, only hinting at the result in the fourth line of the last stanza. Even then one is not fully aware, for the concluding line of the nineteenth century version of the *rondel* is generally a repetition of the first line of the poem, thus fulfilling the etymological sense of the word *rondel*. Here the poem is set up for further ecstasy from the embrace, more sleep and dreams. However, the poet, while beginning to repeat the poem's first line, abruptly breaks off and concludes the cycle of ecstasy: "Et finalement... l'homme est mort!" (p. 90). The dramatic effect of the antithesis in the last line is heightened both by the poem's form and its subject. The constant *tourbillon* of embrace and ecstasy, this dance of love, which provides the lover with an escape from the grief of reality, ends in an embrace of death, thus ending the circular nature of the *rondel* itself.

Although the attitude of Guy-Charles Cros is much different in his poem, "Les autres paradis," first published in 1912, the recognition of the dual aspect of the *poisons* is nonetheless evident. The poet chastises his own kind for being content to remain prisoners of "deux bras de chair." He asks how one can be content with the joys and remorse of such base pleasures when far subtler ones beckon. Certainly, he continues, these "baisers refroidis" and sexual conquest do not equal "un tabac noir et fort." In the last two stanzas the poet urges the enjoyment offered by the "justes divinités":

> Tabac, absinthe, opium, haschisch, éther,
> vous êtes nos justes divinités.
> Vous nous soulevez comme la mer,
> vous nous illuminez comme un ciel cru d'été.
>
> Ah! les seuls poisons lents guérissent
> la folie de nos trop faibles coeurs
> et que nous importent de futurs supplices
> si *maintenant* en nous rien ne connaît la peur? [15]

In a sense one can see here the attitude of de Guaita's lover, who willingly embraced certain death for the ecstasy which the mistress gave. Yet the reader is aware of an implicit irony in the last stanza. Only the "poisons lents guérissent" from the "folie" which prevents enjoying the ecstasy of "*maintenant*." Contrarily, these same "poisons lents," in healing, bring "futurs supplices." And because they are "lents," it is clear that the "*maintenant*" of the future with its "supplices" is destined to be longer lasting than the momentary, fleeting joys of the present.

Jean Ricquebourg, born on Réunion Island in 1868 and friend of both Leconte de Lisle and Léon Dierx, is perhaps best remembered as one of many French colonial writers whose work was inspired by their experience in Indo-China. In the tradition of these writers, Ricquebourg treats opium as a goddess or as the gift of the gods which can open the doors to a mystical, spiritual union or to the *sagesse* of the Orient. In the poem, "La Chauve-souris," the "perle d'opium" is referred to as the "don magique des dieux." Later in the poem, the "chauve-souris," symbol of the *cinq bonheurs* of Oriental philosophy, tries to enter the poet's room and surprises him "couché, possédant [son] idole." However, the drug's exalted role does not deceive the poet concerning the harm brought to the user. This is evident in several poems such as "Sortilèges" and "Cet homme." In the opening lines of "Sortilèges," Ricquebourg symbolizes the horrible country of exile, *Annam*, by a description of the oppressive swamp and its maleficent atmosphere:

> Sur les bords du marais stagnant,
> Assailli d'odeurs méphitiques,

---

[15] Guy-Charles Cros, "Les autres paradis," *Mercure de France*, 96 (1912), 705.

> Harcelé d'un vol bourdonnant,
> Sanguinaire essaim de moustiques,
> Dans l'air humide à la fois chaud,
> J'ai pu détacher de leur tige,
> Qui fléchissait sous le fardeau,
> Des fleurs surpassant en prodige
> La gueule d'où sourd un venin:
> Un suc visqueux en tombait, larmes
> Lourdes qui corrodaient la main.
> —Ainsi, dans tes yeux noirs de charmes,
> Qui tenaient prisonnier mon sort,
> J'ai connu l'horreur de la mort. [16]

Growing in the stagnant swamp, filled with "odeurs méphitiques," and swarms of "moustiques," is a flower of prodigious powers, whose "suc visqueux," euphemistically called "larmes lourdes," surpasses the strongest venim and eats away the hand that gathers it. It seems paradoxical that the "passant" in this wretched land should bother to collect the dangerous juice. In the next lines, however, one sees that the "passant" is "prisonnier" of these "yeux noirs de charmes," from which he has learned the "horreur de la mort."

In view of the background of this poetry, there is much irony in the antitheses inherent in these lines. Traditionally the French colonial writers refer to themselves as exiles, latter day Du Bellays, cut off from their spiritual homeland, forced to mire in this swampy land of death, destined never again to see their native soil, destined to be haunted and destroyed by the vibrant, maleficent spirits of the East. For some, opium provided the means of understanding and entering into harmonious relationship with the eastern spiritual reality. For others, however, it provided only a momentary escape from the fears and horrors of the dark, swampy forests. In this regard, it must be noted that the flower which provides the solace suspiciously grows from this soil of death, that its assuaging juice is referred to as "larmes," and that the exile, seeking release and escape, becomes a "prisonnier" to this flower of death, wherein he seeks refuge.

In the last half of the poem there is a similar arrangement. In the first lines the poet describes the horrors of the country and concludes with his quest for relief:

---

[16] Jean Ricquebourg, *Ciels d'Annam* (Paris, 1936), p. 35. Additional citations from this edition are cited in the text.

> Pays énervant dont l'emblème
> Est un Dragon horrible et tors,
> Sous ton ciel rutilant ou blême,
> Dans tes forêts, amples décors
> Qui s'allument au crépuscule,
> Que la lune voile de blanc,
> Où la sève abonde et circule
> Et s'épanouit trois fois l'an,
> Des fruits à la pulpe grisante
> Sont penchés sur le passant las.
> —Je viens à ta lèvre épuisante,
> En t'attirant de mes deux bras
> Comme on fait de la branche mûre,
> Cueillir l'oubli de ma torture. (p. 36)

Although the "passant" recognizes that the "lèvre" is "épuisante," it brings "oubli" from his "torture." Indeed the ultimate death which he anticipates is in the end a consoling thought, in that it is a lasting refuge ("oubli") from the anguish of his existance. While it is evident that the poet recognizes the destruction wrought by the drug, there is, nevertheless, a difference in attitude, influenced no doubt by the reputation of the drug in the Orient. Inherent in this attitude is a scorn for the physical in deference to all that is spiritual. In this sense, the drug never really becomes a treacherous mistress, since the physical harm she brings is considered inconsequential in comparison with the spiritual solace or, as in other poems, the spiritual enlightenment which she offers.

Finally, there are several passages in Jean Cocteau's diary, *Opium, Journal d'une désintoxication,* which are of considerable interest to this theme. Among his numerous reflections on the drug experience is the writer's characterization of the addict's relationship to the drug. For Cocteau the relationship can be compared with the traditional relationship between the romantic lover and his enchantress, the famous *femme fatale.* In this image are summed up the necessity for the addict to abandon the drug, his reluctance and lack of will to do so, in short, the ironic paradox of his situation. To ask the opium smoker to quit his habit would be like asking Tristan to kill Isolde:

> ...l'efficacité de l'opium résulte d'un pacte. S'il nous enchante, nous ne pourrons plus le quitter... Moraliser l'opiomane, c'est

dire à Tristan: 'Tuez Iseult. Vous irez beaucoup mieux après.' [17]

The irony of Cocteau's statement is greatly reinforced by the Tristan story itself, for the bond between the lovers is not only fatal, but it is Tristan's separation from Isolde which causes his death. Just as Tristan needed the presence of Isolde before his wounds would heal, so does the opium addict need his drug to prevent the horrible syndrome of pains caused by withdrawal. Neither could imagine "killing Isolde" for neither can live without her.

In another passage from the *Journal*, Cocteau again uses the image of the mistress to describe the bitter relationship:

> Il est rare qu'un fumeur quitte l'opium. L'opium le quitte en ruinant tout. C'est une substance qui échappe à l'analyse, vivante, capricieuse, capable de se retourner brusquement contre le fumeur... Bref, il n'existe pas de maîtresse plus exigeante que la drogue qui pousse la jalousie jusqu'à émasculer le fumeur. [18]

Here Cocteau employs the traditional motif of woman's vindictive nature. Enigmatic, capricious and demanding, no revenge is too cruel for the jealous mistress. Returning to the reference to Tristan and Isolde, one is aware of a forceful double irony in the writer's statement, when one considers that the other Isolde (of the white hands) caused Tristan's death because of her jealousy and that habitual consumption of opium is known to diminish the drug-taker's interest in the sexual experience.

The drug experience has been a theme in literature now for well over one hundred years and it is not likely that the current rise in the use of hallucinogenics will be accompanied by a reduction of their importance as a literary theme. This paper illustrates only one use that has been made of this motif. Even so, one can glimpse the fruitful literary potential of an experience which mirrors much of the destiny of man, an experience replete with the irony, antithesis, illusion, and fatal destiny inherent in much of the literature which probes the nature of man's existence and his aspirations.

---

[17] Jean Cocteau, *Oeuvres complètes*, Vol. X (Paris, 1946-51), 60.
[18] *Ibid.*, p. 82.

BYRON AND NERVAL: TWO SONS OF FIRE

JAMES S. PATTY
Vanderbilt University

It is a natural failing of literary critics and historians to suppose that the weight of their commentaries and explanations may ultimately crush the works which they belabor. Certainly the feeling is likely to emerge as one approaches, after so many predecessors, the magical text of Nerval's sonnet "El Desdichado," perhaps the most explicated French poem of recent decades. Fortunately, all true poetry easily disentangles itself from the stifling layers of scholia: it is only on the printed pages of critical editions and other such works that the poem seems to get lost from sight. The poem, we all know when our wits are about us, is elsewhere, alive and well.

Still, there is cause to hesitate when offering yet another comment on the ninth line of Nerval's poem: "Suis-je Amour ou Phébus?... Lusignan ou Biron?"[1] For it is around this line that the most serious discussion has centered, in the commentaries of Kneller and Geninasca, for example.[2] But my present concern is focused even more narrowly than theirs: as the reader might suspect from my title, it is the word "Biron" that will provide my theme. From the work done so far, the following identifications have come forward: (1) on the strength of a

---

[1] Gérard de Nerval, *Œuvres*, ed. Albert Béguin and Jean Richer (Paris, 1952-1956), I, 29. Except as noted, Nerval's works will be cited in this edition, designated simply as *Œuvres*. Frequently cited works (e.g., the major studies of Marie, Richer, and Estève), once fully identified, will be referred to by short titles.

[2] John W. Kneller, "The Poet and his Moira: 'El Desdichado,'" *PMLA*, LXXV (1960), 402-409; Jacques Geninasca, *Une Lecture de "El Desdichado"* (Paris, 1965).

reference to him in *Les Filles du feu* ("Chansons et légendes du Valois" [*Œuvres,* I, 300]), Armand de Gontaut, baron de Biron (1524-1592), a marshal of France killed in battle;[3] Charles, duc de Biron (1562-1602), also a marshal of France (he was the son of the foregoing), executed for treason by Henri IV;[4] (3) a later member of the same dynasty who suffered a similar fate, Armand Louis de Gontaut, duc de Biron (1747-1793), guillotined during the Revolution (it should be pointed out that this particular Biron was usually known as duc de Lauzun — Balzac, for example, consistently uses the latter title);[5] (4) the founder of the Gontaut-Biron dynasty, Gaston Ier de Gontaut Biron, a twelfth-century Crusader;[6] (5) still another ancestor of the Birons, Elie de Gontaut;[7] (6) the Biron (or Berowne) of Shakespeare's *Love's Labors Lost,* who seems to be tenuously connected with the sixteenth-century Birons mentioned earlier;[8] (7), finally, the English poet, who has been proposed in the article by Norma Rinsler cited above and elsewhere.

The multiplicity of candidates and the varied arguments used on their behalf might well induce bewilderment, if not despair, in the reader or student. But when dealing with the ever fascinating sonnets of *Les Chimères* and with other crucial Nervalian texts (*Aurélia,* for example), indeed, perhaps with all of Nerval's work, there are solid reasons for entertaining all plausible suggestions. The point of view of the present study coincides almost wholly with that of such Nerval

---

[3] For example, by Jeanine Moulin in her exegetical edition of *Les Chimères* (Lille and Geneva, 1949), p. 16, and by Norma Rinsler, "Nerval et Biron," *RHL,* LXI (1961), 407.

[4] Norma Rinsler, "Nerval et Biron," p. 407.

[5] *Ibid.,* pp. 407-08. For Balzac's references to the duc de Lauzun, see his *Œuvres complètes,* ed. Marcel Bouteron and Henri Longnon (Paris, 1912-1940), X, 257; XIII, 296; XXI, 391; and XXII, 253.

[6] Robert Faurisson, "Gérard de Nerval: *El Desdichado,*" *L'Information Littéraire,* XX (1968), 94-98.

[7] Jeanne Genaille, "Sur 'El Desdichado,'" *RHL,* XL (1960), 1-10. It should be pointed out that Mademoiselle Genaille does not identify the *persona* of the poem as Biron but as Richard Coeur-de-Lion; Biron, in her view, is merely a comparison with the central figure.

[8] Léon Cellier, "Sur un vers des *Chimères.* Nerval et Shakespeare," *Cahiers du Sud,* No. 311 (1952). Another recent commentator regards Cellier's suggestion as the best; see Marie-Thérèse Goosse, " 'El Desdichado', de Gérard de Nerval," *Lettres Romanes,* XVIII (1964), 111-35, 241-62. For still other suggestions linking Nerval to the Gontaut-Biron clan, see Edouard Peyrouzet, *Gérard de Nerval inconnu* (Paris, 1965), p. 198, n. 32.

scholars as Jean Richer and Norma Rinsler. Richer in particular has shown the fantastic crystallization process by which Nerval built up his personal mythology, drawing on genealogy (false and true), heraldry, archeology, etymology, history, myth, personal experience, literary allusions, alchemy, astrology, the tarot, free-masonry, and many other sources, the whole tied together by audacious syncretism and an inclination to regard every *possible* analogy as valid.[9] Richer himself may occasionally make a far-fetched link, but it is hard to resist the central force of his approach.

This study, then, will attempt to do for Byron what has been done for the various Birons of France. As mentioned, and as might be expected, other scholars have already made this suggestion and have made pertinent remarks designed to bolster it.[10] But no *systematic* attempt has yet been made to establish a bond of identification between Byron and the persona of "El Desdichado," whom I assume to be a projection of the poet himself. This assumption undergirds the methodology used here, whereby the speaker in the poem and the historical Gérard de Nerval are treated as interchangeable. While the present study endeavors to focus, ultimately, on the relationship between Byron and Nerval-Biron, the entire complex of bonds between the two poets will be sketched. Finally, it should be borne in mind that I am not here attempting a synthetic exegesis of the whole sonnet or even of line nine.

One must deal at once with a textual problem. But it turns out that the only variant reveals and rewards, instead of confusing the issue: in the first printing of the poem, in *Le Mousquetaire* of December 10, 1853, "Biron" appears as "Byron." Jean Guillaume, whose discussion of the problem is the most rigorous, regards "Byron" as "peut-être" the result of Alexandre Dumas's editorial intervention; all the manuscripts read "Biron."[11] Fortunately, Guillaume also understands the poetic implications of the two readings: "...la forme 'Byron', applicable seulement au romantique anglais ... est plus restrictive que son homonyme 'Biron', qui concerne et le romantique anglais (cf. le poème de Nerval *A Napoleón. Traduit de Lord Biron*) et tel héros

---

[9] See especially his *Nerval. Expérience et création* (Paris, 1963), *passim*.
[10] Norma Rinsler, "Nerval et Biron," p. 406.
[11] Jean Guillaume, ed., *"Les Chimères" de Nerval* (Brussels, 1966), p. 50, n. 4.

français (cf. *la chanson de Biron,* en appendice à *Sylvie*) et certain personnage de Shakespeare...." [12] As Guillaume indicates, to read "Biron" at the end of Nerval's line is to open broader horizons, for while, to the French reader of the mid-nineteenth century, "Biron" could suggest several possibilities, the spelling "Byron" restricts the field of interpretation. [13] It will be understood at once that Guillaume's approach, in allowing a multiplicity of interpretations, is in harmony with my own.

The textual problem settled, we may turn to the task of establishing another sort of foundation for the present study — a survey of the known facts linking the two men (and the two poets). It is clear that Gérard knew, or knew about, many of Byron's works. Among his early poems still in manuscript, there are two on Napoleonic themes inspired by Byron (As we have seen, one of them even claims to be "traduit de Lord Biron"). [14] Among the *Elégies nationales* (1826) is a poem entitled "Pensées de Byron: élégie," which Nerval reprinted with the "Odelettes" appended to *Petits Châteaux de Bohême* (1852, 1853). [15] More important are the references to the major works of Byron. From a letter to Baron Taylor in 1831, it appears that Nerval, in collaboration with Maquet, wrote a one-act tragedy called *Lara*

---

[12] *Ibid.,* p. 57.

[13] An article from *Le Globe* of October 7, 1829, is revealing on the subject of the ambiguity surrounding the spelling of the poet's name. In a review of Lady Morgan's *Le Livre du boudoir,* we are given a glimpse of the authoress's "premier rout à Londres." She relates how at the party in question she overheard a fragment of conversation between a fashionable young lady and "un très beau jeune homme ayant l'air sombre et distingué par un air de singularité qui tenait le milieu entre la hauteur et la timidité." The young lady asked the handsome young man, "Comment vous portez-vous, lord Byron?" On hearing this, Lady Morgan lets her mind run wild: "Lord Byron! Tous les *braves Birons* de la chevalerie française et anglaise se présentèrent à mon imagination en entendant prononcer ce nom célèbre dans l'histoire...." Thus an Irish lady, on hearing the name "Byron" pronounced, thought at once of the French Birons. Clearly, rich possibilities for ambiguity exist at the graphic and at the phonic level, in English as well as in French. This anecdote, moreover, refers to a family relationship between the Byrons and the French Birons which is occasionally hinted at in biographies of Byron.

[14] See Jean Richer, *Nerval,* p. 55. Edmond Estève in his *Byron et le romantisme français* (deuxième édition; Paris, n.d.), p. 163, mentions still another.

[15] Nerval, *Œuvres,* I, 46-47.

the text of which has been lost.[16] From this point on, there are passing references to *Don Juan, Cain, Childe Harold's Pilgrimage, Manfred,* and *Sardanapalus,* as well as to the poet himself.[17] We might expect that the translator of *Faust* would be more interested in *Manfred* than this bare enumeration suggests, and such is the case: near the beginning of part II of *Aurélia* occurs an unacknowledged quotation from Byron's play: "L'arbre de science n'est pas l'arbre de vie!"[18] Equally intriguing and suggestive, especially in view of the title of *Les Filles du feu* and Nerval's interest in alchemy and "the divinities of fire," is his categorization of Byron as "un fils du soleil."[19]

What Nerval knew of Byron the *man* does not emerge, except dimly and fragmentarily, from such references as these. Before discussing the deeper affinities between the two poets, I would like to bring forward some biographical details of which Nerval (with one or two possible exceptions) was probably unaware, but which would have caught his fancy — with who knows what consequences! — if he had known them. First of all, Byron spent two or three months of his pre-natal life in Paris, for his mother, then in advanced stages of pregnancy, joined her husband there in the late summer or early fall of 1787 and only left the French capital in early December, about a month and a half

---

[16] Nerval, *Œuvres,* I, 740. On the problem of this last text, see Jean Richer, *Nerval,* pp. 140-41 and p. 163, n. 14.

[17] Nerval, *Œuvres,* II, 35, 83, and 1234; for the reference to *Manfred,* see Richer, *Nerval,* p. 248. While this listing of Nerval's references to Byron lays no claim to completeness, it is in order to list here, without comment, some other passing allusions to Byron turned up in the course of this investigation: *Childe Harold's Pilgrimage* — Jean Richer, ed., *Œuvres complémentaires de Gérard de Nerval: La Vie du théâtre,* II (Paris, 1961), p. 491; *Sardanapalus* — *Ibid.,* p. 563; *Manfred, Don Juan,* and Byron himself — Jean Richer, ed., *Œuvres complémentaires de Gérard de Nerval: La Vie des lettres* (Paris, 1959), pp. 7 and 31; Heine compared to Byron — *Ibid.,* p. 72; Shelley and Byron — *Ibid.,* p. 79; performance of Byron's *Werner* by the English actors in 1845 — *Ibid.,* p. 227; an apparent reference to *Lara* — *Œuvres,* II, 26; *Don Juan* — *Ibid.,* 35.

[18] *Manfred,* Act I, scene i, line 12. In his critical edition of *Aurélia,* Richer states that Ballanche also formulates this maxim, but he cites no text in support (see Jean Richer, ed., *Aurélia ou le rêve et la vie* [Paris, 1965], p. 266).

[19] See Norma Rinsler, "Nerval and the Divinities of Fire," *French Studies,* XVII (1963), 136-47. Nerval's phrase about Byron as "un fils du soleil" occurs in his introduction to Heinrich Heine, *Poèmes et légendes* (quoted by Norma Rinsler, "Nerval et Biron," p. 408).

before the poet's birth.[20] Byron's uncle, Captain George Anson Byron was living at Chantilly during this period.[21] Chantilly is, of course, a *haut lieu nervalien*; it is explicitly mentioned on the map which Gérard included in the fanciful genealogy which serves Richer as point of departure in his reconstruction of Nerval's personal mythology.[22] Byron's father died (in 1791) at Valenciennes, a fact which could have been known to Nerval[23] and which would have reminded him of Watteau, a native of that city and an artist for whom Nerval reserves a special rôle as painter of his beloved Valois.[24] Given Gérard's interest in heraldry and genealogy and the *sirène* of line 11 of "El Desdichado," the presence of a mermaid in the crest of the Byron coat of arms would undoubtedly have delighted him.[25] One wonders what his mind would have made of the fact that, according to the poet's leading biographer, it was a certain Lord William Gordon, "pourvoyeur du grand monde," who introduced "Adrienne" (Sophie Dawes) to the duc de Bourbon in London.[26] That Gérard knew of Byron's lameness can hardly be doubted; Norma Rinsler has identified this motif in Nerval's personal mythology, taking as her starting point the lameness of the poet's father.[27] Finally, there is the very etymology of Byron's name

---

[20] Leslie A. Marchand, *Byron: A Biography* (New York, 1957), I, 22. Byron's half-sister Augusta *was* born in Paris, January 26, 1784 (see Peter Gunn, *My Dearest Augusta* [New York, 1968], p. 25).

[21] Marchand, *Byron*, I, 23; Gunn, *My Dearest Augusta*, pp. 25, 30.

[22] Richer, *Nerval*, p. 36. For the capital texts in Nerval, see "Sylvie: souvenirs du Valois," ch. iv and ch. xiii, and *Promenades et souvenirs*, ch. viii ("Chantilly"). In general, see Aristide Marie, *Gérard de Nerval: le poète et l'homme d'après des manuscrits et des documents inédits* (Paris, 1955), ch. iv ("Adrienne"), especially pp. 82-88.

[23] Amédée Pichot, for example, mentions it in his "Essai sur le génie et le caractère de Lord Byron" (*Œuvres de Lord Byron*, trans. Amédée Pichot [Paris, 1823], I, 12), as does Villemain in his article on Byron in Michaud, *Biographie universelle* (Paris, n.d.), VI, 279.

[24] See especially, in *Les Filles du feu*, "Angélique" (cinquième lettre) and "Sylvie," ch. iv (*Œuvres*, I, 209, 268-71). Consult Richer, *Nerval*, p. 317, for other links between Nerval and Watteau. I have not discovered any text which proves that Nerval was aware of the painter's place of birth.

[25] Marchand, *Byron*, I, 5.

[26] I have not been able to identify this person.

[27] See Normal Rinsler, "Gérard de Nerval and the Divinities of Fire," p. 138. It is well to remember that the earlier of the two sixteenth-century Birons was known as "Le boiteux." See Norma Rinsler, "Nerval et Biron," p. 408, for further suggestions along this line. The key text in Nerval is, of course, from "Horus": "Attachez son pied tors...."

to conjure with: Thomas Moore, in his *Life of Lord Byron* (of which three French translations appeared in 1830, immediately after its original publication), [28] vaunts the poet's ancestors in these terms: "In Doomsday-book, the name of Ralph de Burun ranks high among the tenants of land in Nottinghamshire...." [29] Richer's publication of Gérard's fanciful genealogy makes it abundantly clear that the poet's mind reached out for even the most tenuous resemblances in family names, and most especially for those which might be connected with the Labrunies. [30] Gérard would have had no difficulty fitting the name "Burun" into his fantastic scheme.

If we turn to the more obvious affinities and relationships between the two poets, many possibilities arise. Merely as near contemporaries, they shared many experiences and were subjected to many influences tending to create such affinities and relationships. It is necessary to bear in mind that many thousands, perhaps millions, of other men living in the Western world during the first half of the nineteenth century shared the same experiences and felt the same influences, the binding element in the *zeitgeist*. Still, certain motifs prove that Byron and Nerval did indeed live in the same world, motifs so evident in their lives and work as to need no documentation. It suffices to list them: Rousseau, the French Revolution, Napoleon, Hellenism and the Greek War, the Orient. To list such motifs is not, of course, to imply that the two poets handled them in the same way or developed the same attitudes about them. On the other hand, it would not be difficult to show that they were drawn together around these points, rather than separated by them: Nerval and Byron, confronted by the French Revolution and Napoleon, for example, have more in common than, say, Nerval and Joseph de Maistre (and I am not forgetting Maistre the *illuminé*).

There is another name drawn from the pantheon of the time that must be descussed in some detail — Goethe. Men living in the early decades of the nineteenth century often saw Goethe and Byron as the two great literary figures of the age. Chateaubriand, for instance, linked these two names together (and to his own, of course) in his *Essai sur*

---

[28] Estève, *Byron et le romantisme français*, p. 208.
[29] Thomas Moore, *Life of Lord Byron with his Letters and Journals* (London, 1854), I, 1.
[30] Richer, *Nerval*, pp. 33-38.

la littérature angloise (1835): "Lord Byron vivra, soit qu'enfant de son siècle comme moi, il en ait exprimé comme moi (et comme Goethe avant nous) la passion et le malheur, soit que mes périples et le falot de ma barque gauloise aient montré la route au vaisseau d'Albion sur des mers inexplorées." [31] From a somewhat more disinterested source comes the following: "Telles furent la vie et la mort du plus grand poëte des temps modernes, sans en excepter Goëthe (sic), Schiller et Hugo." [32] Thus it seems that Goethe and Byron, in point of sheer preëminence, were frequently linked in the minds of their contemporaries, not that real affinities and influences were lacking: the influence of *Werther* on Byron (and nearly everybody else) and the similarities between *Faust* and *Manfred*, to cite but the most obvious. It is precisely in this latter connection that we find the closest link between Goethe, Byron, and Nerval. As one commentator notes:

> Une scène du second *Faust*, celle qu'une note de Nerval signale comme une allégorie se rapportant — on le suppose, dit-il — au poète Byron, présente Euphorion, fils d'Hélène et de Faust, jeune génie avide de tout connaître qui, renouvelant la tentative d'Icare, vole un moment puis s'abîme sur le sol. [33]

I have been unable to consult the "note" alluded to (presumably a note affixed to the text of Nerval's translation of *Faust*, Part II), but in his preface to the translation Nerval is not, at first glance, so explicit in his reference to Byron: speaking of the mating of Faust and Helen, he says that here Goethe "semble amener sous l'allégorie d'Euphorion la critique des temps modernes." [34] But in what comes next, the resemblance between Goethe's Euphorion and Byron (or perhaps Manfred) becomes more apparent:

> Euphorion ne peut vivre en repos; à peine né, il s'élance de terre, gravit les plus hauts sommets, parcourt les plus rudes

---

[31] Chateaubriand, *Œuvres complètes* (Paris, 1859-1861), XI, 782. The passage is repeated *verbatim* in *Mémoires d'outre-tombe*, XII, iv.

[32] Emile Souvestre, "Notice sur Lord Byron" (Benjamin Laroche, trans., *Œuvres complètes de Lord Byron* [troisième édition; Paris, 1838], p. xvi).

[33] Marie-Thérèse Goosse, "'El Desdichado', de Gérard de Nerval," *Lettres Romanes*, XVIII (1964), 121.

[34] "Préface de *Faust* suivi du second *Faust*" (1840). This passage may be found in Jean Richer, ed., *Œuvres complémentaires de Gérard de Nerval: La Vie des lettres* (Paris, 1959), p. 22.

sentiers, veut tout embrasser, tout pénétrer, tout comprendre, et finit par éprouver le sort d'Icare en voulant conquérir l'empire des airs. [35]

Of course, it is Nerval's position as translator of Goethe's *Faust* that is the basis of this part of my study. And, curiously, Byron has a rôle, admittedly minor, in the Goethe-Nerval relationship (or its legend), for his name appears in the passages from Eckermann which Gérard quotes in his account of the praise which Goethe bestowed on the young and unknown French poet's translation: "Goethe me montra le *keepsake* pour l'année 1830, orné de fort jolies gravures et de quelques lettres très intéressantes de lord Byron...." [36] Still other references reveal that Nerval, like so many others, naturally associated Goethe and Byron, sometimes insisting, however, on their differences as well as on their resemblance. [37]

From Goethe's *Faust* it is logical to go on to other literary relationships between Byron and Nerval (though with two such poets the distinction between life and art, the man and the work, is often blurred, to say the least — in a sense, Byron *is* Manfred and Nerval *is* "Le prince d'Aquitaine à la tour abolie"). In other connections, we have seen that Byron's major poems and dramas — *Don Juan, Childe Harold, Lara, Manfred, Cain,* and *Sardanapalus* — figure in Nerval's work. [38] Two of these works are of special interest here, because their heroes bathe in that world of myth and legend so congenial to Nerval. Obviously, I mean *Don Juan* and *Cain*. On Nerval's identification with the protagonist of the former poem, Norma Rinsler writes: "Pour Gérard, Byron était avant tout le créateur de Don Juan, héros romantique, esprit indépendant et aventureux, type aussi du gentilhomme galant." [39] Very pertinently, with respect to my concerns here, the same critic observes (apropos of Nerval's lost play *La Polygamie est*

---

[35] *Ibid.*
[36] *Ibid.,* p. 30.
[37] *Ibid.,* pp. 7, 272, and Jean Richer, ed., *Œuvres complémentaires de Gérard de Nerval: La Vie du théâtre, II* (Paris, 1961), p. 491. For similar quotations from other writers linking Byron and Goethe, see Estève, *Byron et le romantisme français,* pp. 201-02.
[38] See note 17, *supra*.
[39] Norma Rinsler, "Nerval et Biron," p. 406 (Miss Rinsler details Gérard's interest in Mozart's *Don Giovanni,* as well).

un cas pendable): "L'équivalence plus ou moins inconsciente Biron-Byron-Don Juan est évidemment à l'origine de cette pièce."[40] While the gentle and germanophile Nerval may have found in Faust a more sympathetic model of the lover in pursuit of "l'éternel féminin," one cannot doubt that the glamorous Don Juan exerted a profound spell over him too.

If Faust and Don Juan are types of the unhappy lover, Cain personifies unhappiness itself. Studying the pertinent passages from the *Voyage en Orient* ("Les nuits du Ramazan," chapters vi-vii) and the article "Diorama" (*Œuvres*, II, 1233-36), Richer reveals the place of Cain and his descendants in Gérard's mythological universe: "Cette race de Caïn, dans l'esprit de Nerval, se confond avec celle des demiurges et des grands hommes méconnus que nous avons précédemment étudiée [i.e., Faust, Satan, Karl Moor, Lara, etc.]. Une telle élite est issue des Maîtres du feu."[41]

Yet another literary motif links the two poets in a significant way. Both participated in the general revival of interest in folksongs and ballads. Byron's rôle in this movement is slight, admittedly, and his efforts the mere dabblings of a boy who grew up in the age which knew and loved Ossian, Percy's *Reliques*, and Burns. One of his French biographers, however, speaks of the young Byron's "goût pour les traditions populaires."[42] In Nerval, who translated various ballads by such poets as Goethe, Burger, and Uhland in his *Poésies allemandes* (1830) and who was deeply immersed in the popular traditions of his beloved Valois, the interest in folksongs may be called a literary passion. The crucial text is, of course, his "Chansons et légendes du Valois," published in seven different forms by Gérard.[43] It is there, it

---

[40] *Ibid.*
[41] Richer, *Nerval*, p. 151. Douglas Radcliffe-Umstead has written on this subject: see his article "Cainism and Gérard de Nerval," *Philological Quarterly*, XLV (1966), 395-408. He insists on Nerval's "originality" in the treatment of the Cain theme vis-à-vis Byron: Nerval, he says, "is pushing beyond Dandyism" (p. 400).
[42] Emile Souvestre, "Notice sur Lord Byron," p. viii.
[43] Nerval, *Œuvres*, I, 294-304. See also the texts assembled by Béguin and Richer under the heading "Sur les chansons populaires" (*Œuvres*, I, 456-62) and the appropriate notes by these editors (*Œuvres*, I, 1162-66, 1196-97). As usual, it is helpful to consult Richer, *Nerval*, pp. 323-32. According to Richer, "... Gérard a été en France un véritable initiateur" (p. 323). See also Paul Bénichou, *Gérard de Nerval et la chanson folklorique* (Paris, 1970).

will be recalled, that he refers to the song about Armand de Gontaut, baron de Biron: "Quand Biron voulut danser" (*Œuvres*, I, 300).

Gérard may have been unaware of this aspect of Byron's literary life. It is time to deal with the question of just what he *could* have known and probably did know about the English poet, over and above the specific works already mentioned. Estève's massive study of *Byron et le romantisme français* reveals that the possible sources of Nerval's information are legion. Byron's works, both in the original and in French; individual works and collective editions; poems about Byron (inspired especially by his death in the Greek War); critical articles; translations of the principal biographical materials in English (Thomas Moore, Lady Blessington, Thomas Medwin, John Galt, R. C. Dallas, even Lady Caroline Lamb's *Glenarvon*); paintings on Byronic themes (Géricault, Louis Boulanger, Horace Vernet, and especially, of course, Delacroix); countless reflections of Byron's influence in French poetry, fiction, and drama; special studies of Byron's impact on the major French Romantics — all this and more is heaped up in Estève's book. On Nerval himself, Estève has little to say, for Nerval was still a minor writer when Estève did his work (the original editions appeared in 1907). Suffice it to say that the atmosphere of Romantic France was permeated with Byronic emanations. Those which probably mattered most to Nerval were those to be found in the works (and, to some extent, the lives) of the great French writers of his time. Chateaubriand complained rather peevishly that *Childe Harold* was copied from *René* or, rather more to the point, that Byron failed to acknowledge his debt.[44] Madame de Staël received Byron into the Coppet group during his stay in Switzerland (1816) and greatly admired *Lara*.[45] Lamartine addressed passionate yet admiring reproaches to the English poet in "L'homme" (*Méditations poétiques*, 1820) and presumed to write a sequel to *Childe Harold's Pilgrimage*, "Dernier chant du pèlerinage d'Harold" (1825). Vigny reviewed the 1819 version of Pichot's translation of Byron's *Œuvres complètes* in *Le Conservateur Littéraire* of December, 1820, and, among the many examples of Byron's influence on his poetry, we must note especially that of a passage from *Childe Harold* (IV, xxi) about the stoicism of the dying wolf. Hugo wrote a

---

[44] In a section of his *Essai sur la littérature angloise* (1835), reprinted with some modifications in *Mémoires d'outre-tombe* (see note 31, *supra*).

[45] See Estève, *Byron et le romantisme français*, pp. 54-55.

necrological article "Sur George Gordon, lord Byron" (reprinted in *Littérature et philosophie mêlées,* 1834), splashed Byronic colors over his own *Orientales* (1829), and, perhaps most importantly, assimilated *Mazeppa.* Balzac and Mérimée wrote scathingly of Thomas Moore's biography.[46] Dumas created Byronic heroes in drama (*Antony,* 1831) and fiction (*Le Comte de Monte-Cristo,* 1844-1845). George Sand interpreted *Manfred* in her "Essai sur le drame fantastique" (*Revue des Deux Mondes,* December 1, 1839), and, with suitable changes, modeled Lélia after Manfred, Cain, and Childe Harold, though, obviously, Byron's heroes were not her only models. To complete and crown this digest of Estève's findings, there is the Byronism of Musset, who, in his elegance and dandyism, in his blend of wit and irony with gloom and passion, of cynicism with sentiment, indeed of Classicism and Romanticism, seems almost a French reincarnation of the English poet. In short, on every hand, in the works and the lives of the leading French Romantics, on the surface and deep beneath it, Nerval found the presence and image of Byron.

From all these sources, Gérard would have extracted a Byron strikingly like himself or, rather, like the self he created for himself. What separated them — social rank, for example — could be more than compensated by the French poet's imagination and miraculous powers of wishful thinking: the bourgeois Nerval invented more glamorous ancestors than the noble Byron could actually claim. As for the differences of temperament, the modest and gentle Gérard could look to Byron and see the fulfillment of his own dreams of love and glory. Were they not both poets, both lovers, both unhappy? Whatever else he may be, the person who speaks to us in "El Desdichado" is above all else an unhappy lover and poet. That the "prince d'Aquitaine" is, like his creator and like Byron, a poet is evident from the "luth constellé" of line three and the allusion to Orpheus in the final tercet. That all three poets are also lovers is equally clear: in Nerval's poem, the singer's "star" is dead, the flower which once consoled him is dead, his brow has been kissed by a mysterious queen; on his journeys to the underworld, he transposed on his lyre "Les soupirs de la *sainte* et les cris de la *fée*" (italics mine). It is of course primarily as lovers

---

[46] Balzac, *Œuvres complètes,* XXVIII, 397-98; for Mérimée's article (*Le National,* June 3, 1830), see Pierre Trahard, *La Jeunesse de Prosper Mérimée (1803-1834)* (Paris, 1925), II, 152-60.

that the two poets and Nerval's *persona* are unhappy — after all, the poem is entitled "El Desdichado" (i.e., the unfortunate), and its phraseology and imagery create en overwhelming impression of melancholy and despair: "ténébreux," "veuf," "inconsolé," "Ma seule *étoile* est morte," "le *soleil* noir de la *Mélancolie*," "la nuit du tombeau," "mon coeur désolé" (italics Nerval's). In the crucial ninth line, the love stories evoked are generally tales of frustration and suffering: Psyche endured a long separation from Cupid; Daphne was transformed into a laurel tree just as Phoebus caught up with her; Lusignan discovered Mélusine's shameful secret and so lost her; as for Biron — well, there are many Birons, as I hope to have shown, but most came to a bad end: Armand de Gontaut was killed at the siege of Epernay; Charles de Gontaut was beheaded for treason; Armand-Louis de Gontaut (duc de Lauzun) was guillotined during the Terror; Byron died young in Greece, after having known exile, ostracism, and ennui.

Since it is this last Biron who concerns me here, I wish now to point to various resemblances and affinities between Byron and Nerval of which the latter may have been unaware, but which he easily could have known. Even leaving aside the voluminous biographical materials which swamped France ca. 1825-1830 (Moore, Lady Blessington, Medwin, Galt, etc.), there are many relatively brief biographical sketches accessible to Gérard and in which he would have found ample evidence of moral and spiritual affinities between Byron and himself (and the *persona* of "El Desdichado"). I have studied in particular four documents of this type: (1) Nodier's "Notice préliminaire" for the *Œuvres de Lord Byron*, translated by Amédée Pichot (Paris: Ladvocat, 1823), I, i-xx; (2) Pichot's own "Essai sur le génie et le caractère de Lord Byron" (*ibid.*, pp. 3-183); (3) Villemain's article "Byron" for Michaud's *Biographie universelle*, originally published in 1835, reprinted in later editions of Michaud and in Villemain's own *Etudes de littérature ancienne et étrangère* (1846); and (4) Emile Souvestre's "Notice sur Lord Byron," accompanying Benjamin Laroche's translation of the *Œuvres complètes de Lord Byron* (Paris: Charpentier, 1838), pp. vii-xvi.

Nodier's essay, not really a biography but a general "appreciation" of Byron, sees in him a symptom of an age of upheaval and transition and especially of the collapse of Christianity. Perhaps his central thought is best captured in these words:

> La mélancolie, espèce de maladie mentale dont le nom indique l'origine toute physique, n'avait présenté à l'antiquité classique que l'idée d'une triste infirmité; [in modern times] elle devint une muse. [47]

The vocabulary and imagery Nodier uses are perhaps more telling than his argument: "frénésie," "tombeau," "néant," "frénétique," "maladie sociale," "monument triste," "nos infortunes ... et nos erreurs," "images ténébreuses," "l'Erèbe," "la Nuit," "émanations informes et muettes des tombeaux," "terreur," "morts," "sinistres images," "abstraction indéfinissable et terrible," "pensée corrompue," "fol orgueil," and so on throughout the article.

In the more truly biographical sketches of Pichot, Villemain, and Souvestre, these same ideas and images appear and re-appear, in less lurid terms. After his account of Byron's eccentric and turbulent ancestors, their loyalty to the luckless Stuarts, his father's mistreatment of his mother and his early death, the poet's club foot, the hostile criticism of *Hours of Idleness,* the young nobleman's frustrated loves and betrayed friendships, Pichot summarizes Byron's early experiences in these terms: "Les ennuis de la société pesèrent sur son coeur." [48] In all three sketches, but especially in Villemain's, much is made of the crumbling Gothic picturesqueness of Newstead Abbey. [49] The early death of Byron's father and the young Byron's difficult relations with his mother (who also died when he was relatively young) would inevitably remind Nerval of his own orphaned state. [50] The three biographers all tell essentially the same story and create the same image of the poet: they dwell on his restless travels, his unhappy love affairs, his marriage and the scandal and ostracism which grew out of it. Pride, violence, despair, skepticism, revolt, isolation — such are the recurrent motifs. Several passages seem predestined to catch Gérard's

---

[47] Nodier, "Notice préliminaire" (Amédée Pichot, trans., *Œuvres de Lord Byron* [Paris, 1823], I, vi).

[48] Pichot, "Essai sur le génie et le caractère de Lord Byron," p. 33.

[49] The death's head which Byron transformed into a goblet was the inspiration, directly or indirectly, for a similar prank on Nerval's part in the heady days ca. 1830 (see Aristide Marie, *Gérard de Nerval,* p. 40). Pichot had given the detail on p. 34 of his sketch.

[50] Gérard's relationship with his father, Dr. Etienne Labrunie, has been variously evaluated; see Norma Rinsler, "Gérard de Nerval and the Divinities of Fire," *passim.*

eye. Calling Byron "un fils de l'Orient," Souvestre goes on to observe: "Il y avait en effet chez Byron tous les fiers instincts du Nord mêlés aux aspirations brûlantes du Midi" (p. x). Gérard was later to write: "Lord Byron, qui né dans la brumeuse Angleterre, n'en est pas moins un fils du soleil." [51] The poet who identifies himself with "Le prince d'Aquitaine à la tour abolie" might well have noted the passage (p. xi) where Souvestre writes (apropos of the critics who attacked *Childe Harold*): "Les sarcasmes de Byron ... leur parurent imprégnés d'un poison sans remède, lorsqu'ils virent le poëte vengeur

>   Comme une vaste tour assis dans son orgueil."

Combining this image with the recurring motif of the vast Gothic pile of Newstead Abbey (Pichot [p. 10] refers to "ses ruines"), Gérard might have found in these sketches of Byron's life the germ of that dense and mysterious line which a later poet inserted into *his* vision of a desolate world. [52]

As indicated above, the three biographies, with more or less detail, give essentially the same picture of Byron. Villemain's, however, contains several points that should have been of special interest to Nerval. In describing the literary situation in England just prior to Byron's rise to fame, Villemain has occasion to mention the madness of Cowper, and, despite Villemain's evident lack of sympathy for him, Gérard would certainly have empathized with a fellow-poet "dont l'inspiration, tardive et capricieuse, avait, pour ainsi dire, fermenté, durant *un long intervalle de souffrance et folie où sommeillait son âme....*" [53] Byron's attempt to learn Armenian would surely have created a bond of sympathy between him and the French poet who had pored over various *grimoires* (Dom Pernety, Court de Gébelin, etc.) in his uncle's library at Mortefontaine and whose mind, in a sense, was ever sailing to the East. Villemain writes of Byron's delving into Armenian and some related scholarship: "Cette étude et surtout quelques extraits cosmogoniques de Moïse de Chosroène ramenaient l'imagination du jeune poëte à ces problèmes religieux dont son scepticisme était souvent

---

[51] See note 19, *supra*.
[52] T. S. Eliot, *The Waste Land*, line 430.
[53] Villemain, "Byron," p. 282 (italics mine).

agité, et qui lui ont inspiré le mystère de *Caïn*." [54] Finally, Villemain's insistence on the essential sameness of Byron's heroes and heroines and his explanation of this phenomenon offer a recognizable description of Gérard's own creations and their *raison d'être* (if one makes allowance for a basic difference of temperament — "altier" and "orgueil" do not fit "le bon Gérard"). Byron, says Villemain, had a literary imagination fed by his subjectivity alone and so created but one type of man and one type of woman:

> l'un sombre, altier, dévoré de chagrin, ou insatiable de plaisir, qu'il s'appelle Harold, Conrad, Lara, Manfred, ou Caïn; l'autre, tendre, dévouée, soumise, mais capable de tout par amour, qu'elle soit Julia, Haïdée, Zuléika, Gulnare ou Médora. Cet homme, c'est lui-même; cette femme, celle que voudrait son orgueil. [55]

This passage brings us back to "El Desdichado," for it offers us the same immortal pair: hero and heroine, the unhappy poet-lover and the woman of his dreams, the woman who could console him or who, in some strange past, brought him moments of supreme consolation. The very sameness of characterization brought out by Villemain is only another version of the perpetual identity that Nerval finds everywhere for himself and his beloved. Just as Harold, Conrad, Lara, Manfred, and Cain are all the same and all Byron, so "le ténébreux," "le veuf," "l'inconsolé," the Prince of Aquitaine whose tower lies ruined, and Orpheus are all one and all Nerval. So, too, "[sa] seule *étoile*," "La fleur qui plaisait tant à [son] coeur désolé," "la reine," "la sirène," "la sainte," and "la fée" are the different and yet identical incarnations of Woman whom Gérard pursued as Adrienne and Sylvie in the Valois, as the Queen of Sheba in the Orient, as Aurélia in Vienna, Brussels, and Paris:

> La Treizième revient... C'est encor la première:
> Et c'est toujours la seule....

---

[54] *Ibid.*, 285. Richer, in his *Nerval*, does not mention Moïse de Chosroène (i.e., Moses of Chorene, great Armenian historian of the Fifth Century A.D.) as a source of Nerval's Cainism, but this exotic name and the reference to Cain are well calculated to attract Gérard's attention.

[55] Villemain, "Byron," p. 289.

Thus the pattern at the center of Byron's world is essentially the same as that at the center of Nerval's. I believe I have shown that many of the lesser features — lesser, but still characteristic — of their two worlds are also identical. When the French poet-lover asks: "Suis-je Amour ou Phébus?... Lusignan ou Biron?" is he not inviting us to imagine a dynasty of ill-fated Birons stretching from some princely troubadour of Aquitaine to the great English poet?

GAUTIER'S USE OF COMPARISON IN MADEMOISELLE DE MAUPIN

ALBERT B. SMITH
University of Florida

Critics generally refuse to accord Théophile Gautier talent as a novelist. Even when they admire a work like *Mademoiselle de Maupin*, they are quick to call attention to alleged flaws in its structure. Adolphe Boschot, for example, criticizes the novel for its lack of representational unity (shifts from epistolary form to third-person narrative to dialogue), the lack of clarity in its plot development, and ambiguities in the introduction of characters.[1] René Jasinski taxes Gautier for his failure to organize consistently the elements of the story and to establish proper values among them.[2]

Close study of the narrative discloses that the form which Gautier gives it is eminently appropriate to the theme. Shifts in narrative manner are unobtrusive and have value, moreover, in maintaining the relationship between reader and characters which Gautier evidently desires. The arrangement of the episodes is consistent with the requirements of the action, each major event being introduced to fulfill a specific purpose: either character delineation or plot development, or both.

Character, too, is determined by theme. As I have demonstrated elsewhere,[3] Gautier depicts in his novel two protagonists in search of happiness, d'Albert through possession of an incarnation of ideal

---

[1] Introduction to *Mademoiselle de Maupin*, nouv. éd. revue (Paris, s.d.), pp. xxiv-xxvi.

[2] *Les Années romantiques de Th. Gautier* (Paris, 1929), pp. 313-315.

[3] "Gautier's *Mademoiselle de Maupin*: The Quest of Happiness," *Modern Language Quarterly*, XXXII (1971), 168-174.

female beauty, Madelaine de Maupin through love with a man perfect in his devotion. Consideration of the other characters — whether introduced or simply mentioned — reveals that they, too, desire happiness. Rosette, like Madelaine, wants perfect love, but through a relationship in which sexual enjoyment will be equally as strong as psychic satisfaction. Rosette's aunt wishes above all to regain the joy of maternal love after the death of her son. Even d'Albert's crude manservant is intent on being happy — after his own coarse fashion. Happiness is thus Gautier's general concern in *Mademoiselle de Maupin,* and character is based upon a personage's particular approach to this problem.

In studying the novel, one notices that Gautier makes frequent use of comparison, inviting the reader to see differences of degree or kind among the desires of various characters and among potential sources of satisfaction. Since any approach to happiness implies intensity in the subject's desire, together with his attitude toward objects offering the possibility of satisfaction, comparison can be an especially valuable means for clarifying the nature of a particular approach. It is my aim here to analyze how Gautier uses this means and, by demonstrating his competence, to suggest the need for reconsidering his novelistic talent.

In d'Albert's depiction of his situation and character he makes four comparisons which relate him to others in the pursuit of happiness. The first is between himself and his servant. While d'Albert is bored in the midst of affluence and dreams only of the pleasures he would have in leading a different existence, the servant is content with the material comforts he enjoys in d'Albert's service. Although he is widely traveled, having experienced for himself everything of which d'Albert dreams, he is unimpressed by all that he has seen and done. D'Albert qualifies him as a simpleton incapable of either feeling or reflection and expresses anger that such a dullard should have had the opportunity to take part in exciting adventures while he, the master, has remained at home uninspired.[4]

A few pages farther on d'Albert compares himself with three types: the drunkard, the sensualist, and the gambler (p. 63). These, he says,

---

[4] *Mademoiselle de Maupin,* ed. Adolphe Boschot, nouv. éd. revue (Paris, s.d.), p. 42. Subsequent references will be to this edition and will appear in the body of my text.

have passions which they can satisfy. The drunkard, in his worst degradation, considers himself as happy as a king if he has access to alcohol. The sensualist is literally ecstatic in the presence of a prostitute. The gambler requires only a dirty deck of cards and a gaming table to experience the keenest pleasure. D'Albert envies these men, for he cannot be so easily pleased.

Gautier does not make an explicit comparison between d'Albert and his friend, de C***, yet comparison is evident in the episode which takes place at Mme de Thémines' salon, where de C*** has promised to help d'Albert satisfy his desires (pp. 68-80). By this point d'Albert has focused his dream: he wants a mistress. It is natural, then, that he should consult de C***, who is an expert in the game of love. De C*** cultivates only women who have high social position. While they must also possess superior charm and beauty, they must above all be highly sophisticated in love, with experience in the sexual art and a readiness to enjoy erotic pleasures. De C*** considers the women in Mme de Thémines' salon eminently attractive, "un monde de jolies femmes, —une collection d'idéalités réelles" (p. 68). By contrast, d'Albert is disappointed in them, for he requires more than the sexual desire which they arouse in him.

D'Albert twice compares himself with his correspondent, Silvio. In the first instance he depicts Silvio as fortunate in that he accepts life as it comes, without attempting to create an existence different from the one he enjoys. He is supremely happy in love and seeks no greater satisfaction. While d'Albert does not envy Silvio, he wishes it might be given to him, too, to partake of such felicity (pp. 60-61).

Later d'Albert defines Silvio's happiness. Silvio's relationship with his fiancée is calm and chaste. He is interested not in her physical charms but rather in her beauty of soul. His love is thus pure, depending in no way on such extraneous elements as esthetic appeal or sex to give it value. Though d'Albert desires such bliss, he recognizes that the kind of love which Silvio enjoys could never produce the same sense of well-being in himself (p. 182).

Gautier uses these comparisons as an aid in disclosing d'Albert's character in respect to his ideal. The drunkard, the sensualist, and the gambler, for example, serve to clarify his notion of happiness. By his depiction of the sensualist's and the gambler's emotional reactions, d'Albert implicitly qualifies the feeling which he himself wishes to experience on meeting his incarnated ideal. As for the sensualist, "son oeil blanchit, sa lèvre se trempe; il atteint au dernier degré de son bonheur, il a l'extase de sa grossière volupté" (p. 63); in the gambler moments of keen excitement and nervous spasms mark his pleasure (*Ibid.*). This is what d'Albert desires. The word that he uses in regard to the sensualist — ecstasy — he would apply to his own idea of happiness. His joy when he at last confronts his ideal in Madelaine de Maupin (pp. 204, 256, 366) is scarcely different in quality from that of the men with whom he compares himself.

The greatest value of these comparisons, however, is in emphasizing the extent of d'Albert's desire and in defining its character. Gautier sets up a hierarchy among the individuals whom he compares, basing their placement upon the relative difficulty with which they will achieve full satisfaction. At the lowest point on the scale stands the servant, easily content with material well-being. Next Gautier places the Silvio of d'Albert's first comparison, his low position in the hierarchy determined by the relative ease with which he has found happiness. Somewhat higher stand the drunkard, the sensualist, and the gambler, less easy to please because their passions require specific objects for satisfaction. Yet higher we find de C***. If he resembles the sensualist in his pursuit of erotic pleasure, he is far more discriminating. It is d'Albert who stands at the top of the scale. None of the sources of happiness posited by the others comes anywhere near satisfying him; and it is precisely the function of the hierarchization to demonstrate this fact. By setting his hero against the other men in a hierarchy, Gautier leads the reader to measure the extent of d'Albert's idealism.

Not until the salon episode does d'Albert make explicit the character of his ideal. The comparison with de C*** again serves here. Before this moment one might consider d'Albert as but another young man seeking more or less eagerly to have an affair. Indeed, this is apparently the way in which de C*** views his young friend — as a sensualist only slightly more discriminating than himself. Yet Gautier demonstrates, by contrasting his hero with de C***, that d'Albert's demands are of a different order. While he may be sexually aroused, he states flatly that such excitement as this will not give him the happiness he desires. He furthermore indicates why: these women, though the loveliest that high society has to offer, do not touch his esthetic sense. Only at this moment does it become evident that beauty is what is essential to d'Albert's happiness.

The function of d'Albert's second comparison with Silvio, together with explicit statements to the same effect, is to restrict yet another element from his ideal. By stressing Silvio's love for his fiancée's beauty of soul while regretting his own inability to enjoy Silvio's brand of pleasure, d'Albert implies his own indifference to this quality as an ingredient of happiness. He has already made this indifference explicit: "Je n'ai jamais demandé aux femmes qu'une seule chose, — c'est la beauté; je me passe très volontiers d'esprit et d'âme.... Je préfère une jolie bouche à un joli mot, et une épaule bien modelée à une vertu, même théologale" (p. 133). His desires are exclusive; only in discovering perfect beauty will he have achieved happiness.

In his representation of d'Albert's idealism Gautier also exploits comparison among objects which may be considered as possible sources of satisfaction. Here, too, he sets up a hierarchy. D'Albert's first attempt to find a mistress ends in failure: scarcely one out of a hundred women is passably attractive. Then, when he considers the women gathered in Mme de Thémines' salon, he regretfully acknowledges that they are little more appealing than the others. In fact, only two interest him at all; and they, as we have observed, stir him only sexually. Rosette is his choice among these women; but with her he enjoys nothing beyond refined physical gratification. Something is yet lacking: the ideal which he conceives. Only Madelaine de Maupin stands at the top of the hierarchy, perfect beauty at last incarnate.

By thus employing comparisons among objects as well as among seekers of happiness, Gautier further indicates the reach of d'Albert's particular desires. A man with ordinary demands would easily find, among so many women as d'Albert considers, one who satisfied him. That d'Albert is forced to reject all before he meets Madelaine emphasizes how extreme his idealism is.

Comparison among objects also functions to explain d'Albert's changing emotional state during the course of his search. He sways at first between hopefulness and frustration. But as he considers other women, his frustration grows. The pleasure he enjoys with Rosettte soon turns stale, and he feels more keenly than ever the anguish of unfulfilled desire. It is precisely the comparison between ideal and reality, constantly forcing itself upon his mind, that brings on his growing sense of desperation.

More important yet is the value of comparison in conveying an idea of Madelaine de Maupin's exceptional beauty. Gautier must have recognized early that the subject which he was treating in his novel posed a fundamental and difficult problem: how to make the reader sense such rare beauty as Madelaine's. Indeed, he has d'Albert acknowledge explicitly the inability of language to meet this challenge adequately: "S'il y avait des mots pour rendre ce que je sens, je te ferais une description de cinquante pages; mais les langues ont été faites par je ne sais quels goujats qui n'avaient jamais regardé avec attention le dos ou le sein d'une femme, et l'on n'a pas la moitié des termes les plus indispensables" (p. 257). Obviously Madelaine's beauty cannot be successfully *described*. The novelist in Gautier's situation must use other means, if not to state, then to suggest. Herein lies the value of comparison. Considering Madelaine after having followed d'Albert through his rejections of women progressively more charming, the reader does not need a description of her beauty. Description would in fact weaken the representation. The reader *feels* her perfection. While other devices have also played a role in Gautier's depiction, it is comparison that in large part governs the reader's reaction.

Another type of comparison which figures in d'Albert's self-characterization employs mythological personages. In clarifying the nature of his orientation, d'Albert alludes to the Virgin Mary and Venus (pp. 191-193). While both are beautiful, only the latter attracts his admiration. Mary's beauty is too spiritualized, its cast otherworldly. It is a beauty which orients the viewer toward the immaterial. Venus, on the other hand, appeals to d'Albert precisely because she is terrestrial:

> La Vénus sort de la mer pour aborder au monde, —comme il convient à une divinité qui aime les hommes, —toute nue et toute seule. —Elle préfère la terre à l'Olympe et a pour amants plus d'hommes que de dieux: elle ne s'enveloppe pas des voiles langoureux de la mysticité; elle se tient debout, son dauphin derrière elle, le pied sur sa conque de nacre; le soleil frappe sur son ventre poli, et de sa blanche main elle soutient en l'air les flots de ses beaux cheveux où le vieux père Océan a semé ses perles les plus parfaites. —On la peut voir: elle ne cache rien, car la pudeur n'est faite que pour les laides, et c'est une invention moderne, fille du mépris chrétien de la forme et de la matière (p. 193).

By this comparison d'Albert confirms much that he has been saying about his orientation. He is in no way inclined toward things spiritual.

Enjoyment for him will derive from sensuous pleasures taken in the here-and-now. His appreciation is, furthermore, plastic, his description as if made by a painter or sculptor. This essentially esthetic approach to objects is further evident in his ironic attack on the scorn for form and matter which he sees as fundamental in Christianity. Finally, the comparison confirms his amorality. D'Albert frequently calls attention to his indifference to moral qualities and asserts his hatred of that morality which places constraints on free enjoyment through the senses. He is a thorough-going materialist; his preference for Venus confirms this dominant trait in his personality.

As in his depiction of d'Albert, Gautier also invites the reader to compare Madelaine's desires with those of others seeking a similar means of happiness, and he has her also make comparisons among objects presenting the possibility of satisfaction. In her first letter to Graciosa, Madelaine compares herself with her friend in the question of their attitude toward love (pp. 207-208). Writing of their earlier life and feelings, she emphasizes the ignorance in which they existed. Since neither knew about men's potential as lovers, they formed romantic preconceptions of love, both longing for absolute devotion. But, while Graciosa spent her time dreaming of the flamboyant and the heroic, Madelaine felt a need to know what men were like. Suspecting that they might not be capable of or interested in such devotion as she desired, she assumed her male disguise and ran away from home to observe men in their own environment and in their unguarded moments, so as to discover their attitudes toward the women they professed to love.

Gautier utilizes the comparison between Madelaine and Graciosa to provide an initial characterization of his heroine. In her letter she shows herself to be chiefly interested in the question of perfect love. As she continues to disclose her personality in successive statements, this amorous concern proves to be her overriding preoccupation. She furthermore reveals a fundamental scepticism. While Graciosa merely dreams of an adoring lover, Madelaine sets out to learn for herself whether such a man even exists. As Gautier will show farther on, this sceptical strain is but one aspect of a complex of traits which make up a masculine side of Madelaine's personality. Indeed, it will be this very masculinity which in the end appears as the insurmountable obstacle to her hopes for happiness.

While d'Albert's idealism is predominantly materialistic, Madelaine's is ethical, in that happiness for her will depend on the lover's attitude toward the beloved and toward love (pp. 339-340 *et passim*). If quality of soul matters not at all for d'Albert, it is of paramount concern to Madelaine. We have already considered another character in the novel whose orientation parallels Madelaine's: Silvio. Though Gautier does not explicitly establish a relation between these two, the similarity in their respective approaches invites a comparison which helps to clarify Madelaine's idealism.

Silvio, as we have seen, has found happiness in love. Madelaine never does, at least in the course of the novel, and she despairs of ever finding it. The comparison points up yet another reason why she fails. Silvio has been characterized as a man easily satisfied. Gautier represents Madelaine as incapable of such facile happiness as Silvio enjoys. Her requirements, like d'Albert's, are extreme. By the comparison between her and Silvio, the reader acquires a fuller appreciation of the reach of her desires.

Gautier has Madelaine also make comparisons among objects offering the potential for satisfaction. Like d'Albert, she always considers these from the perspective of her ideal; and in her case, too, the reader recognizes a hierarchization. At the bottom of the scale stand the young noblemen whom she meets immediately after running away from home. Madelaine quickly understands that their only interest is in erotic satisfaction; they care little with whom. They are, moreover, morally despicable, because they are hypocritical. One of them has just left his fiancée, swearing everlasting devotion. On entering the inn where Madelaine meets him, he immediately arranges with the serving girl a meeting for that night, all the while ridiculing his fiancée's serious outlook on love (pp. 222-223). His friends, by applauding him, show themselves to have the same opinions. None of these men, then, could give Madelaine happiness; they have no interest in questions of "soul," and their capacity for devotion is minimal.

Madelaine soon discovers that the young noblemen's attitude is the rule rather than the exception (p. 224 *et passim*). They thus stand as representative of all men, so far as she is concerned. Indeed, only one of the many whom she has observed stands above them in the hierarchy. D'Albert has displayed an admirable honesty in remaining with Rosette long after ceasing to find her attractive. He is manifestly indifferent to the gratification of his carnal instincts. Madelaine finds both his personality and his person reasonably attractive. Above all, he has demonstrated that he loves her sincerely and with his fullest devotion. Yet she cannot accept him as the perfect lover that she demands. The reason is his fundamental materialism. While she recognizes in his esthetic aspiration a certain nobility, she perceives at the same time that such a bent accords no place to that single-minded concentration on the ethical which she requires in love (pp. 354-356).

Rosette, on the other hand, displays exactly the character that Madelaine desires. Rosette's love for Théodore is a perfect example of full, enduring, and single-minded devotion. Recognizing this, Madelaine can only lament that she and Rosette are of the same sex. In Rosette she would have found the felicity she desires (p. 344).

Comparison among objects in the representation of Madeleine's idealism functions, as in d'Albert's case, to emphasize the extent and character of her desires. While it is natural that the majority of men could not approach her ideal, certainly such intense love as that displayed by d'Albert should promise satisfaction. That Gautier has her reject even d'Albert — and for the reasons she gives — demonstrates just how absolute her requirements are. They allow of no adulteration, even in the most adoring lover, by concerns less noble than she demands. Intense devotion for the wrong reasons is as incapable of making her happy as is the essential carnality which she scorns in other men.

Obviously comparison is not the only device which Gautier uses in *Mademoiselle de Maupin* to clarify his protagonists' quest of happiness. It is, however, an extremely useful one for defining their particular ideals and the quality of their desires. Gautier's talent lies not only in this functional exploitation of comparisons but also — and especially — in the manner in which he introduces them. They are always natural and timed appropriately to carry the maximum effect. The relationship which Gautier establishes between progressively attractive objects and his protagonists' growing frustration that not even these can give full satisfaction, is a mark of the novelist's conscious preoccupation with form and of his competence in structuring his narrative. His talent is further evident in his use of comparison to have his characters *demonstrate* the personality which they have already said they have or will say is theirs. D'Albert's and Madelaine's presentation of their respective situations and desires is essentially confessional. But telling proves nothing. Demonstration is necessary if the reader is to consider them trustworthy as autoanalysts. By reporting his reaction to the beauties in Mme de Thémines' salon, d'Albert implicitly demonstrates the degree of his desire, which he has already stated is extreme. At the same time he reveals something about his idealism that we do not know. Nothing up to the salon episode reflects his indifference to sex: the reader has no reason not to infer that d'Albert's desire for a mistress involves a simple desire for sexual satisfaction. The comparisons which Gautier invites with de C*** and causes his hero to make between reality and ideal serve to eliminate sex as a motivation in d'Albert's conduct and to make clear that beauty is his dominant preoccupation. The capability with which Gautier handles such comparisons — the economy of his means in making them serve more than one function, his exploitation of them as organic parts of his narrative, and his effective timing of their introduction — suggests that he is far from untalented in building an effective narrative. Further structural analysis, not only of *Mademoiselle de Maupin* but of other novels and stories as well, would show him to be an eminently competent craftsman.

THE *HOMO DUPLEX* IN NINETEENTH-CENTURY FRENCH LITERATURE

JAMES M. SMITH
Emory University

The theme of the *homo duplex,* or the doubling of the personality, occupies a prominent place in nineteenth-century French literature. Several striking examples may be found in the writings of the Romantics. In the latter half of the century incidence of the theme is even more widespread. It is the purpose of this study to identify principal types of the *homo duplex,* to examine their origins and to propose an explanation of the more frequent occurrence of the double in post-Romantic French literature.

The French treatment of the theme owes its origins in part to German literature, in which the *Doppelgänger* was fully and variously developed. The more characteristic development of the *Doppelgänger* was external: that is, the double appeared as a separate being, capable of independent action. In one manifestation of the theme, the *Doppelgänger* involved a pair of friends, whose selves were so closely associated that in effect they shared but one soul in their two bodies, one the *alter ego* of the other. In other treatments the double was the creation of a wizard, in the form of a golem or mandrake, who did the bidding of his master. Still another popular variation on the *Doppelgänger* motif was the shadow double, as in Chamisso's *Peter Schlemihl,* in which the hero sells his shadow to the devil, only to have the former, that is, his second self, turn against him, thwarting his actions.

Less frequent in German literature of this period is the inner *homo duplex,* that is the disintegration or division of the personality, often under the stress of violent emotional shock, into opposing component elements, usually two in number and most often representative of good and evil. The two inner selves are characteristically successive, alternating in the individual, as in the case of Dr. Jekyl and Mr. Hyde, rather than occupying his psyche simultaneously.[1]

In French literature of the nineteenth century, one finds both external and inner treatments of the theme. The external treatment reflects for the most part the enduring interest, among the Romantics as well as among later writers, in the mysterious and the fantastic, with occasional and somewhat superficial psychological implications. For example, in his *conte* "Le chevalier double," Théophile Gautier tells of a knight, Oluf, born under a "double star," with a double personality. Once, in the darkness, he is confronted with a strange knight — his double. They fight and Oluf feels the wounds he gives as well as those he receives. He kills the spectre, and one of the stars under whose sign he was born disappears.

Alfred de Musset himself was said to have seen his double, while at Fontainebleau with Madame Sand. The latter had so unnerved Alfred with a recitation of her previous loves that he roamed about the forest in a daze, finally going to sleep at the bottom of a ravine. He was awakened by a man singing, a besotted man with a hideous face, who so terrified him that Musset fell to the ground, for he recognized the face as his own.[2] In Musset's "Nuit de décembre" the "étranger vêtu de noir" is often considered the poet's other self, who appears before him to console him. And in the last scene of Musset's *Les caprices de Marianne,* Octave says, at the tomb of Coelio: " 'Coelio était la bonne partie de moi-même.... Ce tombeau m'appartient; c'est moi qu'ils ont étendu sous cette froide pierre....' "[3]

Gérard de Nerval, in his life as well as in his works, which are in the main autobiographical, presents striking examples of the *homo duplex.* During his frequent and tragic seizures of madness he was sometimes visited by his *alter ego,*[4] and in his *Voyage en Orient,*

---

[1] On the *Doppelgänger* see Ralph Tymms, *Doubles in Literary Psychology* (Cambridge: Bowes and Bowes, 1949); and Otto Rank, *Don Juan: une étude sur le double* (Paris, 1932).

[2] Cf. Frances Winwar, *The Life of the Heart* (New York, 1945), p. 146.

[3] *Œuvres complètes* (Paris, s.d.), p. 401.

[4] Cf. Aristide Marie, *Gérard de Nerval, le poète, l'homme* (Paris, 1914), pp. 172-3.

Hakem, the hero of a tale contained therein, returns to his palace to see himself, that is, his double, marrying his sister. Similarly, in the last part of the *Aurélia*, Gérard himself sees his double marrying his sweetheart.

Among the post-Romantics several examples of the external *homo duplex* are to be found. In Rimbaud's prose piece entitled simply "Conte," a Prince "Galopait fièrement. Un Génie apparut, d'une beauté ineffable.... Le Prince était le Génie. Le Génie était le Prince." [5] Guy de Maupassant presents in "Le Horla" a combination of the theme of the external double with that of the vampire legend: " '...Quelqu'un accroupi sur moi, et qui, sa bouche sur la mienne, buvait ma vie....' " " 'Ce ne pouvait être que moi?' " [6] In *Double*, of Francis Poictevin, a woman awakes in a cold, deserted wilderness, unable to move. She slowly remembers that she has died. Suddenly her double appears before her, but even this is only an apparition, her real double having been freed at her death and fled to a more luminous world. [7] In the same work the hero dreams that his double appears to him in a mirror, with independent actions and attitudes.

In *L'ange et la sphinge*, of Edouard Schuré, we find a variation of the theme of two individuals with a single soul. The hero, Konrad, a knight turned monk, feels a strange affinity for a knight whose portrait hangs in his monastery. It seemed to him that they were the same person, and so they were. The living Konrad is a reincarnation of the Konrad in the painting, brought back to life to expiate the sins of the latter: " 'Lui et moi, nous étions la même personne...,' " declares the monk. [8]

Probably under the influence of Poe's "William Wilson," Henri de Régnier, in "Le seuil," presents a figure who digs a pool in sand, gazes into it and sees not his own face but the bloody visage of his mystic brother, his other self, from whom he tries to escape, to no avail. He then kills himself. [9]

---

[5] *Illuminations* (Paris, 1922).
[6] *Œuvres complètes* (Paris, 1938), VI, 229-30.
[7] *Double* (Paris, 1889), p. 118.
[8] *L'ange et la sphinge* (Paris, 1897), p. 137. In Schuré's *Le Double* the hero is haunted by his double, who appears before him, taunts him and interferes with his actions.
[9] *Poèmes: 1887-92* (Paris, s.d.).

In all of these treatments of the double we find two bodies, spectral or corporeal, sharing one soul.

Occurrences of the inner *homo duplex* in nineteenth-century French literature present a development more interesting and more characteristic of the French treatment of the theme, especially among post-Romantic writers. Unlike the outward manifestations of the double, which served importantly as plot elements, here the treatment is more analytical than narrative and is used more as a device to establish or explain character than one with which to develop or further plot structure. An important distinction must be made, furthermore, between the German and French developments of the inner *homo duplex*: among the French writers treating the subjects the two selves characteristically occupy the psyche simultaneously rather than consecutively. [10]

The inner development is more national in its origins. The rising Romantic movement had prepared a compatible terrain for the more introspective *homo duplex*. Rousseau had scrutinized his own actions and emotions, engaged in endless self-analysis. His Romantic heirs in general indulged in similar self-searching, often exaggerated to the state of neurosis. In Musset's autobiographical *Confession d'un enfant du siècle,* Octave, the hero, plumbs his ego, as does Sénancour's Obermann; Lamartine, Hugo and, to a lesser extent, Vigny, vivisected their hearts and presented them, still beating, to the public. At the end of Constant's *Adolphe,* the hero of which is also a victim of unwholesome self-probing, we find:

> Je hais cette vanité qui s'occupe d'elle-même en racontant le mal qu'elle a fait, qui a la prétention de se faire plaindre en se décrivant, et qui, planant indestructible au milieu des ruines, s'analyse au lieu de se repentir.... [11]

Exaggerated self-analysis, which by definition requires that one part of the ego observe the acts of another part, leads quite naturally

---

[10] Examples of the latter treatment occur in French literature in the period under consideration, for example in Marcel Schwob's *Cœur double* and in Maupassant's "Un fou"; but such examples are neither characteristic nor frequent.

[11] *Adolphe,* ed., William Morton Dey (New York and London, 1918), pp. 115-6.

to a doubling of the personality. Walter Pater pointed out as a special characteristic of Romantic eras "a consciousness brooding with delight over itself." [12]

In the post-Romantic period infinite interest in self is often expressed in an intense cultivation of sensations, characteristically followed by a cold and deliberate analysis of them. The Decadent hero, epitomized by Des Esseintes of Huysmans' *A rebours*, shows a more detached and at the same time more refined interest in his sensorium, upon which he performs exquisite experiments, than did the more simply organized Romantic hero. One of the best examples of this is found in the trilogy of Maurice Barrès, *Le culte du moi*. Philippe, the hero, cultivates his intellectual self and his sensory self; the former observes and analyzes the latter:

> Nous possédons là un don bien rare de noter les modifications de notre moi, avant que les frissons se soient effacés sur notre épiderme. Quand on a l'honneur d'être, à un pareil degré, passionné et réfléchi, il faut soigner en soi une particularité aussi piquante. Raffinons soigneusement de sensibilité et d'analyse. [13]

Fin-de-siècle literature provides many examples in which one part of the personality watches and observes the other. In *La Faustin*, of Edmond de Goncourt, the actress heroine declares:

> Voyez-vous, j'ai une chose qui ne me trompe pas.... Quand mon talent donne bien.... je m'écoute.... j'ai du plaisir à m'entendre.... je jouis de moi-même.... je suis en même temps et l'actrice et un peu mon public. [14]

In *Monsieur de Phocas*, of Jean Lorrain, the hero, after killing a man, states coolly to the police that he had felt himself doubled and that it seemed as though he were watching a play which he were directing himself. [15] Robert Greslou, in Bourget's *Le disciple*, also claims to have a dual personality, one part the spectator and the other the actor. In one of Barbey d'Aurevilly's *Diaboliques*, "La vengeance

---

[12] "Winckelmann," *Renaissance Studies* (London, 1910), p. 211.
[13] *Un homme libre* (Paris, 1937), p. 13.
[14] *La Faustin* (Paris, s.d.), p. 148.
[15] *Monsieur de Phocas* (Paris, s.d.), p. 399.

d'une femme," a decadent nobleman has "la faculté de se regarder faire et de se juger à mesure qu'il agit...." [16] Remy de Gourmont associated old, refined civilizations with doubling of the personality: "L'homme est un animal qui a le privilège de se regarder agir; et plus il est ancien dans la civilisation, plus il est cultivé, plus il se regarde avec complaisance." [17]

In Gourmont we find a *homo triplex,* an elaboration and embroidery on an established theme typical of the *fin-de-siècle.* In his novel *Sixtine,* he writes of the male protagonist, the writer d'Entragues:

> Sa triplicité, division scolastique bien élémentaire, il l'expliquait ainsi: une âme qui veut, une âme qui sait l'inutilité du vouloir, une âme qui regarde la lutte des deux autres et en redige l'iliade. [18]

Villiers de l'Islé-Adam also presents a tripling of the ego, in *Tribulat Bonhomet*: everyone is made up of a surface, or outer, being, dominated in turn by an inner being, the real being, which is usually animal in nature and more or less concealed by the outer or social being. To these parts of the ego Villiers adds a third element, the soul. At death the physiognomy becomes either markedly bestial or markedly spiritual, depending on which of the two inner natures, beast or soul, is ultimately the stronger. Bonhomet is made to exclaim: " '...Ce serait *Homo triplex,* qu'il faudrait dire.' " [19]

One significant element in the development of the inner *homo duplex* in France was, then, an abiding absorption in self. Another source was the revival of the concept of Original Sin and the corollary insistence on the moral duality of man. Joseph de Maistre, in his *Soirées de Saint-Pétersbourg,* both reflects and strengthens this revival:

> Dans l'état où [l'homme] est réduit, il n'a pas même le triste bonheur de s'ignorer: il faut qu'il se contemple sans cesse, et il ne peut se contempler sans rougir; sa grandeur même l'humilie, puisque ses lumières qui l'élèvent jusqu'à

---

[16] *Les diaboliques* (Paris, 1922), p. 280.
[17] *Le chemin de velours* (Paris, 1924), p. 45.
[18] *Sixtine* (Paris, 1928), p. 165-6.
[19] *Œuvres complètes* (Paris, 1923), III, 161.

l'ange ne servent qu'à lui montrer dans lui des penchants abominables qui le dégradent jusqu'à la brute. [20]

Xavier de Maistre put forth a similar idea, though it was not specifically related to Original Sin:

> ...L'homme est composé d'une âme et d'une bête.... On s'aperçoit bien... que l'homme est double.... C'est à la bête qu'il faut s'en prendre, à cet être sensible, parfaitement distinct de l'âme, véritable *individu,* qui a son existence séparée, ses goûts, ses inclinations, sa volonté.... [21]

Baudelaire, who was influenced by Joseph de Maistre, [22] continues to stress the moral dichotomy of man: "Il y a dans tout homme, à toute heure, deux postulations simultanées, l'une vers Dieu, l'autre vers Satan." [23] Even as a child, Baudelaire tells us, he felt two contradictory sentiments within his heart: "l'horreur de la vie et l'extase de la vie...." [24] To Baudelaire the *homo duplex* is essentially a statement of the conflict between man's baser instincts and his longing for the ideal, between the burden of sin imposed upon man since the Fall and the possibility of Redemption through suffering and Grace: "Dans la brute assoupie un ange se réveille." [25]

In writing of Chateaubriand's René, in 1848, Sainte-Beuve went to the heart of the theme, especially as it occurs in the latter half of the century: one part of the personality, the conventional, older, more experienced part, sits in judgment over the other, like an evil eye which disconcerts it, which prevents it from acting:

> Quand on est René, on est double; on est deux êtres d'âge différent, et l'un des deux, le plus vieux, le plus froid, le plus désabusé, regarde l'autre agir et sentir; et, comme

---

[20] *Soirées de Saint-Pétersbourg* (Paris, s.d.), I, 80.
[21] "Voyage autour de ma chambre," *Œuvres complètes* (Paris, s.d.), p. 16.
[22] Cf. Mother Mary Alphonsus, *The Influence of Joseph de Maistre on Baudelaire* (Bryn Mawr, Pennsylvania, 1943).
[23] "Mon cœur mis à nu," *Journaux intimes* (Paris, 1938), p. 62.
[24] *Ibid.,* p. 88.
[25] "L'aube spirituelle," *Les fleurs du mal* (Paris, 1922). Cf. Joséphin Péladan, *Le vice suprême* (Paris, 1886), p. 250: "L'homme est deux: esprit et brute, d'où deux existences parallèles et simultanées...." Cf., also, the quotation from Villiers de l'Isle-Adam, *supra.*

un mauvais oeil, il le glace, il le déjoue. L'un est toujours
là qui empêche l'*autre* d'agir tout simplement, naturellement,
et de se laisser aller à la bonne nature. [26]

Baudelaire recognized this, asking: "Qui parmi nous n'est pas un *homo duplex?* ...Toujours double, action et intention, rêve et réalité; toujours l'un nuisant à l'autre...." [27] In *Le double,* of Edouard Schuré, we read:

> Il y a souvent dans l'homme deux consciences opposées....
> Elles se combattent sans se vaincre. Impossible de faire taire
> l'une ou l'autre. Chacune va son train logiquement, infaillible-
> ment, démolissant l'œuvre de l'adversaire, sans que nous puis-
> sions l'arrêter, si bien que nous ne sommes plus qu'un théâtre
> de ruines et de destruction. [28]

The same idea is found in Villiers' *Tribulat Bonhomet,* in which Dr. Lenoir says: " '...Cet être extérieur, seul accessible et perceptible, n'a-t-il pas toujours en lui son spectateur, son contradicteur, son juge?' " [29]

Philippe, the decadent hero of Barrès' *Un homme libre,* complains of the difficulty of freeing the better part of his ego from the baser part. He finds it necessary to give up the inactive life of solitude in which he had been cultivating his *moi,* for " 'la partie basse de mon être, mécontente de son inaction, troublait parfois le meilleur de moi-même. Parmi les hommes je lui ai trouvé des joujoux, afin qu'elle me laisse la paix.' " " 'D'ailleurs, mon *moi du dehors,* que me fait! ...Ce qui importe uniquement, c'est mon *moi du dedans*....' " [30] Huysmans' Durtal, as presented in *La cathédrale,* is, by implication at least, a *homo duplex.* The struggle within him between his desire to believe and his pride, which stands in the way, amounts to a doubling of the personality. Here again we find one part of his being observing and interfering with the actions of the other part:

---

[26] *Chateaubriand et son groupe littéraire sous l'empire* (Paris, 1889), p. 345. This study was delivered as a series of lectures, at Liege, in 1848-9; it was first published in 1860.

[27] *L'artiste* (Paris), January, 1859.

[28] *Le double* (Paris, 1899), p. 144.

[29] Pp. 157-8. Cf. Maurice Barrès, preface to *Un homme libre,* p. iv: "Il y a dans ma conscience un moqueur, qui surveille mes expériences les plus sincères et qui rit quand je patauge."

[30] Pp. 230, 165.

> Dès qu'il entrait dans une église ou s'agenouillait chez lui, il sentait le froid lui geler ses prières et lui glacer l'âme, il discernait les attaques sourdes, les assauts muets d'un ridicule orgueil.[31]

He, too, suffers from hyper-analysis: " 'Ce que je suis las de me surveiller, de tâcher de surprendre le secret de mes mécomptes et de mes noises.' "[32] In André Gide's *Les faux-monnayeurs*, we find a later occurrence of the theme:

> "Quoi que je dise ou fasse, toujours une partie de moi reste en arrière, qui regarde l'autre se compromettre, qui l'observe, qui se fiche d'elle et la siffle, ou qui l'applaudit. Quand on est ainsi divisé, comment veux-tu qu'on soit sincère?"[33]

Of the dual personality one element is at times the executioner and the other the victim, thus fusing sadism and masochism into one exquisite sensation of pain and pleasure in the same person. The most noteworthy instance of this is the "Héautontimorouménos," in Baudelaire's *Fleurs du mal*:

> Je suis la plaie et le couteau!
> Je suis le soufflet et la joue!
> Je suis les membres et la roue,
> Et la victime et le bourreau!
> Je suis de mon coeur le vampire....[34]

Echoes of this are found in the following passage from *Sixtine*, of Remy de Gourmont:

> L'art de se mettre lui-même en croix, de se stigmatiser, comme un visionnaire, de mener en d'effroyables tortures, vers une agonie lente, son coeur labouré de morsures, l'art du bourreau de soi-même....[35]

---

[31] *La cathédrale* (Paris, 1930), I, 56.
[32] I, 293.
[33] *Les Faux-Monnayeurs* (Paris, 1926), p. 469.
[34] Cf. Baudelaire, "Mon cœur mis à nu," *Journaux intimes*, p. 54: "Il serait peut-être alternativement victime et bourreau." Cf., also, Albert Jhouney, "La reine," quoted without source in Charles Morice, *La littérature de tout à l'heure* (Paris: Perrin, 1889), p. 331: "Si tu veux être Lucifer et sa victime, / La tentatrice et la séduite...."
[35] P. 284.

One factor in the dichotomy of the *homo duplex* would seem to lie in the deep cleavage between bourgeois society and a significant number of writers, especially in the latter half of the century, who were engaged in a deliberate attack on accepted patterns of ethics, aesthetics and social customs. Baudelaire's antipathy toward the bourgeoisie is clearly documented in his writings, as well as in his somewhat childish antics calculated to startle his complacent compatriots. Yet Baudelaire, whose background was bourgeois, was saddled with a sense of guilt for not achieving the orderliness, calm, *mesure* and untroubled religious devotion which were his heritage. [36]

The Goncourt brothers, who, despite the particle before their name, came from bourgeois stock, shared Baudelaire's anti-bourgeois bias and like him sought deliberately to distinguish themselves from their less exquisitely organized contemporaries by deviating from the ways of the middle class. [37] Flaubert, like most of his major characters, was torn by conflicts between his desires and inclinations and the incapacity to fulfill them. His romantic longings in a materialistic age go far to explain his literary production. [38]

---

[36] Baudelaire's *Journaux intimes* yield various passages in which this sense of remorse and anxiety is clear. From "Fusées" we quote: "Fais tous les jours ce que veulent le devoir et la prudence." "Trop tard peut-être." "Je me jure à moi-même de prendre désormais les règles suivantes pour règles éternelles de ma vie:

"Faire tous les matins ma *prière à Dieu, réservoir de toute force et de toute justice, à mon père, à Mariette et à Poe,* comme intercesseurs; les prier de me communiquer *la force nécessaire* pour accomplir tous mes devoirs, et d'octroyer à ma mère *une vie assez longue* pour jouir de ma transformation; travailler toute la journée, ou du moins *tant que mes forces me le permettront;* me fier à Dieu; ...faire de tout ce que je gagnerai quatre parts, —une pour la vie courante, une pour mes créanciers, une pour mes amis, et une pour ma mère; —obéir aux principes de la plus stricte sobriété...."—pp. 46, 49.

[37] Throughout their *Journal* (Paris: Flammarion, s.d.) the antibourgeois bias of the Goncourts is explicit. For examples, see: I, 213, 215, 244; II, 178, III, 82; IV, 229. For the influence of this attitude on their aesthetic, see Pierre Sabatier, *L'esthétique des Goncourt* (Paris, 1920).

[38] Flaubert noted within himself two opposing beings. Cf. the following passage taken from his *Correspondance* (Paris: Charpentier, 1900), II, 84: "Il y a en moi deux bonshommes distincts: un qui est épris de gueulades, de lyrisme, de grands vols d'aigle, de toutes les sonorités de la phrase et des sommets de l'idée; un autre qui creuse et qui fouille le vrai tant qu'il peut, qui aime à accuser le petit fait aussi puissamment que le grand, qui voudrait faire sentir presque matériellement les choses qu'il reproduit."

In Barbey d'Aurevilly, the publication of whose *Diaboliques* (1874) resulted in the author's being prosecuted by the government on charges of outraging public morals (just as Baudelaire, Flaubert and the Goncourts had been prosecuted), we find the familiar conflict with the world surrounding him, which frustrated fulfilment of his lofty aspirations and quixotic fancies. All of his adult life Barbey deliberately cultivated an attitude which was based primarily on an inversion of accepted values, which was, in turn, in conflict with his own Norman common sense.[39] Thus we find again, by implication at least, the familiar pattern: one part of the personality observes and judges the actions of the other.

Basic conflicts between the writer and his age, though not always resulting from the same elements, may be found also, among many others, in Leconte de Lisle,[40] Villiers de l'Isle-Adam,[41] Rimbaud,[42] and Jean Lorrain.[43]

---

[39] Cf. Jean Canu, *Barbey d'Aurevilly* (Paris, 1945), especially pp. 40-42, 53, 69, 76, 97, 133-4, 195, 204-5, 208, 226, 352, 357, 407-8.

[40] Concerning Leconte de Lisle, whose mother was orthodox in religious practice and whose father was not a believer, Irving Brown has written in *Leconte de Lisle* (New York, 1929), pp. 6-8: "In the French poet the two natures [intellectual and emotional] are at times sharply distinct and even antagonistic. The struggle between the heart and the brain is extremely acute in this poet.... It is the will to believe in the supernatural... which is torn away by his intellect.... This tragedy of two incompatible temperaments... is expressed throughout the poetry of Leconte de Lisle."

[41] Villiers, who found the bourgeois world surrounding him highly distasteful, withdrew fairly successfully into a brilliant realm of fantasy, of his own creation. On the inner conflict of Villiers, see Max Daireau, *Villiers de L'Isle-Adam, l'homme et l'œuvre* (Paris, 1936), pp. 10-11: "Et non pas le combat que se livrent, depuis des temps immémoriaux, l'Esprit et la Matière, mais l'effort constant de l'Esprit pour se soustraire à la Matière, lutte sournoise où... il refuse de capituler..., sacrifiant sa sensibilité aux lois inhumaines de son idéal...."

[42] In *L'aliénation poétique* (Paris, 1946), p. 128: Jean Fretet sees in Rimbaud a split personality: "Rimbaud ne serait-il pas plutôt double? ...une adhésien totale et un refus total dans un même moment et d'un seul mouvement." Cf. Benjamin Fondane, *Rimbaud le voyou* (Paris, 1933), p. 121, where Rimbaud is referred to as "vécu malgré lui, par les deux puissances contradictoires qui se disputent son âme, [et qui] ne peut se décider pour aucune."

[43] Jean Lorrain, of solid bourgeois stock, early conceived an intense dislike for middle-class smugness and lack of imagination. Endowed with an exceptionally vulnerable sensibility, he sought to create a façade to hide and protect his inner being. So successful was he that he very nearly became the decadent debauchee that he claimed to be. Yet there occur at times in Lorrain longings

Despite their inversions of established values, almost all of these men were brought up in more or less conventional circumstances. It would seem inevitable that they retain an underlying stratum of conventionality, a residuum of their early training, which, though passive, sat in judgment on their actions, emotions and thought processes which departed from the normal.[44] This may explain the greater incidence of this aspect of the theme — in which one part of the double sits in judgment over the other, often interfering with its activities — in the second half of the century, when the conflict between poet and public became more acute.

---

for healthy, simple appetites and even feelings of remorse. Cf. Georges Normandy: *Jean Lorrain* (Paris, 1927), especially pp. 27, 45, 55, 68, 78, 81, 105, 119, 133.

[44] Cf. Remy de Gourmont, *Promenades littéraires* (Paris, 1904), I, 184: "Malgré la profonde influence que le romantisme a exercé sur l'esprit français, il est resté classique, ami de la mesure, de la règle, d'une simplicité digne."

RAMÓN CARNICER Y BATLLE (1789-1855)
CONDUCTOR, DIRECTOR, COMPOSER

STERLING A. STOUDEMIRE
University of North Carolina

Italian opera, in its modern concept, was introduced into Spain by Philip V for his own entertainment and, simply by accident, that of his satellites. The first performances were in celebration of royal weddings or birthdays and were presented in the palaces, mainly in the Palacio del Buen Retiro. In the public theaters opera was to appear much later.[1] "El domingo de Carnaval de dicho año (1738), día en que se inauguró el nuevo teatro de los Caños del Peral, puede considerarse como la fecha *oficial* de la instalación de la ópera italiana en Madrid, puesto que por primera vez se representaba en un local decoroso, ejecutada por artistas de reputación y con el aparato escénico que reclamaba. Se hizo la ópera *Demetrio*; la concurrencia, que fue numerosa, salió satisfecha del espectáculo."[2] The text of this opera was by Pietro Metastasio, the music by Johann Adolf Hasse, and the production was directed by Farinelli, the famous *sopranista,* who the year before had been enticed to Spain and away from other crowned heads of Europe who were competing for his service. It is most likely that Queen Isabel Farnesio engineered the whole plan without the suspicion of her husband, hoping that Farinelli would make some impression upon the moody and morose Philip. Farinelli was employed

---

[1] For a study of the introduction of Italian opera in Spain, see Emilio Cotarelo y Mori, *Orígenes y establecimiento de la ópera en España hasta 1800* (Madrid, 1917).

[2] Luis Carmena y Millán, *Crónica de la ópera italiana en Madrid desde el año 1738 hasta nuestros días* ... con un prólogo histórico de Francisco Asenjo Barbieri (Madrid, 1878), p. 22.

specifically, and paid handsomely, to sing for the king and to produce Italian operas for the court's wide circle of nobles, French and Italian as well as Spanish. Five Italian operas were presented in the Caños del Peral in 1738-1739, but thereafter public performances were not permitted and Farinelli devoted his time to the Coliseo de las Comedias in the Buen Retiro. The series began on May 9, 1738, with a production of *Alessandro nell' Indie,* text by Metastasio and music by Francesco Corselli, in celebration of the wedding of Charles, to become the third, and María Amalia of Saxony. It is more than probable that all festivities had been planned by Queen Isabel.[3] Farinelli continued to produce operas in the palace theaters and came to be a favorite at court as long as Queen Isabel was living, after the death of Philip V and through the reign of Fernando VI. Queen Isabel died in 1758, Fernando VI in 1759, and his brother Carlos III, the so-called "best of the Bourbons," succeeded to the throne. One of the first acts of the new king was to exile Farinelli, who had been in Spain twenty-two years and who had made that Bourbon court famous for its Italian opera.[4]

The first public presentation of Italian opera in Madrid was in 1787 when again performances were permitted in Los Caños del Peral. These productions continued down to 1810 when it was decided to raze this old theater in order to make way for an imposing new building which would be dedicated solely to opera. The site was not cleared until 1818, however, and many obstacles delayed the construction with the unhappy result that the Teatro Real did not open its doors until 1850 with a performance of Donizetti's *Favorita.* The Teatro del Príncipe and the Teatro de la Cruz had presented Italian operas, along with their routine repertory of *comedias, refundiciones,* translations, etc., from 1783 to 1848. The Teatro del Circo also presented Italian operas from 1842 to 1850, when the Teatro Real assumed this responsibility and artistic obligation.[5] The Teatro Real, at first regarded as el *suntuoso teatro,* soon was recognized as something of an architectual tragedy because of its poor acoustical quality and, as a result, it was closed in 1925 to be reopened October 13, 1966, after

---

[3] Carmena, p. 10.
[4] Sterling A. Stoudemire, "Metastasio in Spain," *Hispanic Review,* IX (1941), 184-186.
[5] Carmena, pp. 47-52.

major renovation and after having remained closed for forty-one years.

In this complex history several native Spaniards have been associated with the Italian opera in such a degree that they were regarded as "Italian composers," the most successful and the one to exert great influence on the Spanish theater in both Barcelona and Madrid for more than thirty years was Ramón Carnicer y Batlle.

Ramón Carnicer, the son of a tailor, was born in Tárrega in the Province of Lérida and baptized on October 24, 1789. At the age of seven he began to study music under Don Buenaventura Feliú, head of the Chapel at Tárrega, and when a vacancy occurred in the famous choir of the Cathedral of Seu de Urgel, Ramón's parents succeeded in securing the seat for their son. The boy was subjected to a rigorous examination conducted by the Chapel Master Bruno Pagueras, organist Codorech, violinist Feliz Roig, and three priests. Demonstrating a sound knowledge of the fundamentals of music and possessing a beautiful voice, Ramón was accepted as a member of the choir and there he remained as first *tiple* until his voice began to change, almost seven years later. He had begun to study the organ and counterpoint in 1800 and his progress was so rapid that he was appointed cathedral organist for *días ordinarios*. In 1806 he went to Barcelona to study with Chapel Master Francisco Queralt and Carlos Balaguer, organist of the Cathedral. At that time the Italian opera in Barcelona was flourishing and through curiosity young Carnicer began to attend just to see what opera was like. He was unhappy with what he discovered, but his friends soon convinced him that there were other kinds of music, that fugues, canons, and other types of Church music did not form the whole picture. In order to learn more of this new (to him) art, Carnicer began to study the Italian language and to compose music for Italian lyrics. [6]

Italian and Italians had dominated the opera in Spain and as a result a royal order of December 28, 1799 had decreed that in the

---

[6] *Gaceta musical de Madrid*. Redactada por una sociedad de artistas bajo la dirección de D. Hilarión Eslava. Año I, Núm. 8, 25 de marzo de 1855, pp. 57-59. (The article on Carnicer is signed "Por R." Perhaps it was written by *R*afael Hernando, one of three students appointed to prepare the "pompa fúnebre." This article, the chief source of biographical information on Carnicer, was assembled by his associates and published as a memorial a week after his death. The parish records at Tárrega show that Carnicer was baptized on October 24, 1789. Printed records list this as the date of birth.

future "las óperas extranjeras deberían cantarse en idioma castellano y por intérpretes españoles, a la vez que los bailes extranjeros quedaban prohibidos." The order was reaffirmed on March 11, 1801, making the prohibition effective for all Spain. Barcelona, traditionally alert to oppose the central government and ever ready to demonstrate her independence, defied the order and continued to present Italian opera, at the very time Ramón Carnicer was deeply engrossed in his study of this art. This prohibition lasted until January 25, 1808, when another royal order lifted the ban on foreign languages, and opera in Italian returned to the Madrid theaters.[7] This relaxation regarding foreign influence and monopoly was premature in view of political developments that came later in the year: in February, French troops occupied Pamplona and Barcelona, Carlos IV abdicated on March 19, and General Murat at the head of his French army entered Madrid on March 23. The next day Fernando VII returned to Madrid amid the great rejoicing of all the people and was recognized as king by almost everybody except the French ambassador. Napoleon was of another opinion, however, and immediately Fernando was lured across the border to southern France, forced to abdicate, and Joseph Bonapart, "Pepe Botellas," was appointed king of Spain. Violent reaction was not long in coming. On the famous *Dos de Mayo* the Spanish people rose up and began their own war, a guerrilla operation against the emperor's troops, one that was to last six years and was to forecast the collapse of Napoleon's power in Europe. During these difficult years the Spanish people had little occasion to be concerned about a choice of languages for the opera. Early in 1814, Fernando was released and permitted to return to Madrid where he immediately established an unbending despotism that was to last almost twenty years.[8]

In 1808, when Carnicer was just beginning to understand the Italian opera, Balaguer died and shortly thereafter Napoleon's troops occupied the city. The situation became intolerable for the sensitive Carnicer, not yet twenty years old, and he fled to Mahon on the Island of Menorca where accomodations were almost non-existent and, when

---

[7] José Subirá, *Historia de la música teatral en España* (Barcelona, 1945), p. 170; and F. Virella Cassañes, *La ópera en Barcelona, Estudio histórico-crítico* (Barcelona, 1888), pp. 51-52, 81-82.

[8] Clarence E. Chapman, *A history of Spain* (New York, 1948), pp. 406-409, 494.

available, little better than primitive. The young exile was permitted to live in a Franciscan monastery until he could find quarters elsewhere. The prior was pleased to learn that his guest was an accomplished organist and Carnicer was invited to play for the "rosario y gozos de San Antonio, cuya novena empezamos hoy sin tener más organista que un ciego que no puede acompañar." [9] Carnicer came to be something of a sensation in this new position and almost everybody in the city went to hear him play. As a result there developed in Mahon an interest in the study of music that had not been evident previously. Carnicer accepted several piano students but his work was seriously handicapped since there were only three or four pianos in the city. In less than a year, however, there were more than forty instruments available, some brought from Mallorca, others from London. Carnicer had the good fortune to meet many older and well-educated persons who had come to Mahon to escape the torture of Europe. Among them was a learned German, Carl Ernest Cook, who had studied with Mozart and who was willing to demonstrate the newest techniques in playing and teaching piano. It was at this time that Carnicer began to transcribe Italian operas for the piano, apparently one of the first composers to interest himself in this practice.

When the Emperor's troops were withdrawn from Barcelona in 1814 Carnicer returned home. On August 20 of that year he was married to Doña María Magdalena España. In 1815 he was placed at the head of a committee to organize concerts for the purpose of raising funds to be used in constructing a monument in memory of seven martyrs who were hanged by the French in 1809. The venture was so successful that thereafter, in spite of his youth — he was only twenty-six — Carnicer found himself designated to serve in like capacity for other public campaigns for concerts and festivals. In 1816 the people of Barcelona expressed a desire to elevate their theater to the artistic level of the Italian organization for indeed they were embarrassed that a foreign art in Barcelona should surpass their own. If they were to have Italian opera, they would present it themselves in their own theater, even if they had to employ foreign singers. The first public meeting was presided over by Captain General Castaños, and a committee, composed of Gaspar de Remisa, Francisco Larad, and

---

[9] *Gaceta musical*, p. 59.

Antonio Viguer, commissioned Carnicer to go to Italy to employ singers for the new project. Carnicer suggested that the first requirement was to secure the services of an orchestra director who was a strict disciplinarian as well as a good musician and conductor, one who would require the musicians to attend rehearsals regularly. At Carnicer's suggestion the committee employed Pietru Generali as director and soon the orchestra at the Teatro de Santa Cruz was regarded as one of the best. Carnicer himself was *Maestro al cimbalo* and in 1817 was named director of the Italian company he had brought to Barcelona. [10]

The first Italian opera to be presented by the new company was *Adele di Lusignano*, by Carnicer himself, on May 15, 1819, in honor of the Infanta Luisa Carlota, the day she arrived in Barcelona to marry the Infante Francisco de Paula Antonio. The opera had a surprising run of twenty days. At this time Carnicer had been composing for Italian texts and had written several arias that had been introduced into other operas, as well as an overture for Rossini's *Barbieri di Siviglia*, which had been presented in Barcelona, July 16, 1818, and preferrred by some critics to the one written by Rossini later. Other operas presented during that season were *Clotilda* by Coccia (August 19, 1819), *La Gazza Ladra* by Rossini (December 12, 1819), and *Il Turco in Italia*, by Rossini (June 9, 1820). For two years Carnicer remained as director of this company. [11]

Up to this time Carnicer's compositions had been chiefly of a religious nature: an oratorio, *La muerte de Abel*, several Masses, hymns, etc., almost exclusively for convents and monasteries in and near Barcelona. One of his close associates records that Carnicer made a careful examination and estimate of these compositions and, coming to the unhappy decision that they had no lasting value, he destroyed them. In 1820 he went to Italy a second time to obtain the services of Italian singers for the Barcelona opera. Also during this period, in spite of his full-time duties as conductor and director, he managed to compose and present three operas: *Adele di Lusignano* (May 15,

---

[10] *Ibid.*

[11] José Subirá, *La ópera y los teatros de Barcelona*, 2 vols.; Núm. 8 y 9 de "Monografías Históricas de Barcelona" (Barcelona, 1946), I, 79-80; and F. Virella Cassañes, p. 110.

1819), *Elena è Constantino* (July 16, 1821), and *Don Giovanni Tenorio* (June 20, 1822), all in the Teatro Principal.[12]

Carnicer's ability came to be recognized in all the capitals of Europe; he was invited to be guest conductor in Madrid during the season of 1823-1824 and in the next two years he visited London and Paris several times in search of talent for his theater. This European reputation brought him an order to come to Madrid in the capacity of conductor and director, and Soriano Fuertes states that the request was quite precise: "Por ser necesario para la formación de la compañía de ópera."[13] This royal order, dated March 20, 1827, brought Carnicer to Madrid and placed him in charge of Italian opera in the Teatro del Príncipe and the Teatro de la Cruz, a position he was to hold to almost the middle of the century.[14]

Mesonero Romanos chronicles with misgivings the popularity of the Italian opera at this period, stressing especially the vogue of Rossini. In one of his most popular and discerning essays, *La filarmonía*, written in March, 1933, he traces the meteoric rise of Rossini whose first opera in Madrid, *L'Italiana in Algeri*, had been presented on September 29, 1816, in the Teatro del Príncipe, almost a decade before Carnicer assumed his new position:

> El entusiasmo inexplicable que aquella brillante producción causó en esta capital fue un anuncio de los gratos momentos que el público podía esperar del autor del *Barbero de Sevilla*. Sin embargo de la escasez del espectáculo no fue perdido para un público naturalmente filarmónico. Y a medida que aquél iba adquiriendo vigor, veíase desterrar entre los aficionados el estilo monótono y amanerado de la antigua escuela, para dar lugar al sentimiento y vida de la nueva. La afición del público iba creciendo al par que sus conocimientos, y era menester complacerle si se quería dar calor a aquel movimiento. La empresa teatral de 1821 hubo de pensar sin duda

---

[12] Joaqun Merás, *Calendario lírico-italiano, extracto de datos adquiridos por el autor á la vista de irreprochables documentos, épocas célebres, apertura de teatros, estrenos de óperas, compositores, artistas líricos y noticias de interés directo para el teatro italiano*, recogidas y ordenadas por Don ... (Madrid, 1877), pp. 30, 37, 40.

[13] Mariano Soriano Fuertes, *Historia de la música española desde la venida de los fenicios hasta el año 1840*, 4 vols. (Madrid, 1855-1859), IV, 295. F. Virella, p. 111.

[14] *Gaceta Musical de Madrid*, pp. 59-60.

de este modo, decidiéndose a volver a presentar a los madrileños el espectáculo de la ópera italiana de que aun se conservaba reminiscencias, aunque remotas. Siguió así la ópera, más o menos boyante, hasta que en 1825 se ajustó la compañía *Montresor*, desde cuya época no fue una afición la del público sino un furor filarmónico. El mérito de los cantantes, la nueva pompa con que se exornó el espectáculo, lo escogido de las funciones que se presentaron, fue cosas de trastornar todas las cabezas, y llegó a tal punto el entusiasmo, que no solamente se lo imitaba en el canto, sino en el gesto y modales. [15]

Soriano Fuertes recalls that many European composers were required to work with Italian lyrics at this time. In Germany and in France there were serious and successful attempts to neutralize this foreign influence; such efforts in Spain were less effective. "El teatro nacional fué abandonado y aun despreciado; las mejores obras de nuestros clásicos poetas se tenían por monótonas é ínsulas; y la novedad italiana en vez de ser estimada para sostener nuestras mayores glorias literarias, destruyó nuestro teatro, y aumentó contra nosotros el sarcasmo extranjero, oscureciendo nuestro brillantez pasado, y esclavizando nuestro porvenir." [16]

November 12, 1829, almost three years after Carnicer had been required to come to Madrid, María Cristina de Borbón, accompanied by her parents, the King and Queen of Naples, came to Spain and Spaniards of all stations were jubilant in their welcome to Fernando VII's new queen, his fourth. María Cristina immediately began to demonstrate a serious interest in the artistic life of her new nation, and at her suggestion the Real Conservatorio was established. On June 23, 1830, Francisco Piermarini was named the first Director and, Ramón Carnicer was appointed *Maestro de composición* at an annual salary of 20,000 reales. The staff was large: professors for all instruments, an instructor in Spanish, one in Italian, one for the dance, as well as secretaries, cooks, laundresses, etc. Students applying for admission to the Conservatory had to be not less than twelve years old and no more than fifteen, and each applicant had to present to the

---

[15] Ramón de Mesonero Romanos, *Escenas Matritenses* (*Panorama matritense, escenas matritenses, tipos y caracteres*), estudio preliminar, bibliografía y notas de Federico Carlos Sáinz de Robles (Madrid, 1945), pp. 239-241.

[16] Soriano Fuertes, IV, 285-286.

admissions officer a birth certificate, a letter of recommendation from his parish priest, one from his music teacher, a certificate of vaccination, and even a letter from the mayor of his town. [17] This first public act of Queen María Cristina was an indication of the influence she was to exert on Spanish art, politics and royal intrigue for many years, first by her own magnetic personality, then through her daughter Isabel II, and much later through various channels while she was living in Paris in exile down to her death in 1878. [18]

Fernando's three previous queens had died young and only the second, his cousin María Isabel of Portugal, had participated in the public life of her people. María Cristina was a different breed. "Fernando, estimulado por el ejemplo de su esposa, quiso también fundar algún establecimiento de instrucción que respondiese a necesidades de otro género, y creó, por esos mismos días, la Escuela de Tauromaquia en Sevilla." [19] (Out of fairness to Fernando we must remind ourselves that he established the Museo del Prado, largely with his own money and his own priceless collection of paintings.)

It was early in 1831 that Rossini went to Madrid as the guest of the rich banker Alejandro Aguado in order to visit his wife's niece, Josefa Pérez y Colbrán, the wife of Joaquín Espín y Guillén, who was to serve later for many years as the director of the chorus in the Teatro Real. In addition to a gala performance of *Il Barbieri*, with the royal family in attendance, at least seven Rossini operas were presented during the season (*La Cenerentola; Elisabetta, Regina d'Inghilterra; Mathilde di Shabràn, Mosè in Egitto, Otelo, Semiramide* and *Zelmira*) totaling more than forty performances. Not only was Ramón Carnicer the conductor, he presented his own opera *Colombo* at least eight times. Rossini was then only thirty-nine years old and had already

---

[17] Soriano Fuertes, IV, 328-333.
[18] Theo Aronson, *Royal Vendetta: The Crown of Spain, 1829-1965* (Indianapolis, 1966), pp. 3-42.
[19] Ramón de Mesonero Romanos, *Memorias de un setentón, natural y vecino de Madrid*, Escritos por el Curioso Parlante, 2 vols. (Madrid, 1926), II, 96-98. "The two years which followed Ferdinand VII's wedding (his second marriage) to his niece the Portuguese Infanta María Isabel, on September 29, 1816, until her death on December 26, 1818, were decisive for the restoration and completion of the Prado Museum, thanks to the help of the short-lived queen." F. J. Sánchez Cantón, *Prado, Madrid* (Milan, 1968), p. 13.

presented his last opera (*Guillaume Tell*) in Paris a year and a half earlier. At least twenty-two of Rossini's operas had been presented in Madrid and with his visit there was renewed interest in his work, but by this date Bellini and Donizetti were his serious competitors. Mesonero goes on to point out that in the court of Fernando VII "Esta afición de la sociedad matritense hacia la filarmonía no era como ahora (1880) la expresión de una moda pasajera y de *buen tono*, sino un verdadero culto, una devoción entusiasta hacia el arte que tan preclaros genios ostentaba a la sazón un Rossini, un Donizetti, un Bellini, un Meyerbeer." He pays tribute to Carnicer, describing him as one of the great and popular directors of the time.[20]

The Conservatory, located on the Plaza de los Mostenses, was opened on April 2, 1831, and Carnicer composed a part of the music for the elaborate opening exercises, attended by the royal family. On the first of September una Escuela de Declamación was added to the Conservatory. On March 6, 1832, in celebration of the birth of María Luisa Fernanda, second daughter of Fernando VII and María Cristina, to become the wife of the Duke of Montpensier, was presented the two-act "ópera," *Los enredos de un curioso*, text by Félix Enciso Castrillón and music by Carnicer and others. The students also presented a program for the royal family, the first number being *Un capricho sobre temas españoles*, with full orchestra.[21]

The artistic life of Madrid, stimulated and encouraged by María Cristina, Italian by birth but Spanish by choice, moved smoothly and often excitingly until the death of Fernando VII in 1833. Isabel was

---

[20] *Ibid.*

[21] Soriano Fuertes, IV, 343-346. *Los enredos de un curioso* was the first zarzuela of the century and had been presented at the Conservatorio de Música, in February, 1832, by the students of the voice classes. It was called "melodrama" since the word "zarzuela" had fallen into disuse and was thought to be improper. The book was written by Félix Enciso Castrillón; the music was composed by Pedro Albéniz, Baltasar Saldoni, Francisco Piermarini and Ramón Carnicer. (A curious coincidence is that one of the most popular zarzuelas of a later day, *Luisa Fernanda*, text by Federico Romero and Guillermo Fernández-Shaw, music by Moreno Torroba, was presented for the first time in Madrid on March 26, 1932, in the Teatro Calderón.) The next zarzuela was presented two months later, *El rapto*, with text by Mariano José de Larra and music by Tomás Genovés. There was no other zarzuela until 1839, *La novia y el concierto*, text by Bretón de los Herreros and music by Basilio Basili, who had come from Italy in 1827 as a singer. He remained to teach music and Italian, and married the famous actress Teodora Lamadrid. Subirá, *Historia de la música teatral*, pp. 172-173.

only three years old. Not even her strong-willed mother was able to stem the wave of dissatisfaction, inside and outside the Royal family, that swept Spain into a disastrous civil war. The earlier repudiation of the Salic Law made it possible for a woman to ascend the throne, but this arrangement was not acceptable to the king's brother, Don Carlos, even in a nation famous for its competent, powerful and respected queens. The Conservatory, which had produced many fine musicians and actors, including Julián Romea, also suffered. [22] The number of scholarships for needy students was reduced sharply and the Conservatory was forced to move to cheaper quarters in the Calle de Alcalá. Later it was moved again, most properly, to the Teatro Real. [23]

Ramón Carnicer remained as chief conductor in the Príncipe and Cruz continuously from the time of his arrival in Madrid in 1827 until 1845, except for guest appearances in other theaters and a two-year desertion to the Teatro del Circo, which had been constructed in the Plaza del Rey in 1834 in the form on a circus for the sole purpose of presenting equestrian shows. Due to the small number of theaters in Madrid — there were only two — and to the great demand for dramatic performances that had developed in the public — an interesting application of the law of supply and demand in the field of Art — the Circo was renovated in such fashion that it could accommodate conventional plays and operas. A brilliant Italian company inaugurated the renovated theater on June 21, 1842, with a performance of *La Vestale*, (music by Mercadante, text by Cammarano). The Circo continued to present Italian opera until the Teatro Real was dedicated with a performance of Donizetti's *La Favorita*, on November 19, 1850. [24] An intriguing footnote to the gala opening of the Circo is that Ramón Carnicer was manager and conductor during

---

[22] Mariano José de Larra says of Julián Romea, who made his first appearance on the Madrid stage in *El testamento*, translated by Ventura de la Vega from Eugène Scribe's *Le Testament de Polichinelle*, April 21, 1833, "No se necesita preguntar de quién es discípulo. Sabemos por una parte que pertenece al Conservatorio de María Cristina, que por lo visto empieza a dar frutos, y por otra basta oírle para reconocer en él su maestro, el primer actor Latorre, profesor de Declamación en aquel Establecimiento." *Revista Española*, 23 de abril de 1833, in Larra, *Artículos de crítica literaria y artística*, Clásicos Castellanos, 52 (Madrid, 1923), p. 88.

[23] Soriano Fuertes, IV, 350-354.

[24] Carmena y Millán, p. 93.

the seasons 1842-1843 and 1843-1844, when more than twenty-five separate Italian operas were presente to enthusiastic audiences: thirteen by Donizetti, four by Bellini, three by Verdi, and only two by Rossini. Felice Romani was librettist for five of these operas. From August 10, 1842, to April 20, 1844, no Italian opera was presented in the Príncipe or the Cruz, for aparently those theaters could not function without Carnicer and could not compete with the excellent Italian company working at the Circo. The small bilingual texts that were printed specifically for the first performance of these operas usually list the names of the singers, the composer, and the director or conductor but by 1830 the name of the librettist is often omitted. Many of these texts bear the interesting notation "Maestro, Director Don Ramón Carnicer." [25]

Ramón Carnicer's career as composer of Italian operas extends over twenty of his thirty years as director and conductor. His first three operas, as indicated above, had been presented in Barcelona: *Adele di Lusignano* (May 15, 1819), text by Felice Romani. This opera had been composed first by Michele Carafa. [26] This was followed by *Elena è Constantino*, text also by Romani, July 21, 1821 and later, July 16, 1827, in the Teatro del Príncipe, Carnicer's first opera in Madrid. [27] *Don Giovanni Tenorio* ossia *Il Convitato di pietra* was presented on June 20, 1822. This writer has not been able to locate a printed copy of the text nor has he been able to learn the name of the librettist. [28] Carnicer's next opera was not presented until more than seven years later when he was well established as director and conductor in Madrid. *Elena y Malvina*, [29] text by Romani, was pre-

---

[25] Carmena y Millán, pp. 107-120, 141. The library of the University of North Carolina holds more than two hundred titles of these Italian-Spanish texts; the present writer has perhaps fifty others.

[26] Merás, *Calendario* ..., pp. 9, 20, 37, 65; and Alfred Loewenberg, *Annals of the Opera, 1597-1940* (Cambridge, 1943), p. 332.

[27] *Helena y Constantino*, ópera semiseria en dos actos, que se ha de representar en El Teatro del Príncipe de esta Córte (Madrid, 1827). (Bilingual Text).

[28] Loewenberg (p. 342) says the librettist is "unknown." Gendarme de Bévotte in his "Liste de Don Juans" at the end of vol. II of his *La Légende de Don Juan*, 2 vols. (Paris, 1911), does not mention the Carnicer opera. This writer has been unsuccessful in his search for a copy of the text.

[29] *Elena y Malvina*, melodrama semiserio en dos actos, que se ha de representar en los Teatros de esta Córte (Madrid, 1829). (Bilingual text).

sented first at the Príncipe, February 11, 1829. About two years later, January 12, 1831, *Colombo*,[30] text also by Romani, was presented at the Príncipe. This text had first been composed by Morlacchi, and presented in Genoa, June 21, 1828.[31] *Eufemio di Messina* appeared at the Príncipe, December 14, 1832.[32] *Ismalia* ossia *Morte ed Amore*,[33] text also by Romani, was presented at the Teatro de la Cruz, March 12, 1838. This text had first been composed by Mercadante in 1832. These seven operas appeared over a period of almost twenty years, silhouetted as high peaks against a spectacular career as conductor, director, producer and composer. Clément states that Carnicer wrote an opera *Ipermestra*,[34] but Peña y Goñi is of the opinion that Clément is referring to an opera by Saldoni, warm friend and disciple of Carnicer's.[35]

Carnicer had been composing for Italian lyrics even before the first performance of his *Adele*. On October 16, 1818, he inserted an aria in *Agnese*, by Buonvoglia and Paer, which had first been presented in October 1809, in Ponte d'Altaro, based on Amelia Opie's *The Father and the Daughter* (1801).[36] This opera was also presented early (September 14, 1829) in Carnicer's career in Madrid. He had also composed many miscellaneous pieces, arias, etc. which were introduced into more than twenty operas, four by Rossini, three by Pacini, others by Bellini, Donizetti, Cimarosa and other well-known composers of the period. To this we should add the overture to *Il Barbieri di Siviglia* (1818), *Adolfo e Chiara* (1818), several symphonies, festal pieces for

---

[30] *Colombo (Cristóbal Colón)*, melodrama serio in due atti (Madrid, diciembre de 1830). (Bilingual text). Loewenberg, p. 358.

[31] Loewenberg, p. 366.

[32] *Eufemio di Messina* ossia *I Saraceni in Sicilia*, Melodramma serio in due atti ... que se ha de representar en los Teatros de esta Corte (Madrid, diciembre de 1832). (Bilingual text).

[33] *Ismalia* ossia *Morte ed amore*, Melodramma in due atti, Teatro de la Cruz, Marzo de 1838 (Madrid, [1838]). "Beneficio del señor Ramón Carnicer." (Bilingual text).

[34] Félix Clément and Pierre Larousse, *Histoire lyrique ou dictionnaire des opéras* (Paris, n.d.), p. 363. "*Ipermestra*, Opéra italien, livret de Métastase, musique de Carnicer, compositeur espagnol, représentée à Saragosse, en 1843."

[35] Antonio Peña y Goñi, *La ópera española y la música dramática en España en el siglo XIX, apuntes históricos* (Madrid, 1881), p. 149.

[36] Loewenberg, p. 304.

the Royal family, many hymns, some of them scored for full orchestra, etc. [37]

In 1843 Carnicer was commissioned to write a Requiem Mass for the elaborate funeral of one Safont, a rich banker who was drowned in a river near Madrid. With Carnicer conducting, the Mass was played flawlessly by two hundred musicians. [38] For composing and conducting the Mass and a *nocturno*, Carnicer requested a fee of 40,000 reales. The son, José Safont, insisted that the bill was exorbitant and refused to pay. Carnicer referred the matter to the court and an investigating committee of three composers was appointed to make a recommendation regarding the fairness of the fee. After much wrangling the committee, upon the recommendation of Indalecio Soriano Fuertes, the father of the famous musicologist, the Safont family was required to pay the fee as charged. [39] After 1845 Carnicer was not very active in the theater but down to his death he remained a faithful friend and sponsor of actors and musicians. He died 17 March 1855 at fifty-six Calle de Santa Isabel, where he had lived for many years, only a short distance from the Príncipe and the Cruz where he had worked so long and which he loved so deeply. Among his many honors, he had been made a caballero in the Real Orden de Carlos Tercero. Even though for most of his life he had been in lucrative positions, he had never been wise in handling financial matters and he died poor. Nevertheless, since he had been something of a popular idol and sponsor of young actors and singers, he was given a funeral proper in Spain for such a figure. [40] A number of Military bands played alternately in the funeral procession, and in the *duelo* with the family were many of Carnicer's colleagues from the Conservatory and theaters, as well as many students and admirers. The funeral oration was pronounced by Hilarión Eslava, who was to become one of Spain's most famous musicians as well as musicologist. [41]

Saldoni, also to become a famous musicologist, who entered the Conservatory when it was first opened and for a number of years was

---

[37] A complete list of Carnicer's musical compositions can be found in *Gaceta Musical de Madrid*, p. 304.

[38] Basilio Basili, one of Carnicer's best students, tells of the disagreement over the fee in *Pruebas de peritos en el pleito seguido entre el Excmo. Sr. don José Safont y el compositor de música, D. Ramón Carnicer* (Madrid, 1844).

[39] Peña y Goñi, pp. 150-152.

[40] Soriano Fuertes, pp. 353-354.

[41] *Gaceta Musical de Madrid*, pp. 59-60.

closely associated with Carnicer, records that the master on occasion would work all night preparing lessons and exercises for his students, refining his own compositions, and carefully studying and analyzing the scores of the operas he was to conduct. He was kind and gentle, but he could be firm and even severe, if the situation demanded, for it was his desire and even his requirement to get perfection from his students and his orchestra. Saldoni says he gave piano lessons to Elena, Carnicer's daughter, and that Carnicer had a brother who was a famous guitarist who died in Sevilla "hacia 1866, según nos dijo un sobrino." [42]

Carnicer, born in a small town in the province of Lérida, the son of parents of modest circumstances who early recognized his ability and placed him in the local choir at the age of seven, then in the Cathedral School at Seo de Urgel, and finally in Barcelona at the age of eleven, for forty years was active and influential in the theatrical life of Spain. He was the first to introduce serious study of the piano to Mahon, then to establish and regularize the Italian opera in Barcelona, bringing famous singers to his theater, and then to Madrid, at the command of the king, in 1827, where he was active for twenty years. It is not Carnicer the composer of church music or even of operas in whom we are interested at the moment, for most of his compositions have long been forgotten, but Carnicer the director and conductor who exerted great influence in the Príncipe and the Cruz. In that spot he had the opportunity to see everything presented on the Madrid stage from the time of his arrival in 1827 to 1845, and as an interested spectator and critic, on to 1855. The first performance in Madrid after Carnicer's arrival, after the recess for Lent, was *Del rey abajo, ninguno* (April 15, 1827), followed by *Cuentas veo, tantas quiero* (April 17), *La segunda Celestina* (April 19), *El pastelero de Madrigal* (September 21), all *refundiciones* by Dionisio Solís. These were interspersed with Italian operas and new plays. It must have been with more than passing interest that in the next year (1828) Carnicer read Bretón's *El furor filarmónico*. [43] This *sátira,* in tercets, did little to stem the tide of enthusiasm for the Italian opera for in

---

[42] Baltasar Saldoni, *Diccionario biográfico-bibliográfico de efemérides de músicos españoles,* 4 vols. (Madrid, 1868-1881), II, 120-124.

[43] Manuel Bretón de los Herreros, *Obras,* 5 vols. (Madrid, 1883-1884), V, 17-28. Bretón mentions names of singers, composers and titles of operas in this *sátira.*

that same year fourteen operas by five composers, totaling 125 performances, appeared on the Madrid stages, most of them conducted by Carnicer. He had a part in the great vogue of Rossini and he likewise played an important role in the rise of Bellini and Donizetti. He was also witness of Romanticism from the first performance of *La conjuración de Venecia* to *Don Juan Tenorio* and on to *Traidor, inconfeso y mártir*. His retirement in 1845 came at the time when Verdi was first introduced to Madrid. Carnicer had the great satisfaction to see the Teatro Real open its doors with a gala performance of Donizetti's *La Favorita* (November 19, 1850). Many visions must have passed through the memory of this Catalan who had so long been a prominent figure in the Madrid theater: Tárrega, Seo de Urgel, Barcelona, Mahon, Napoleon, Rome, Paris, London, Madrid, Príncipe, Cruz, Circo and now the fine new building where his Conservatorio would be housed.

In the season of 1854-1855 fourteen operas were presented in the new theater: seven by Verdi, three by Donizetti, one each by Bellini, Petrella, Pacini, Meyerbeer. The season opened with *Il Trovatore* (October 28), and closed with Donizetti's *Lucia,* presented on March 15, repeated on the sixteenth and seventeenth.

On March 17 Carnicer died and the Teatro Real was closed for the remainder of the season.

No más, no más callar; que ya en mi seno
Tanta bilis no cabe, Anfriso mío,
Y tanta indignación, tanto veneno. (p. 17)
... ...
Ni el comprender la letra á mí me vence.
Si cuando no debía *Otelo* canta,
lo mismo es en toscano que en vascuence. (p. 24)

A SKETCH BY CONSTANTIN GUYS, AND AN ACCOUNT OF HIS RELATIONSHIP WITH THE GONCOURT BROTHERS

ALISON M. TURNER
Raleigh, North Carolina

The pen and wash sketch reproduced opposite is of unusual interest to those who love French art and literature of the nineteenth century. It is by the enigmatic French artist Constantin Guys, the draughtsman so highly vaunted by Baudelaire in his essay "Le peintre de la vie moderne," one of the most illuminating and prophetic pieces of art criticism of the last century.[1] The sketch opposite came into my possession in a way that would have delighted the artist, who sought all his life to remain personally anonymous and the details of whose adventurous life are largely unknown to us. He seldom signed his works, and he would not allow Baudelaire to use anything but his initials in writing about him.

My painting, "Chevauchée Matinale," is one of his rare signed works and is dated 9/bre, '53.[2] It was discovered quite unexpectedly by my mother amongst my grandmother's possessions after her death in 1950 and given to me shortly thereafter. We know nothing of its origin, though my mother conjectures, since it was found among family papers and sketches, that it might have been kept because it was of personal interest to my grandmother, possibly even being a sketch of her

---

[1] This essay first appeared in the *Figaro* in instalments on 26 and 28 November and 3 December, 1863. As Baudelaire's diaries show, it was largely written earlier, between November 1859 and February 1860.

[2] Probably *novem* (= *neuf*) / *bre*, 1853, but possibly September, being the ninth month.

mother and grandfather, Anna and William Steuart Trench, and a friend.[3] His sons, Thomas and Townsend, drew and painted somewhat in the style of Guys, and may have had lessons from him, though this is pure speculation. They lived in Queen's County (now Laoighis) in Ireland. It is an established fact, however, that Guys was at one time engaged as a French tutor to an English family. He gave lessons to the grandson and granddaughter of Thomas Girtin, the famous English watercolourist, in London from 1842 to 1848.[4] Sometime during this period he also joined the staff of the newly founded *Illustrated London News* as draughtsman.[5] In 1848 he left for Paris to witness the events of the revolution on behalf of the *Illustrated London News*. A letter of his to Gavarni in March 1848[6] indicates that he was secretly thinking of leaving the journal, and we have no further knowledge of his movements until 1852, when we have an indication that he was at one occasion in Paris. On 14 September, 1853, he is writing from Paris to a friend concerning a publishing project. In 1854 we know that

---

[3] I have often wondered, in studying other paintings by Guys, whether in view of his mnemonic technique remarked on by Baudelaire in his essay, Guys did not perhaps frequently duplicate figures for the sake of balance, since it is very common in his works to find two very similar figures or even pairs of figures, apparently seen from different angles and with only minute differences of dress. In this case the two women in my picture, whose horses are also remarkably similar, may be one and the same, merely recalled visually in two different positions.

[4] F. P. Barnard, "Constantin Guys — Twelve unknown drawings," *Artwork*, No. 22 (1930), pp. 83-93. Professor Barnard is the son of Mary Girtin, one of the two children tutored by Guys.

[5] See the article entitled "Second Empire Elegance; Exhibition at the Marlborough Gallery," *Illustrated London News* 229 (7 July, 1956): 24, which includes details of payments made to Guys by the *ILN* between 1845 and 1847.

[6] Reproduced in an article by Luce Jamar-Rolin, "La vie de Guys et la chronologie de son œuvre," *Gazette des Beaux-Arts* 48, Series 6 (July 1956): 78. This article is a most helpful and scholarly attempt to write a life of Guys based as far as possible on documentary evidence, including several previously unpublished letters of Guys, Baudelaire's correspondence with him, and Guys' dated pictures. It also contains the first attempt to date drawings by Guys according to the fashions portrayed in them, but on the admission of the author his conclusions are only tentative in view of Guys' mnemonic technique and his habit of retouching sketches or even repeating certain subjects at later dates (p. 90). There are certain minor inaccuracies in the article, in particular the volume numbering of Baudelaire's correspondence with Guys, and the date of Gautier's *Notice* to the *Fleurs du Mal* is wrongly given as 1888 — it should be 1868.

he was again with the *Illustrated London News* as he was sent by them as an artist-reporter to the Crimean War. So it is conceivable that sometime between 1848 and 1853 he could again have sought private employment as a tutor, or it may simply have been as a guest or casual acquaintance of the Trench family that he executed the rapid sketch which found its way into my family's possessions.

At all events, this was an extremely lucky find, as it was painted by Guys at the height of his artistic powers.[7] Though apparently very casually executed, it is a much more finished and carefully composed work than some of his sketches, and does not suffer from the occasional clumsiness or excess of line to be found in some of his earlier works, nor from the harsh, almost caricature-like effect to be found in his later period. It is fresh, light, full of movement and life. By this time Guys had learned to capture only the essential gesture and to convey it by means of a delicate wash of colour and incredibly swift, sure strokes of the pen. But anything that one can say about Guys' skill has already been said so much better and with so much greater intensity of feeling by Baudelaire that it is far more rewarding to turn briefly to his essay and to see Guys' work through his eyes:

> Ainsi, M. G., traduisant fidèlement ses propres impressions, marque avec une énergie instinctive les points culminants ou lumineux d'un objet (ils peuvent être culminants ou lumineux au point de vue dramatique), ou ses principales caractéristiques, quelquefois même avec une exagération utile pour la mémoire humaine; et l'imagination du spectateur, subissant à son tour cette mnémonique si despotique, voit avec netteté l'impression produite par les choses sur l'esprit de M. G. Le spectateur est ici le traducteur d'une traduction toujours claire et enivrante....[8]
>
> ...Pour tout dire en un mot, notre singulier artiste exprime à la fois le geste et l'attitude solennelle ou grotesque des êtres et leur explosion lumineuse dans l'espace.[9]

---

[7] It was exhibited by the Marlborough Gallery in London in their "Constantin Guys" exhibition of June-July 1956, and was also one of the twenty-four pictures chosen to represent Guys' work in the Phaidon Press edition of Baudelaire's critical works, *The Painter of Modern Life and Other Essays*, translated and edited by Jonathan Mayne (London, 1964).

[8] Charles Baudelaire, "Le peintre de la vie moderne," *Œuvres complètes*, ed. Bibliothèque de la Pléiade (Paris, 1961), p. 1166.

[9] *Ibid.*, p. 1169.

It is this final phrase, with its mysteriously existential quality of perception, that haunts me when I look at the three riders of my picture. It so exactly describes the effect of Guys' work — the breathtaking suddenness of the appearance of his subject, its dramatic illumination and the sense of its transitoriness and imminent dissolution in space. This quality is enhanced in the work in question by the simplicity and breadth of the background. Equally apt in Baudelaire's criticism is his phrase "une exagération utile pour la mémoire humaine," if one observes the manner in which Guys has portrayed the movement of the horses' legs. This distortion for the sake of emphasis has frequently been observed by other critics of Guys' work. What a world of difference between this *instantané* seen through the eye of an artist and a nonselective photographic *cliché*!

My admiration for Guys' work led me to try to discover more about the life and personality of the artist. Disappointingly, no new or startling information about his life has come to my notice, nor have I been able to unravel the reason for his mysterious desire for anonymity, though, as will be seen, everything seems to point to a family or personal problem rather than to professional modesty. In tracing his association with the French literary world of the nineteenth century, I have found that Guys' association with Baudelaire (as reflected in the latter's afore-mentioned essay, and in his letters) has already been the subject of much critical study [10] and has been well documented by Luce Jamar-Rolin in his article on Guys. [11] However, I have also come across numerous references to Guys in the Goncourts' *Journal* and evidence of his influence on two of their novels. Some of this information has been presented elsewhere in studies of Guys, [12] but it is incomplete and deserves more comprehensive treatment and discussion. Since the passages concerning Guys in the *Journal* contain

---

[10] See for example Margaret Gilman, *Baudelaire the Critic* (New York, 1943); Introduction by Jonathan Mayne to Charles Baudelaire, *The Painter of Modern Life and Other Essays*, pp. ix-xvii.

[11] Jamar-Rolin, pp. 88-94.

[12] Jamar-Rolin's article contains various brief references to Guys' association with the Goncourt brothers, but does not trace the much more complete evidence available in the edition of the *texte intégrale* of the *Journal* in 1956, since this was the year his article appeared. Further mention is made of Guys' relationship with, and influence on the Goncourts in Gustave Geoffroy, *Constantin Guys, L'historien du IIe Empire* (Paris, 1920), Chapters V and IX, but this evidence is very general and insufficiently documented.

the most vivid record of his extraordinary personality that we possess and help to complete the evidence of his whereabouts at different periods of his life, they will be quoted in full. In the course of this examination, Guys' influence on the Goncourts' novels *Charles Demailly* and *La Fille Elisa* will be considered.

An outline of what we know of Guys' mysterious life [13] will help to provide a background to the Goncourts' highly impressionistic description of the artist's personality.

Constantin Guys was born in Flushing on the 3rd of December, 1802 (often erroneously given as 1805), the son of François-Lazare Guys and Elizabeth Bertin. His father was at that time *commissaire de marine*. We know virtually nothing of his early life, except one remarkable detail, which Guys himself told Mary Girtin, his pupil in the Girtin family, and which, if true, may very well be the cause of his almost psychopathic desire for anonymity. At the age of sixty, his father, a severe, harsh man, married a sixteen year old girl, to whom one of his sons was engaged. This was the cause of violent family quarrels and hatreds. Constantin's brother soon died, and Constantin appears to have broken with his family. [14] He led a restless, nomadic existence, journeying to every part of the globe, as we know from the account given by Nadar, and which is substantiated by a study of his drawings, done in France, England, Holland, Spain, Italy, Greece, Turkey and the Crimea. He is believed to have taken part in his early twenties in the Greek War of Liberation under Byron's leadership (in the Goncourts' account there is evidence to support this, as we shall see), and to have joined a French cavalry regiment from 1824 to 1830 (his marvellously accurate portrayal of horses and military uniforms would seem to substantiate this). We know virtually nothing of his life in the 1830's. In the 1840's, as we have seen, he seems to have combined the jobs of private tutor and of draughtsman to the *Illustrated London News*, and in 1854 he was sent by this journal to the

---

[13] Based on the following sources: Jamar-Rolin, *passim*; Geoffroy, *passim*; Claude Roger-Marx, *Constantin Guys* (Paris, Collection des Maîtres, 1949); Clifford Hall, *Constantin Guys* (London, 1945); Catalogue of Constantin Guys Exhibition (London, 1956), with preface by Bruno Streiff. Much of their evidence is based on what Guys himself told Nadar (famous for his experiments as photographer and balloonist), who was perhaps his closest friend, and who wrote his obituary notice in the *Figaro* of 15 March, 1892.

[14] Jamar-Rolin, p. 71. However, according to Nadar's account, Guys did receive a small pension from his cousin Barthélemy later in his life.

Crimea. Towards the end of the 1850's he seems to have taken up a more or less settled existence in Paris, intermittently working for various illustrated journals, and to have become quite widely known in the Bohemian and literary circles of the Second Empire. There is growing evidence in his letters and drawings that he was living a precarious hand-to-mouth existence, and was gradually slipping lower and lower on the social scale, as witnessed by the increasing number of brothel scenes and dearth of pictures of the high society that he so often portrayed during his middle years. The final years of his life became more and more pitiful and in 1885, at the age of 82, he was run over by a cab on leaving Nadar's house, and one leg was badly broken. Destitute, he was taken to the Maison Dubois, a home run by *L'Assistance publique*, where he spent the last seven years of his life largely riveted to his bed, with scarcely any contact with the outside world. He finally died at the age of 89 on 13 March, 1892. In 1895 two posthumous exhibitions of his work were held in Paris.

Guys' relationship with the Goncourt brothers seems to have begun in 1858 and continued intermittently into the 1870's. There is no reference in their *Journal* to their having entertained Guys at their own house; it seems that he was a casual acquaintance whom they met chiefly at Gavarni's,[15] and judging by Edmond's harsh denigration of Guys' work in a diary reference of 1895 à propos of the posthumous Guys exhibitions, they must have considered his acquaintance an increasing social liability. However, we do owe them a remarkable portrait of Guys the man, as interesting a piece of literary portraiture as Manet's visual portrayal of Guys in his old age.

In the Goncourt *Journal*, there is a reference to Guys in 1856, which shows that they were already familiar with one facet of his work at that date:

> Ces femmes à vingt sous: non les terribles créatures de Guys, mais une tournure et une langue de lorettes.[16]

---

[15] Gavarni, French draughtsman and caricaturist, intimate friend of the Goncourts, who wrote his life (*Gavarni, l'homme et l'œuvre*, 1873). In 1947 he was invited on Guys' recommendation (see Jamar-Rolin, pp. 71-75) to join the staff of the *Illustrated London News*.

[16] Edmond et Jules de Goncourt, *Journal*, texte intégral établi et annoté par Robert Ricatte, 22 vols. (Monaco, 1956), 2:20, dated "un samedi de juillet."

Their next reference to Guys follows two years later after a visit to Gavarni, and seems to indicate they have not yet met Guys, but that he is already well-known in certain circles as a *raconteur*:

> Il [Gavarni] nous parle de Guys, de ce conteur animé et pittoresque, des héros de ses histoires. Il doit un jour dîner avec un certain homme que voici....[17]

There follows a story about an Italian gambler called *La Mouche* — a story which starts amusingly and becomes wildly improbable. It would scarcely be worth mentioning were it not that it is taken up again in association with a prototype of Guys in the Goncourts' novel *Charles Demailly,* as we shall see in discussing the next entry concerning Guys in the *Journal.*

This entry is by far the longest on Guys, and much the most interesting. In reading this impressionistic verbal portrait of Guys, one must bear in mind that Guys may have been carried away by his love of a good story to add extra zest to his autobiographical sketch, and that we are also dependent upon the Goncourts' fidelity to their original model:

> Nous trouvons, chez Gavarni, Guys, le dessinateur de l'ILLUSTRATION anglaise, le dessinateur à grand style et à lavis enragé des scènes bordelières, le physionomiste moral de la prostitution de ce siècle.
> C'est un étrange homme, qui a roulé sa vie dans tous les hauts et les bas de la vie, couru le monde et ses hasards, semé de sa santé sous toutes les latitudes et à tous les amours, un homme qui est sorti des garnis de Londres, des châteaux de la *fashion,* des tapis verts [18] d'Allemagne, des massacres de la Grèce, des tables d'hôte de Paris, des bureaux de journaux, des tranchées de Sébastopol, des traitements mercuriels, de la peste, des chiens d'Orient, des duels, des filles, des filous, des roués, de l'usure, de la misère, des coupe-gorge et des bas-fonds, où grouillent comme dans une mer toutes ces existences échouées, tous ces hommes sans nom et sans bottes, ces originalités submergées et terribles, qui ne montent jamais à la surface des romans.
> Un petit homme sorti de tout cela avec l'énergie, une énergie terrible sous ses moustaches grises; étrange, varié,

---

[17] Goncourt, *Journal,* 2:209-10.
[18] *tapis verts,* gambling dens.

divers, changeant de voix, et d'aspect, se multipliant et se renouvelant, faisant oublier un moment le grognard que vous avez à vos côtés, et dans sa causerie emportée et avec sa physionomie qui mue, changeant de masque et en changeant encore, entrant dans tous les personnages qu'il vous peint; boitaillant le long du chemin et battant contre vous, poussé par le vent et sans cesse, d'un coup de plat de main sec et nerveux relevant ses manches sur ses bras osseux, diffus, verbeux, débordant de parenthèses, zigzaguant d'idée en idée, déraillé, perdu et se retrouvant, ne lâchant pas une minute votre attention, vous tenant toujours sous le coup de sa parole éclatante, peinte et dont le tapage est comme visible aux yeux, comme celui d'un tableau. Éloquence bavarde, singulière, fortunée, où tout à coup, votre attention qui va lui manquer, il la ramasse avec une image de voyou, une métaphore d'argot; où tantôt apparaît, dans le désordre et le miroitement un grand mot de la langue des penseurs allemands; où tout à coup, l'objet est défini par un mot de la *technie* de l'art, comme un bas-relief de lord Elgin.

Et ce sont mille choses qu'il évoque ainsi, dans cette promenade de souvenirs, où il jette de temps en temps des poignées d'ironie, des croquis, des souvenirs, des paysages, des tableaux, des profils, des aspects de rue, des carrefours, des trottoirs où flaquent des savates de *marcheuses*; des physionomies de villes trouées de boulets, saignantes, éventrées, des ambulances où se pressent les rats. Puis au revers de cela, — comme dans un album, au revers d'un dessin de Decamps, une pensée de Balzac, — il sort de la bouche de cet homme des silhouettes sociales, des aperçus sur l'espèce française et sur l'espèce anglaise, tout nouveaux et qui n'ont pas moisi dans les livres, une philosophie comparée du génie national des peuples, des satires de deux minutes, des pamphlets d'un mot.

C'est Janina [19] prise et ce ruisseau barboteux de chiens, qui coule entre les jambes de Guys.

C'est Dembinski avec une chemise bleue, jouant sa dernière chemise, jetant un louis, son dernier louis, sur un tapis vert et sans pâlir, le poussant jusqu'à quarante mille francs.

Puis c'est le château anglais, la haute futaie, la chasse, trois toilettes par jour et bal tous les soirs, une vie d'em-

---

[19] Janina, now more commonly Ióannina, the capital city of the department of this name in Greece. Reference to this name in the context in which it occurs would seem to give substance to the legend that Guys was involved as a young man in the Greek War of Liberation, as does the reference in the first paragraph to the "massacres de la Grèce."

pereur menée, conduite, payée par un monsieur qui s'appelle Simpson ou Thompson. C'est le voyage éclaboussant à l'étranger de ce marchand de la Cité, dont le fils de dix-huit ans inspecte dans la Mediterranée les 18 bateaux de son père, dont pas un n'a moins de deux mille tonneaux: "Une flotte, dit Guys, comme l'Égypte n'en a jamais eu." C'est nous, qu'il compare à l'Anglais: "Avez-vous jamais vu à Londres un Français qui ne fît rien, qui fût là pour dépenser de l'argent, bien tranquille dans une belle voiture? Les Français voyagent pour se distraire d'un chagrin d'amour, d'une perte au jeu ou pour placer des rouenneries... Mais là, un Français dans une calèche, un Français qui ne soit ni acteur, ni ambassadeur, ni cuisinier, avec une femme, une femme comme notre mère ou notre sœur, une femme qui ne soit ni une putain ni une actrice ni une couturière, on n'en a jamais vu!"

Puis le voilà qui nous parle peinture, qui nous parle des peintres, qui nous parle des paysagistes, de cette innombrable représentation de la nature sans action, de l'amour de la friture: "Jamais de gants, jamais aux Italiens! Ils n'aiment pas la musique, ils n'aiment pas les chevaux, — parce qu'ils n'en ont pas. Le soleil, la campagne et encore la friture!" [20]

Though the details of Guys' adventures may be spiced with the exaggeration of a good *raconteur*, there is, however, a thoroughly convincing nucleus of truth in the Goncourts' portrait of the man. It corresponds to and completes the portrait of the artist drawn for us by Baudelaire in his essay. What chiefly concerned Baudelaire was the manner in which Guys went about his work, the effect that he produced and the subjects he chose to illustrate. What interested the Goncourts was Guys' personality and his skill as a conversationalist — a verbal draughtsman. There is no indication that they personally ever considered him to be a great artist — rather the reverse. It seems, in fact, as further extracts from their diaries will show, that they felt his merits as an artist had been unjustifiably exaggerated. They appeared to be familiar with only one aspect of his work: his portrayal of prostitutes and brothel scenes.

Nevertheless, the two accounts marvellously complement one another, and the whole man emerges more clearly from a synthesis of the two portraits. Though Baudelaire does insist that Guys is first and

---

[20] Goncourt, *Journal*, 2:221-23. The final paragraph is presumably a derogatory reference to the realist school of painting of Courbet and his admirers. "Aux Italiens" would of course be the *Théâtre des Italiens*.

foremost a man of the world ("M. G. n'aime pas être appelé artiste. N'a-t-il pas un peu raison? Il s'intéresse au monde entier; il veut savoir, comprendre, apprécier tout ce qui se passe à la surface de notre sphéroïde"),[21] he is, however, mainly concerned with giving us a portrait of the artist. He stresses Guys' role as an *observer,* rather than as a participator or a conversationalist, and he tells us a considerable amount about Guys' artistic procedures and also about the subjects of his drawings. Here the two accounts of Guys converge, because Baudelaire's description of Guys at work reveals an impetuousness and a tremendous outpouring of nervous creative energy ("...un feu, une ivresse de crayon, de pinceau, ressemblant presque à une fureur. C'est la peur de n'aller pas assez vite....").[22] These are two of the chief characteristics of the Goncourt portrait ("...une énergie terrible sous ses moustaches grises..., ...d'un coup de plat de main sec et nerveux relevant ses manches sur ses bras osseux, diffus, verbeux, débordant de parenthèses, zigzaguant d'idée en idée, déraillé, perdu et se retrouvant..." etc.).[23] And the subjects of Guys' drawings as outlined by Baudelaire are also, broadly speaking, the subjects of his conversation — high life, low life, military life, and anything foreign or exotic. He is not interested in the humdrum and everyday; the bourgeois holds no interest for him except as a subject for ridicule.

Even Guys' habit of "zigzagging from idea to idea" in his conversation finds its echo in Baudelaire's description of Guys' way of working on as many as twenty drawings at the same time, taking up first one, then another, and gradually increasing their intensity of tone. This is well-rendered impressionistically in the Goncourts' account by the manner in which various subjects are introduced, dropped, and then reintroduced with further detail (the vague "massacres de la Grèce" becomes the specific "Janina prise..."; "des tapis verts d'Allemagne" is, as it were, the background wash for the later sketch, "C'est Dembinski...sur un tapis vert...").

Both portraits confirm the truth of Baudelaire's observation that Guys was primarily a man of the world. His conversation and his art were but two complementary means of expression, into which he could channel the intensity of his feelings about the world around him.

---

[21] Baudelaire, *Œuvres complètes,* p. 1158.
[22] Baudelaire, *Œuvres complètes,* p. 1168.
[23] Goncourt, *Journal,* 2:221.

In reading the Goncourts' portrait, one is struck by one essential difference of tone as compared to Baudelaire's later account — the Goncourts seem to observe Guys with a kind of dispassionate amazement, even with a certain amount of amusement. One can sense, however, that Baudelaire's encounter with Guys was on a much deeper level, and his portrait expresses a genuine admiration and human sympathy lacking to the Goncourts' description. In fact, Baudelaire's enthusiasm is, if anything, too exuberant, as it blinds him to the limitations of Guys' art, but it is an error on the right side.

The Goncourts were sufficiently impressed with the personality of Guys, if not with his art, to use their character sketch of him as the basis for their portrait of Laligant in their novel *Charles Demailly*.[24] This is stated in a diary entry of 31 March, 1861: "Laligant, prototype: Guys." In the same day's entry, they state that their novel contains "...deux genres de personnalités qu'il faut bien distinguer: des portraits, et des personnages créés et amplifiés d'après un prototype." However, the character of Laligant scarcely corresponds to this definition, as it is so close to the prototype as to be almost indistinguishable, much of it being taken word for word from their original sketch of Guys in the *Journal*. A few imaginative details are added chiefly to make Guys sound even more of an adventurer than he was, but all of it is in keeping with the original.[25] The story of *La Mouche* (no longer an Italian, but a Croatian refugee) is told by Laligant at table — almost exactly as Gavarni had related it, as a story of Guys', to the Goncourts.

Guys' extraordinary powers of conversation are again mentioned in a diary entry of 28 January, 1859, concerning Gavarni:

> Gavarni...n'a de chatouillement intime, de récréation de son terrible labeur, que quand il a la conversation de ces

---

[24] Laligant is also spelt Lalligant, Lalignant, in the *édition définitive* (Paris, 1926), pp. 145-50. We shall use the spelling given by the Goncourts in their diary reference.

[25] At one point Laligant's tremendous flow of words is compared to "la parole de Diderot," an interesting addition which has not escaped the notice of Robert Ricatte, whose critical works on the Goncourt brothers are well known. He points out the influence of Diderot's *Le Neveu de Rameau* on the Goncourts' description of Laligant, where it is even more marked than in the sketch of Guys in the *Journal*, written shortly after a recent reading of *Le Neveu* (Robert Ricatte, *La création romanesque chez les Goncourt* (Paris, 1953), p. 127 and n. 64).

> gens qu'il appelle les *riches,* les êtres *pleins de fait,* par opposition à ceux qu'on baptise avec un mot, "homme d'esprit," "bon garçon," etc; ces originaux complexes, résumé et assemblage d'un tas de choses comme Aussandon, Guys, natures étranges, organisations qui vous démontent, langage concret, hommes dont "la vie se passe à être un objet d'étude et de jouissance pour l'intelligence de ceux qui boivent avec eux, sans qu'il reste rien de cela dans une œuvre écrite ou peinte." [26]

The next reference to Guys in the *Journal* is over ten years later, on 25 November, 1871, a year after the death of Jules:

> Peindre, dans mon roman de la prostitution, la grandeur macabre qu'ont rendue les crayons de Rops [27] et de Guys. [28]

The novel referred to here is of course *La Fille Elisa* (1877), the Goncourts' study of prostitution and of the sufferings and evils of criminal detention. A most interesting and comprehensive study of the sources of this novel has been made by Robert Ricatte in his *Genèse de la Fille Elisa.* [29] The possible influence of Guys' work on the novel has not escaped him. In a detailed examination of various passages from the novel, he shows the probable extent of this debt to Guys, which he considers much greater than that to Rops. [30] These are his conclusions:

> ... l'art de Guys a laissé dans *La Fille Elisa* des traces plus générales. Il a fixé aux yeux d'Edmond un certain type bestial de prostituée, et à l'inverse il lui a enseigné la poésie de certaines de ces créatures; surtout il l'a aidé à voir les attitudes des filles avec un œil plus artiste, à discerner sous les gestes professionels de subtiles arabesques, à organiser ses figurantes en des groupes savamment construits et baignés dans les magies du clair-obscur. [31]

A year later, on 19 November, 1872, at a time when a serialized version of the Goncourts' *Gavarni, l'homme et l'œuvre* was appearing

---

[26] Goncourt, *Journal,* 3:98-99.
[27] Félicien Rops (1833-1898), French caricaturist and line engraver.
[28] Goncourt, *Journal,* 10:44.
[29] Robert Ricatte, *La Gènèse de la Fille Elisa* (Paris, 1960), pp. 140-53.
[30] *Ibid.,* p. 143.
[31] *Ibid.,* p. 153.

in *Le Bien Public* (from 18 June, 1872, to 4 March, 1873), Edmond became inadvertently involved once more with Guys, in an affair that seems to have warped his subsequent judgment of Guys' work, as we shall see in a highly biased and unfavourable criticism of Guys in his *Journal* on 22 April, 1895. Apparently on 5 November, 1872, there had appeared in the serialized *Gavarni* the account of Guys taken from the *Journal* of 23 April, 1858. [32] The rest can be told in Edmond's own words:

> Ne jamais faire de réclame aux bohèmes ou, alors, les prendre nageant dans l'outre-mer avec des nimbes de pairs de France!
> Nous avions rencontré deux ou trois fois, chez Gavarni, Guys; et ma foi, il nous avait tout simplement ravis avec l'originalité de sa parole. Nous marquons complètement cette admiration, que nous faisons de lui, dans notre volume sur Gavarni. Mais enfin, le caractère de cet homme, c'est d'être un des particuliers qui ont le plus pataugé dans les troisièmes dessous de la société européenne. Il fallait dans ce portrait, pour qu'il eût la moindre ressemblance, dire que Guys avait couru des filles, habité des garnis, mangé à des tables d'hôtes. Au dernier moment, poussant le scrupule à ses dernières limites, j'avais retiré le nom et biffé sa qualité d'aquarelliste.
> Aujourd'hui m'arrive Nadar, qui me demande, officieusement et assez gentiment, de retirer un tas de phrases soulignées. Au premier mot, allant au-devant de la demande de Nadar, je lui dis que n'ayant eu aucune intention d'être désagréable à Guys et bien au contraire, je suis tout prêt à effacer entièrement le portrait dans le volume de Plon. Cette satisfaction radicale ne satisfait qu'à demi Nadar, qui me pousse à garder le portrait, en l'adoucissant, en l'édulcorant. Au fond, on voudrait la réclame, et Nadar m'a même insinué que Guys ne serait pas fâché que je dise un mot de ses aquarelles. Oh! la susceptibilité des bohèmes! J'oubliais de dire que ce duel en herbe m'est arrivé le 19, pour le jour de ma fête." [33]

If, in contradiction to what Edmond states here, but as Ricatte tells us in his footnote to this affair, Edmond publicly used Guys' name in giving details of his life as an adventurer, he must have known that he would deeply offend Guys. He must have been familiar

---

[32] See the note by Ricatte (Goncourt, *Journal*, 10:118, fn.1).
[33] *Ibid.*, p. 118.

with Baudelaire's essay on Guys and the latter's stated desire for anonymity, and at the same time he could not have failed to know the real identity of the subject since he knew him personally already. One can only surmise sadly that Edmond knew that Guys had not the means at his disposal to prosecute him for defamation of character, and that anyway this would only further expose his identity. The whole affair seems to point again to the conclusion that it was not for questions of professional modesty that Guys had chosen to remain anonymous, but because of personal reasons in connection with his past, or because of his present mode of life.

However, it seems that Guys and Edmond de Goncourt still continued to meet socially on occasion, as on 24 April, 1873, Edmond recounts how he has recently seen Guys at Philippe Burty's:

> Ce soir, chez Burty, Guys nous conte l'arrivée de Gavarni à Londres. Il débarquait en casquette, sans un chapeau, sans un habit, dans l'impossibilité de faire une visite, de dîner dans une maison. Il nous le peint hostile à toute relation, et recevant très froidement d'Orsay, que lui, Guys, avait décidé à lui rendre visite: "Mais il n'y a rien à faire avec ce sauvage!" lui dit d'Orsay.
> Cependant, il lui fait obtenir une audience du secrétaire du Prince Albert, auquel Gavarni présenta une soixantaine d'aquarelles, qui ne furent pas achetées par le prince, mais furent vendues à vil prix à un usurier.
> Sur les dispositions artistiques de Gavarni en Angleterre, le récit de Guys est très contradictoire. Tantôt, il nous le montre ne voulant que passer quelques jours à Londres et disant que ce qu'il fera sera moins bien fait que par les gens du pays. Tantôt, il nous le montre très pris, très empoigné par ce qu'il voit et très désireux de le reproduire avec son accent.
> Un grand nombre de dessins sur les événements de 1848 sont faits d'après les dessins de Guys. A l'arrivée des dessins au LONDON NEWS, les feuilletant, Gavarni, saisi par le caractère, le pittoresque de tel ou tel crayonnage, disait: "Je prends celui-là!" et du croqueton faisait un dessin terminé pour la gravure.[34]

One can see that Edmond was only interested in Guys' account in so far as it gave him further information on Gavarni. But for us

---

[34] Goncourt, *Journal*, 10:125-26.

the account is interesting for the further light it sheds on Guys' movements and his contacts in high circles in England while working for the *Illustrated London News*.

The next reference to Guys in Edmond's *Journal* does not appear until 1895, two and a half years after Guys' death. It is the highly prejudiced account of Guys' work mentioned above:

> Je fais aujourd'hui les deux expositions de Guys, l'exposition de la rue Laffitte, l'exposition Petit.
> La critique de l'heure présente veut en faire un grand monsieur. Mais non, Guys est un dessinateur rondouillard et le plus sale enlumineur de la terre.
> Guys n'a vraiment qu'une valeur, c'est d'être le peintre de la basse putain dans le raccrochage du trottoir. Il a rendu la provocation animale de son visage, sous ce front mangé par d'écrasants bandeaux, la lasciveté de la taille sans corset, le roulis des hanches dans la marche, le retroussage ballonnant de la jupe, la tombée des mains dans les poches du petit tablier; l'attache dénouée du chapeau au chignon, l'excitation lubrique de son dos et de ses bras nus, en la mollesse et l'avachissement de l'étoffe qui l'habille, — et cela dans les eaux verdâtres d'une aquarelle de Morgue.

Granted that Edmond does at least give Guys the credit for effectively painting the bestiality of a certain type of prostitute, it is still a fairly devastating piece of criticism, and the insulting tone ("tubby little draughtsman ... dirtiest illustrator on earth") leads one to the regrettable conclusion that Edmond has let his personal feelings distort his critical judgment. The passage is, however, of interest in showing how familiar Edmond was with the details of one type of Guys' work, and lends support to Ricatte's conclusions that Edmond was indeed quite strongly influenced by Guys' drawings in his portrait of prostitution in *La Fille Elisa*.

Perhaps Edmond was unable to do justice to Guys because of his *parti pris* in favour of Gavarni — these days considered the lesser artist of the two. Baudelaire's superiority of critical judgment in matters of art is nowhere more clearly illustrated than in his ability to discern in Guys a truly original artist without unnecessarily denigrating Gavarni.[35] Time has proved him right and Edmond wrong, as can

---

[35] "Tel qu'il est, Gavarni est un artiste plus qu'intéressant, dont il restera beaucoup." (Baudelaire, "Quelques caricaturistes français," *Œuvres complètes*, p. 1010.)

be seen from the following extract from the latter's *Journal* of 9 November, 1895:

> Cet homme de talent qui s'appelait Baudelaire a dit parfois des énormités, ainsi que le jour où il appelait Guys le peintre de la vie moderne, et Gavarni le peintre de la chlorose. [36]

The last reference to Guys in Edmond's *Journal* is a brief "obituary" on Guys' art. It is a note of 24 November, 1895, on the sale of certain of Nadar's pictures: à Manet, à Daumier, "...et les dessins de Guys, sauf trois ou quatre, se sont vendus des vingt, des trente francs." [37] Little did Edmond foresee how sought after Guys' work would become seventy-five years later, once his true value as a precursor of the Impressionist painters was established.

The Goncourts' testimony adds nothing to our appreciation of Guys the artist, but it sheds precious light on the personality of the man. The shadowy, anonymous figure of Guys is brought vividly alive in their evocative description of his appearance and his conversation, particularly in the unforgettable synesthetic phrase "sa parole éclatante, peinte et dont le tapage est comme visible aux yeux...." [38]

---

[36] Goncourt, *Journal,* 21:128. The reference to Gavarni is from "L'Idéal," *Les Fleurs du Mal*: "Je laisse à Gavarni, poète des chloroses, / Son troupeau gazouillant de beautés d'hôpital."

[37] Goncourt, *Journal.* 21:133.

[38] Goncourt, *Journal,* 2:221.

TABOUROT'S SIEUR GAULARD: THE GRATIFYING DUNCE

F. W. VOGLER
University of North Carolina

It is unlikely that any writer since Honoré de Balzac could be said to have been influenced by the prose fiction of Etienne Tabourot, "Seigneur des Accords," a contemporary of Montaigne's who was known to his immediate posterity as the "Burgundian Rabelais." Even for Balzac, the use of Tabourot as a source is to be seen only in one of his least well-preserved works, the tediously archaizing *Contes drolatiques*.[1] In his analysis of Balzac's debt to Tabourot, Wayne Connor has shown that Balzac borrowed material primarily from *Les Escraignes dijonnaises*, a plebeian successor to the *Decameron* and the *Heptameron* in that its stories are told by members of a group of humble tradesmen, laborers, and housewives from a Dijon neighborhood. Thanks to a single spark of internal evidence, Balzac's use of the term *Bourguignotte*, Connor suggests that Balzac may have been familiar with a still more obscure work of Tabourot's, *Les Contes facecieux du Sieur Gaulard, Gentilhomme de la Franche-Comté Bourguignotte*, first published in 1585 and reprinted in several later editions of Tabourot's works during the first two-thirds of the seventeenth century.[2]

The *Contes facecieux* constitute an extended literary portrait of an ostensibly dimwitted provincial nobleman, whose absurd exploits are recounted in a long series of seldom-connected short anecdotes,

---

[1] Wayne Connor, "The Influence of Tabourot des Accords on Balzac's *Contes drolatiques*," *Romanic Review*, 41 (1950), 195-205.
[2] *Ibid.*, p. 198.

averaging some four or five per duodecimo page. According to Tabourot's modern biographer, Georges Choptrayanovitch, this work more than any other reveals Tabourot's skill as a *conteur*.[3] Such a judgment is remarkable indeed in light of Choptrayanovitch's unfavorable description of the *Contes facecieux* in his next paragraph:

> Comme le titre l'annonce, ce recueil contient des facéties insipides, des banalités, des histoires scandaleuses. C'est une collection de grossièretés. Tout ce que Tabourot connaissait de bas, de grossier, de cru, il l'attribue à un personnage légendaire plutôt qu'historique.[4]

For Choptrayanovitch, Gaulard was created by a merciless satirist as an incarnation of silliness and stupidity. In order safely to lampoon the provincial nobility, it was expedient for Tabourot to make his dunce-figure a member of the Franc-Comtois gentry, therefore non-French and particularly uncosmopolitan; Choptrayanovitch is probably correct in this assumption, for the political and social significance of the setting is repeatedly suggested in Tabourot's references to the support given to the King of Spain by the nobility of Gaulard's province. It is probably true as well that Gaulard was a product of Tabourot's imagination, with certain autobiographical reminiscences but without any specific real-life model. Tabourot was free to develop this character as it pleased him, but exactly what purpose he had in mind is really not altogether clear. It is at this point that Choptrayanovitch seems to have overlooked an important aspect of Tabourot's characterization, for he finds only bitter, even violent satire in these anecdotes:

> Gaulard, ce Franc-Comtois ridicule et bafoué, est une énorme caricature, à travers laquelle Tabourot vise les vices et les ridicules de tous ses pareils, les seigneurs ignorants et vaniteux, les dévots crédules aussi bien que les Francs-Comtois détestés, et enfin ses contemporains de tous rangs et de toutes classes.[5]

---

[3] *Etienne Tabourot des Accords (1549-1590): étude sur sa vie et son œuvre littéraire* (Dijon, 1935), p. 171.

[4] *Ibid.* There is actually far less coarseness in the *Contes facecieux* than Choptrayanovitch indicates, and such restraint is noteworthy on the part of a "Burgundian Rabelais" who was capable of the most exuberant crudity in his writing.

[5] *Ibid.*, p. 180.

Yet the very first paragraph of the *Contes facecieux* creates a mood that is not bitter, not violent, not at all that of an *énorme caricature* satirizing the faults and foibles of Tabourot's contemporaries:

> Il y a des personnes de si bonne paste, & heureuse rencontre, qu'ils semblent estre nais pour faire rire les autres: & voit-on bien que Nature les a douez d'une si gracieuse simplicité, que vous lisez en leurs visages, & jugez par leurs paroles qu'il ne faut rien prendre de mauvaise part d'eux. Aussi les voyez-vous ordinairement bien venus en toutes compagnies, & cheris de la Fortune: de sorte qu'ils vivent joyeusement, bien vestus, bien nourris, sans envie, sans ambition, sans amour, sans procés, & sans debtes. Et si davantage un trait de liberté contre quelqu'un leur eschappe, on ne s'en offense jamais, mais on en rit gracieusement, comme on voit bien que cela leur vient en la bouche sans malice. [...] Aussi telles gens ont cela de propre, qu'ils ne prennent pas en mal si l'on se gaudit d'eux, mesmes en leur presence, encores que quelquesfois ils le connoissent bien: & sont contens le plus souvent d'en rire les premiers, s'accoustumans par là, à sçavoir dissimuler les affaires du monde.[6]

If this preamble can be accepted as providing the key to Tabourot's intention in creating Gaulard, his collection of anecdotes reveals a person quite different from the outrageous buffoon found by Choptrayanovitch. Here instead is a man whose role in life is to give pleasure to others by allowing them to feel superior to him. He does this, however, less by his actions than by his ingenuous observations about the daily happenings in his life. The comic element is thus primarily verbal rather than visual.

Examples can be found on nearly every page of the *Contes facecieux* to support this view of an inoffensively amusing Gaulard. When he is caught in a drenching rain, the humor of the situation lies not in his bedraggled appearance but in his explanation that it was merely "une petite pluie seche qui est tombee sur [lui] environ deux ou trois heures."[7] Likewise, when he is unlucky enough to contract a mild

---

[6] Etienne Tabourot, *Les Contes facecieux du Sieur Gaulard, gentil-homme de la Franche-Comté Bourguignotte*, in *Les Bigarrures et Touches du Seigneur des Accords, avec les Apophtegmes du Sieur Gaulard, et les Escraignes dijonnoises* (Paris, 1662), p. 179f.

[7] *Ibid.*, p. 193.

case of venereal disease in an encounter with a prostitute, an unexpected comical twist is provided by Gaulard's rueful acknowledgment that God's punishment has surely been visited upon him... for having forgotten the girl despite his promise to remember her.

At every turn, it would appear, Gaulard manages to delight those around him (although not necessarily modern readers) with some disconcertingly naïve remark. During a sermon, he sputters angrily that he will never agree to put up with the social equality of souls in paradise as described by the preacher. A friend complains of moles' ruining a fine meadow of his with their burrowing; Gaulard promptly suggests that he have it paved. After agreeing not to say anything to anyone about a morsel of gossip which is then shared with him, he announces that he will at least *write* about it to his friend the Seigneur des Accords, who collects and publishes that sort of material. When invited to visit the residence of an abbot, he assures his prospective host that he will stay for only two or three weeks and that meals will be no problem as long as partridge, turkey, and beef are always provided. An artist commissioned to do Gaulard's portrait is instructed to have his likeness read aloud from a book — *son et lumière!* In petitioning the King of Spain for a favor, he justifies his appeal by claiming that he and all his ancestors have died in Spain's military service. When told of plans to extend the city walls of Paris to include the Saint-Germain district, Gaulard enthusiastically endorses the project because it will bring visitors lodging out there closer to the center of the city and its activities. When informed as he is on several occasions of the death of a kinsman or acquaintance, Gaulard either rejects the news as false (surely whoever it was would have informed him personally!) or else gravely wishes the deceased a long and happy life.

Even Gaulard's social inferiors are permitted to feel better endowed with common sense than he, but here again this is usually due to Gaulard's expression of absurd ideas rather than to his actual conduct. His cook could probably easily endure his master's abusive tone when reproached for providing only ordinary fare, never savory epigrams with dessert, as was reported to have been done not long before at the house of one of Gaulard's innumerable cousins. And his secretary would be unlikely to take offense at Gaulard's order to insert at least a half dozen *etc.* at the end of every dictated letter after the secretary has explained to his amazed master that the term is used to indicate a closing *formule de politesse*. An innkeeper's reaction could only have been one of amusement to Gaulard's demand that a noisy fountain in the street outside his room either be moved or burned. Even his barber must have sniggered at Gaulard's angry ultimatum that he be sent at least a "Maistre Clerc" if the master barber himself is unable to come to his house, a reaction very similar to that of Monsieur Jourdain when offered a song by his music master's pupil.

At times, though, it appears that Gaulard may well be feigning naïveté in order to maintain his image as a dependable laughingstock in any group. When an Italian makes a sweeping gesture in describing a landscape, Gaulard asks him to lower his arm so as not to block the view. A Comtois just back from Spain uses the Hispanism *baiser les mains*, and Gaulard, promptly washing his own, invites him to proceed. On another occasion, Gaulard apparently dumbfounds his interlocutor, an enemy who has come upon him while unarmed and relieving himself in a ditch; when his foe chivalrously declares that he will not attack until Gaulard has finished and can defend himself, he is told that he might as well go away, for there is no chance of Gaulard's finishing as long as the other man is in sight.

If Gaulard can be considered to be a kind of professional booby, his creator Tabourot must be manipulating his character for something more than just anti-*hobereau*, anti-Comtois satire. For all his silly pretentions of rank and culture, Gaulard does not take a dead-serious view of himself or of life in general and is thus able to lead the sort of cheerful, unreflective existence of those "chéris de la Fortune" described in Tabourot's preamble. Tabourot himself believes that others would do well to allow a little frivolity in their too-earnest lives, or so he claims:

> Ce [other collections of amusing anecdotes] que je desire infiniment voir en ce malin siecle, pour regaillarder les esprits tous effarouchez de nos François, qui ne sont en peine, que pour avoir voulu trop contrefaire les severes, & appliquer contre leur naturel leurs esprits, à rechercher cinq pieds en un mouton.[8]

---

[8] *Ibid.*, p. 221.

As was mentioned earlier, reprintings of this work were available in France well into the second half of the seventeenth century. It is quite possible that the bibliophile La Bruyère was familiar with it; at any rate, his *Caractères* demonstrate the progress made in the art of caricature in the space of a century, with Classical focus and density replacing the loosely articulated, repetitive catalogue of Tabourot's sixteenth-century form. In that evolution lies the kinship — by no means remote — between Gaulard and Ménalque.

PHILOGYNY AS AN ELEMENT IN MAUPASSANT'S WORK

A. H. WALLACE
University of Tennessee

Maupassant was not showing us a Romantic "femme fatale" when he repeatedly told tales in which the woman gained ascendency over the man. His admiration for woman grew out of personal contact and observation, not from fear inspired by a superstitious cult. Among the strangely few men who enjoyed Maupassant's unstinting admiration, most had chosen celibacy and so were relatively safe from acts of weakness that so often characterize a husband's behavior and which would have lowered them in his esteem. Flaubert, of course, was so far in the vanguard of this select few as to be the god of the microcosm. To Maupassant marriage was a form of servitude which the female refused to accept because she recognized it as such, and to which the male submitted while deluding himself with the notion that he was free, the master. The calm demeanor and unflinching resolve of Maupassant's mother inspired early his admiration for woman and caused him to question the myth of male superiority. Madame de Maupassant's influence upon her son can never be accurately evaluated, for the more one ponders his work the more one is struck with her presence in the character of heroine after heroine. Far more accurate assessments can be made of the influence of Maupassant's father in shaping the son's prejudicial view of husbands as self-centered weaklings who deserved cuckolding, and of the role his disappointment in his father had in determining him to seek in Flaubert a father who was not weak or unworthy of the charge. And yet, paradoxically, we find Maupassant writing near the end of his days in favor of marriage. The cruel spark of loneliness ignited this twilight mania in a man who had spent most of his career satirizing or openly denouncing the institution. Celibacy confirmed the strange and haunting terror that was typical of Maupassant's bouts with insanity. He speaks of his terror of loneliness in a letter to his mother: "J'ai peur de l'hiver qui vient, je me sens seul, et mes longues soirées de solitude sont quelquefois terribles. J'éprouve souvent, quand je me trouve seul devant ma table avec ma triste lampe qui brûle devant moi, des moments de détresse si complets que je ne sais plus à qui me jeter."[1]

It should be stated that Maupassant did not always write with the aim of inciting sympathy for the married woman's plight or of excusing her extramarital affairs. *Une Famille* typifies a number of stories whose aim is clearly to decry how marriage destroys friendship between old male cronies and to express his repugnance at how the wife is always certain to drag her husband down to her level. These stories, with their strange male prejudice, lack the power of those which speak with admiration of woman. What vitality they have results from a sudden and ephemeral anger, and not from the slowly nurtured conviction that lends the moving power and lasting vitality to his writings which praise woman.

The magnificent courage and nobility of woman in time of war and defeat inspired what many consider to be his greatest story, *Boule de Suif*. War was a fact of Maupassant's life. This makes his praise of woman's behavior as contrasted to the less admirable, often even cowardly, behavior of her counterpart the more striking. But it does not seem out of character to the one who has opened his eyes to the apparent philogyny in his other works. Philogyny is not merely a tone in Maupassant, it is the basic trait of his attitude concerning the human species.

The prostitute Rachel, in *Mademoiselle Fifi*, behaves in the way that epitomized for Maupassant the *effective* disdain of the conquered. Women can deal with a derisive effectiveness above man's capacities, Maupassant believes, because they have learned how as long-suffering prisoners of male conventions. You think you're raping the women of France, sneers the proud Rachel to the sadistic Mademoiselle Fifi (Wilhelm d'Eyrik): "Moi! moi! je ne suis pas une femme, mais je suis une putain, c'est bien tout ce qu'il faut à des Prussiens."[2] Her

---

[1] Guy de Maupassant, *Œuvres complètes* (Paris: Louis Conard, 1907-1910), IV, cxxvii.
[2] *Ibid.*, X, 23.

stabbing of him and the ringing of the bells which had remained silent in the face of his ironic threats to be the cause of their ringing again or have the townsmen's blood are almost anti-climatic, following as they do in the wake of her success in making the Prussian feel the littleness ascribed to him and his kind by those he had conquered but could not break.

The Comtesse de Brémontal's sensitivity, her love of poetry and her melancholy surroundings are all reminiscent of Laure de Maupassant. She too is abandoned by her husband, whose seignorial, Norman bravado causes his whimsical mind to place military service above his duty to remain and protect his pregnant, defenseless wife. Even so she behaves with disdainful composure in the face of threats by the Prussian officer who has taken over her house. So effective is her contempt that the Prussian suffers the ignominy fatal to all conquerors' pride. Maupassant had great plans for this novel to be entitled *L'Angélus*. It was to be his masterpiece in the genre. His dedication to the project and the magnitude of the idea he had in mind can be guessed at from notes sketching what was to follow the events described above: the Countess' boy would be born on Christmas a cripple in one of the chateau's outbuildings, his disfiguration the result of his mother's having been brutalized by the Prussian. The religious connotations are perhaps a little too obvious, but it must be kept in mind that the story came to him as something that had to be written only when he was already hopelessly in the grip of his tragic malady. No one can say what he might have done with the theme had he been in good health.

The tragic fate of the lovely Irma of *Le Lit 29* has none of the mawkish sentimentality of so many stories of its kind. While showing us how war so tragically truncates those seemingly perfect affairs, Maupassant shows us simultaneously how imperfect are most of the males in such affairs. The lady-killer, Captain Epivent, was happy to rattle the medals on his chest in fury at an enemy who had had the gall to rape his woman then take her life. Nonetheless he was unhappy to find that his beautiful mistress was alive and had syphilis. Unhappy because he would have to go to see her to satisfy the world that he was who he said he was, unhappy that he would somehow have to tarnish the image of himself that he sought to publicize. His visit to her begins on an ironic note, and demonstrates clearly her selfless love for him: she expresses pride in his medals, and does not waste time in complaining about her condition. Only when he pressed her did she reveal the patriotism that had prompted her to refuse treatments for the infection a Prussian had brought her: she had taken it upon herself to spread the infection amongst the hated army of occupation, using her beauty as a lure. It was what she could do to avenge her country's lost pride. She had known she would end up here, but it had been worth it. "Et je les ai empoisonnés aussi, tous, tous, le plus que j'ai pu." [3] The Captain leaves with the purpose of never returning. But he cannot play the hero before the people. Though he ignores her letter of entreaty, he has to go to save face when the hospital chaplain comes after him. Maupassant's description of her contempt for her former lover removes any doubts as to his dedication to emphasizing the sharp contrast between the pusillanimity of the male, with his illusory strength, and the strong courage of the female, with her alleged frailties. Irma's choice of a name for the man she was dismissing was forged in the mind of a creator burning with a sense of outrage at men blinded to the truth by their stubborn, ego-inspired anti-feminism. "... Va donc, *capon!* Plus que toi, oui, j'en ai tué plus que toi, plus que toi." [4] (Italics mine.) She died the following day.

Berthine of *Les Prisonniers* is a healthy peasant girl whose vengeance against the invaders is blunt, unsophisticated and as final as a wily Norman peasant's business transactions. She allows them in her house, tricks them into her basement from which escape is impossible, and then convinces them that surrendering to the local constabulary, ignominious though it may be, is the choice for them. Evidence that Maupassant did not deem a male capable of this sort of clear design and execution is the fact that he presents an exceedingly satirical and damaging picture of the ostentatious, bungling militia commander who joyfully accepts the total credit for the capture.

One sees the same admiration for the concise manner in which women exact their vengeance against the enemy in the story about the mad woman — insane from grief because she had befriended the Prussians, being an innocent in politics, prior to learning that their army had killed her son — and how she beguiled her Prussian "guests" into signing their names on a piece of paper and then incinerated

---

[3] *Ibid.*, XXIX, 82.
[4] *Ibid.*, 88.

them in her house as they slept soundly, sure of her friendship. She wanted their signatures as proof to their loved ones that they were dead and that *she* and she alone had been responsible for their deaths. Her steady dedication to her purpose is admirable, even if one does not like her aim. Maupassant liked her aim, but more important, it is consistent with his philosophy to depict woman as being the one capable of the kind of discipline necessary to overcome the greatest obstacles.

The high place *Boule de Suif* occupies in French literature is merited, for it presents woman's courage and resolve with such power and art as to have few parallels. It is because it is the clearest and most moving presentation of Maupassant's admiration for female strength in times of dire disillusionment that we have saved a discussion of it until now. Defeat breaks the souls of most of the men it tries. And those strong survivors of the initial shock, upon viewing the tragic shambles of their fellow-beings' broken spirit, often knuckle under to despair themselves. The few who can look upon such tragedy and still remain whole are the real heroes who cause men to pick up their pride and begin again. A person familiar with Maupassant's life and work will know why he chose a prostitute for this super-human accomplishment. But one must see his treatment of woman in the proper light and must be familiar with every line he wrote about her to reconcile his ambivalence regarding woman as a general class, for the question continually arises as to how he could have set a course in his own life which seemed oriented upon degrading her. We have to come to the conclusion that the woman he met in the bordello he found to be the consummation of all the qualities he considered important and admirable: we have Boule de Suif as evidence. His second reason for choosing her is quite as evident. There was no better way for Maupassant to continue his effective needling of society's pride in its conventions, in particular the ones that tended to assign a priori the virtue of acting heroically to the male and faintheartedness and ineffectual sentimentality to the female. And even more pointedly, he could mock the conventional stigmatizing of prostitutes as socially destructive and morally inferior. The lovely figure we see emerging from the wretched world that spawned, abused and reviled her, even giving her the name, Boule de Suif, to show its mockery, is the brain-child of a loving and admiring creator, whose philogyny is evident.

Maupassant knew that the best place for the greatest to show themselves was in a world where what had posed as greatness had been revealed as fraud — the world of defeat where wound-licking is often mistaken for struggle. Boule de Suif comes upon a scene where people are more concerned with adapting to defeat and calling it by another name than with refusing to be servile. It is a world where her refusal to accept the defeat the others took for granted both sets her apart from the common herd and brings her into conflict with it. She would not have been able to utter eloquent words about idealism, but she possessed it and the courage to realize its goal. Maupassant wastes no time in stamping her with the mark of superiority. The coach has scarcely begun its journey before his concise artistry has revealed to us that the other passengers, and especially the women, with their conventional morality leading at best to the delusion of the rectitude of their ambitions for peace and material prosperity, are indeed impoverished human spirits beside this brave, engaging prostitute. Maupassant thus wins our esteem early and causes us to be more wary of the others. Loiseau, the wine merchant, spouts the kind of clichés typical of the articulate among the society with which Maupassant found himself at loggerheads. One of his pronouncements which removes the other women's hypocritical compunction against accepting food from a prostitute is the type thing one finds in Flaubert's *Dictionnaire des idées reçues*. Boule de Suif's ignorance of their absurd clichés sets her above them in our minds. Her fellow passengers are shown from the beginning as people who have nothing for the times but talk. Boule de Suif would never articulate the accepted idea that "dans des cas pareils tout le monde est frère et doit s'aider," but she would act in such a way as to fulfill its promise. With this brief incident Maupassant has shown us the larger meaning of his story and how the meaning of his story transcends the boundaries in which he had given it light. Maupassant could not have been more effective in drawing the line between the others and Boule de Suif. The latter returns to life what she takes from it and more, and in so doing she is neither a conventional prostitute, nor a conventional human being, she is a woman and a superior human being.

Later, at the inn, in the scene in which the other traveling companions quarrel over what they think would be the right thing for Boule de Suif to do, Boule de Suif herself has figuratively ascended to an empyrean where the pettiness of her erstwhile companions is not permitted to trouble her choice of action. Maupassant shows considerable artistry in the symbology of having Boule de Suif upstairs in the inn, separated from the others physically by some small distance, while her spiritual separation from them is so vast, as vast as the distance between positive and negative. By means of this symbol, Maupassant is able to say again what he is saying with the whole story. The terrible pettiness of rationalizing to which we all resort brands itself upon our minds as they deliberate: "Puisque c'est son métier, à cette gueuse, de faire ça avec tous les hommes, je trouve qu'elle n'a pas le droit de refuser l'un plutôt que l'autre."[5] Maupassant makes us see the real question that we all must face with such startling clarity that we know we are in the presence of a master. Through Boule de Suif's unerring understanding of what it means to give herself to the enemy, we come to understand what it means for us to give ourselves to the enemy. And, moreover, we come to understand that in giving themselves to everything most people give themselves to nothing, and that the enemy will settle for nothing but the greatest as his price. Maupassant, like us all, mourned in the face of the realization that so often the sacrifice of the greatest only causes those who benefit from the selfless act to respond by a show of their utter unworthiness. He chose a woman to show us his admiration for the unique strength of the great. And as if to dismiss the male race from consideration for such a role, he shows us that the only self-anointed revolutionary, and the only one who complains of Boule de Suif's lot, when it comes time to revolt against the others whose deliberations he has condemned, does not act. He talks. Maupassant thereby is able to demonstrate again how the times called for deeds, and the bitter disappointment he felt over the behavior in general of his countrymen. "Je vous dis à tous que vous venez de faire une infamie!"[6] And the next day Cornudet eats with the others from whom only inefficacious words had ever separated him and continues deluding himself by singing the "Marseillaise." If *Boule de Suif* is truly Maupassant's masterpiece, it owes the honor to the insistent admiration for woman which receives its finest artistic expression and compression in the story. The theme is not new, nor does it end here. Philogyny is omnipresent in his writing.

---

[5] *Ibid.*, IV, 56-57.
[6] *Ibid.*, 69.

Madame de Maupassant's fear that that very genius of which she was so proud would be the cause of an ever-widening gulf between her and her son, though such a fear often proves well founded, need not have tormented her. In Maupassant's creative output alone her influence is apparent, more apparent than it was to either mother or son. She perhaps could not see her success for the troubling fantasies her mind served up to her as she watched him move restlessly about Europe and Africa and as she watched him become more and more a recluse because of his art and his illness. The novels especially provide us with portraits of women who are in so many ways like Laure de Maupassant. The problems these women face and their superiority in dealing with them seem to have been inspired by his observations of his mother's life.

In *Notre Coeur* we see a bitter rendering of a situation which Maupassant must not have viewed as a very large exaggeration of that of his mother. He speaks of the heroine, Michèle de Burne: «Mariée avec un vaurien de belles manières, un de ces tyrans domestiques, devant qui tout doit céder et plier, elle avait été d'abord malheureuse." [7] Like Laure de Maupassant, Madame de Burne was not the kind of woman who would allow herself to become enslaved by the shallow ambitions and vanity of an inferior husband. The difference in the way Maupassant causes Madame de Burne to work out her problem is the fictional aspect; the aggravation of the problem by a complacent and indifferent husband and by the social milieu that tries to justify rules meant to make the superior accept what the mediocrity takes for good remain the same. The same problem is treated in the other Maupassant novels. Each time the solution is different. We see that Maupassant, like his teacher, Flaubert, undertakes a study of the series of environmental forces that encircle woman so tightly as to cause her to attempt to break out of the sterile circle so fatal to her own ideas of her happiness and destiny. Maupassant's heroines resemble Emma Bovary because we find them in the identical situations, not in their dealing with them. That they do deal with them, either through a stoic acceptance of fact or by establishing themselves as mistresses of their social fate, shows how they are different from Flaubert's heroine. When death removed Madame de

---

[7] *Ibid.*, XII, 7.

Burne's primary problem she vowed never again to put herself in the compromising position marriage called for. But she needed men. She needed to dominate them and succeeded in doing so. Then André Mariolle came into her life bearing the same determination as she not to allow himself to fall in love. But a paltry investment of her emotions shattered his resolve to remain independent. Her easy conquest of him resulted from Maupassant's conviction that the male is the weaker of the two sexes when it comes to achieving the destiny he has set for himself. Mariolle was a non-writing talker about writing. Maupassant believed males were more frequently talkers than doers. He was not nearly so harsh on females, although he did have the novelist, Gaston de Lamarthe, whom some have seen as Maupassant himself, tell the weak Mariolle: "Voyez-vous, mon cher, la femme n'est créée et venue en ce monde que pour deux choses, qui seules peuvent faire épanouir ses vraies, ses grandes, ses excellentes qualités: l'amour et l'enfant." [8] Maupassant was fond of dropping this line with acquaintances who took it as evidence of a misogynism which does not appear justified considering all of the evidence to the contrary. Lamarthe is probably closer to expressing his creator's conviction when he argues that the realist-naturalist novelist in suppressing the poetic quality of existence and dealing only with life's grim realities is to blame for woman's turning upon her weaker counterpart: "Or, mon cher, plus d'amour dans les livres, plus d'amour dans la vie. Vous étiez des inventeurs d'idéal, elles croyaient à vos inventions. Vous n'êtes maintenant que des évocateurs de réalités précises, et derrière vous elles se sont mises à croire à la vulgarité de tout." [9] How strongly this suggests Maupassant's great depth of understanding of both *Madame Bovary* and of the realist-naturalist movement in literature! Mariolle's failure to reach any of the admirable goals he had set for himself is a presaging of his surrendering of all of his male prerogatives. Maupassant's hatred for inadequacies in the male flows into the book with as much force as his admiration for the female's ability to turn the tables on an environment fostering the conventions that threaten her individuality. This dual emphasis is one of the weaknesses of the book. More than the latter half of the book consists of studies of Mariolle which make it more and more apparent that such a weak prize is

---

[8] *Ibid.*, 144.
[9] *Ibid.*, 146.

hardly worth the effort of Madame de Burne and that there is no possibility that there will be any dramatic reversals or conflict to revitalize the story. Maupassant does give us an interesting reversal of himself in the character of Mariolle. Are we to assume then that his success in the arts being the opposite to his hero's failure, his success with women was just as clearly the opposite? Probably he meant for us to. But that scarcely is sufficient to justify our admiration for the novel. "Les arts l'ayant tenté, il ne trouva pas en lui le courage nécessaire pour se donner tout à fait à l'un d'eux, ni l'obstination persévérante qu'il faut pour y triompher." [10] Mariolle's algolagnic relationship with a serving girl, whom he had read to him from *Manon Lescaut* each night, evidences the strange almost maniacal proclivity Maupassant developed in later years for debasing the male. It is so exaggerated as to be boring. He did very well in reducing man to a low state in all of the excellent treatments of cuckoldry in his work. Perhaps he spent his artistic capacities to deal with the subject in those fine efforts.

Fort comme la Mort is the only novel of Maupassant that treats woman with disdain. The book is a dull one which describes how the hero Bertin, terrified by the thought of growing old, abandons his mistress, Madame de Guilleroy, and attaches himself to her daughter, Annette, as if he could obtain from her youth his nearly depleted vitality. Maupassant, as is well known, was inordinately troubled by the prospect of growing old. This novel is not a good one, and it may be because it does not have the proper artistic detachment that he was able to achieve with incredible efficiency in his stories about madness. He had, as was usual with him, dealt with the same problem in *Fini*, a story which is practically incorporated into the novel. It is clear that Maupassant's first purpose was to study the problem of aging and that the weaknesses or strengths of the persons who were undergoing the process were not a point of issue. Therefore, we only point to this novel with its dependent and fainting female to allay any suspicions that we are avoiding discussions of stories which might be considered to contradict the assertion that Maupassant was a philogynist. Bertin is, besides, quite in character. He certainly cannot be offered as evidence of any erosion of Maupassant's general contempt for the male — not when he has to be shown the foolishness of his

---

[10] *Ibid.*, 205.

idea that a man in his forties can play like a lover in his twenties simply because he does not want to think of growing old. Maupassant was too aware of how typically bourgeois this notion of Bertin's was, and so angered by it that he destroyed his hero in a maudlin operatic scene that followed his having been run over by a coach. The ending is typical of the novel, weak.

Christiane Andermatt, the heroine of *Mont-Oriol*, another disappointing novel, represented a personification of the author's cry of despair over the growing conviction that there was no such thing as an ideal love or marriage. Though, as Sullivan suggests, it is the weakest of his novels, it provides still more evidence of Maupassant's admiration for woman. Here, more than in most cases, the admiring treatment of the heroine is resultant to Maupassant's failure to find much worthy of consideration in the man. Here she wins his praise by default so to speak. If the "main characters are mere clichés, uninteresting as individuals," [11] then it becomes apparent that a part of the blame for the bad book has to be laid upon his habitual preoccupation with presenting the female in an advantageous limelight. His election of Christiane as worthy of expressing his almost total disillusionment with the dream of two beings finding the ideal in each other, however, hardly justifies the suggestion that she has no individuality.

> ... Quand elle avait cru que leurs chairs et leurs âmes ne faisaient plus qu'une chair et qu'une âme, ils s'étaient seulement un peu rapprochés, jusqu'à faire toucher les impénétrables enveloppes où la mystérieuse nature a isolé et enfermé les humains. *Elle vit bien que nul jamais n'a pu ou ne pourra briser cette invisible barrièrre qui met les êtres dans la vie aussi loin l'un de l'autre que les étoiles du ciel.* [12] (Italics mine)

Maupassant frustrates her by instilling in her mind the illusion that a great love is possible, before shattering her hopes with the revelation that her lover, Paul Brétigny, in spite of his poetic idealism, is hollow and vain like all men. She is defended from those who would condemn

---

[11] Edward D. Sullivan, *Maupassant the Novelist* (Princeton, N. J., 1945), 98.

[12] Maupassant, *op. cit.*, XVIII, 410.

her cuckolding of her husband in typical Maupassantian fashion: Andermatt deserved it. The sarcastic tone of Maupassant's description of the Jewish financier, Andermatt, so clever in business and wrapped up in deals as to be oblivious to anything else, is doubtless unworthy of his creative powers. But his blindness is not unlike that of M. Roland of *Pierre et Jean*. His inability to conceive of the possibility of his being a cuckold, and so accepting his wife's pregnancy with the faith of the complacent husband stereotype is hardly more exaggerated than that of his counterpart in *Pierre et Jean*, who is rarely thought of as a mere cliché. Here, as elsewhere, it is not the woman who is to blame for the failure to achieve the ideal union of two souls. It is Paul Brétigny with his cowardice and brutal indifference to her once he discovers he is the father of her unborn child who fails because of his inveterate male weakness. Maupassant does not intend to show us that Paul, or man, in dealing harshly with a woman he professes to love, acts with the firmness of a woman when she thwarts her mate from exercising his mythical seignorial dominance over her; his intention is just the opposite, to show us that his brutality and indifference are but weak substitutes for a clear-cut action.

Christiane's outcry at the instant she learns her baby is a girl recalls Emma Bovary: "Ah! mon Dieu!" [13] But she cannot abandon the baby because it is going to be subject to the prejudices and limitations imposed on it by a male-dominated society. She resolves to show Paul her sovereignty and then to dismiss him. Maupassant paints a cruel picture of the weak lover being denied even a glimpse of the baby. But his heroine, by the manner in which she demonstrates that she has come to grips with her fate and has asserted her individuality, excites one's admiration. The men in her life are indeed but clichés, but she remains in the mind as a symbol of Maupassant's philogyny.

L'Inutile Beauté is an ironic title fashioned by Maupassant who expresses his anger at the stupid bestiality which had created the conventions that made it a virtue to corrupt the beauty of a woman and a crime for her to seek to defend it. The accepted idea that it was a disgraceful and unnatural waste for a beautiful woman not to bear children receives all the fury of a writer who had been coached in fury against bourgeois mediocrity by the master, Flaubert. Maupassant's philogyny makes him fashion the idea that a woman's rebellion

---

[13] *Ibid.*, 391.

against the deformities of pregnancy is more natural than unnatural — a dogma which for him was incontrovertible.

Maupassant's heroine, the Comtesse de Mascaret, has set out to prove that the supposed Holy-Writ that declared a beautiful woman was all the more required to perpetuate the species than a plain one had not come from heaven but was a fraudulent document forged by the male ego. The author's readiness to do battle with this convention, which comes closer to being accepted by the opressed victims than any other male ordinance, and which has received repeated anointings by religions, shows that Maupassant was willing to risk everything in the cause of his philogyny. Maupassant was infamous for his frank emphasis upon woman's utility as a means to sexual gratification and pleasure. That he seemed to prefer her in this role to that of mother made a great deal of difference to his critics who pointed to his frequenting of bordellos as a sign of his degenerate and corrupted life. But to observe his actions merely as the basis for drawing pristine moralizations is to miss the point: Maupassant had a genuine respect for prostitutes who sold their beauty to give pleasure, which he considered every bit as noble a sacrifice as motherhood. It also followed therefore that a beautiful woman, no matter what her station, had every right to oppose the legalized annihilation of her beauty by a husband who cared only for his name and his pleasure. So many observers found Maupassant's behavior paradoxical to such a degree that they could see little but hypocrisy in his defence of woman. There is really no paradox, and to assume that there is one obscures his message and makes it impossible to see such *nouvelles* as *Boule de Suif*, *La Maison Tellier* and *L'Inutile Beauté* in the light required to interpret them properly and to fit them into the over-all pattern of his works.

Maupassant's scorn for the male plays a most important role in shaping the philosophy that produced *L'Inutile Beauté*. The hero's pusillanimous cry that the law is on his side achieves the purpose Maupassant intended: it makes us wonder if it is not a shame that conventional marriage laws serve men who are so weak as to have nothing of a more noble cast to keep their wives at home. This *nouvelle* is a sober appraisal of a kind of dominant male for whom all laws which serve to assure his position of sovereignty are sacred, despite evidence that many of them may break higher laws which eventually will bring his civilization down upon his head. The Count of Mascaret's children interest him only as proof of the moments he had been master over his wife. His wife interests him mainly as an object to be dominated and left to vegetate. He is hence a perfect prey for her scheme to get even by telling him the children are another man's.

Maupassant's thesis in the story is an interesting expression of his aesthetic idea that all beautiful things are the result of the imagination which is both mankind's unique blessing and greatest curse. A curse because it is the instigator of frustrated and endless searching for an ideal love, a blessing because it is the crowning glory of the work of a few great men worthy of elevating the status of mankind. To him the great irony is that the ones who discover and protect beauty are treated as miscreants while the ravishers of it are supported by the pack. It is again noteworthy how Maupassant's admiration for woman places her not only in harmony with vital elements of his philosophy, but extends to her the role of representing them in his work.

The novel, *Bel Ami,* has been much praised by critics. Its hero, Duroy, seems to present a relief from all of Maupassant's males whose weaknesses draw his condemnation. But a close scrutiny of both the hero and its principal heroine, Madame Forestier, will erase any notions that Maupassant's attitude towards the male and female has made an about-face. Madame Forestier is like Maupassant's mother and the ideal woman we have seen portrayed elsewhere in the terms she lays down as prerequisite for her accepting Duroy's proposal: "Mais il faudrait aussi que cet homme s'engageât à voir en moi une égale, une alliée, et non pas une inférieure ni une épouse obéissante et soumise." [14] Bel Ami wants to marry the widow of his publisher, because such a marriage will assure his rise in society. He never enjoyed the supremacy over her which custon allowed, because his creator, even in describing one male who managed to get his way in his life, was not willing to suggest that he would not meet in woman more than his match. Duroy is never allowed by his creator to escape the certainty that his success is due to the fact that he had been her puppet: she wrote his best material. She was the ventriloquist without which he had no voice. Maupassant has his co-workers deride him in order to show that even he is not capable of gaining ascendency over a resolute

---

[14] *Ibid.,* XII, 291.

woman: "Tu ne serais rien sans elle." [15] And as if to make more certain the subservience of the male, Maupassant dwells upon the sufferings of his hero occasioned by the suspicion that his wife is cuckolding him, a manifestation of the author's desire to show the male up as weak and dependent in contrast to the female. He shows that his divorce of her is a desperate attempt on his part to be free of her superiority. And he gives to him a new wife who is from the same mold as Emma Bovary, a wife whose dreams, like Emma's, made her an easy prize, and not one to be publicized as a conquest worthy of the dominant member of the species: "Suzanne aussi songeait; et le grelot des quatre chevaux sonnait dans sa tête, lui faisait voir des grandes routes infinies sous des clairs de lunes éternels, des forêts sombres traversées, des auberges au bord du chemin, et la hôte des hommes d'écurie à changer l'attelage, car tout le monde devine qu'ils sont poursuivies." [16] Here, as elsewhere in Maupassant, it is evident that woman is to be admired.

Though, as has been previously demonstrated, Maupassant regards marriage as an imposition upon the male, he is not in sympathy with his problems simply because the male holds the option of changing the conventions regarding marriage and steadfastly refuses to use his option. The female receives his admiration and sympathy because she has no options. In *Sur l'Eau*, his attractive autobiographical sketches, Maupassant makes it clear that he is firmly committed to demonstrating how it is that woman is victimized by marriage far more than man, and that he has no conventional admiration for the institution: "Un prêtre autorisait en latin, avec un gravité pontificale, l'acte animal, solennel et comique qui agite si forte les hommes, les fait tant rire, tant souffrir, tant pleurer

… … … … … … … … … … … … … … … … … …

service funèbre de l'innocence d'une jeune fille." [17]

The evidence of Maupassant's philogyny provided by the novel, *Une Vie*, is so obvious as to have caused a number of critics to comment upon its appearance there. We have, therefore, saved the most conclusive evidence until the last. The placement here of the discussion does not, however, rest upon this fact alone. For the novel is, in

---

[15] *Ibid.*, 347.
[16] *Ibid.*, 540.
[17] *Ibid.*, XXVIII, 102-103.

many ways, autobiographical. From it a critical reader can piece together the answer to many of the puzzles that present themselves to the Maupassant scholar. It is no wonder that Maupassant's sense of moral outrage at the fact that nineteenth-century French society conspired to crush the vitality from woman and leave her stripped of the right to be an individual is so prominent here. For the inspiration for it came in part from his observations of his mother's life. The attitudes expressed by the author in the novel magnify the influence that Laure de Maupassant had upon her son to the point that we cannot fail to take her influence into account in criticizing his work.

The setting of the novel is in the same general locale where Maupassant spent his childhood. The father-husband of *Une Vie* is remarkably like the man Maupassant must have considered his father to be. The air of hostility that developed between Jeanne and her husband is not unlike that which developed between Gustave and Laure de Maupassant. Viewing these obvious similarities between the situation in *Une Vie* and the dominant situation of Maupassant's childhood could lead one into the bog of oversimplification. We have, therefore, been careful in our choice of passages with the hope of shedding some further light on Maupassant's strange relationship with his parents.

It can be safely suggested that Jeanne's impatience to be released from the monastic school she has been attending derives from the emotions Maupassant himself experienced at being cooped up for several years in a school. The manner in which he presents her thoughts at the prospect of escaping is too authentic not to have been inspired by memories of the Séminaire d'Yvetot. Jeanne's love of the sea gives Maupassant a chance to voice his own: "...et elle se promettait une joie infinie de cette vie libre au bord des flots." [18] For Maupassant the Elysian Fields were the moving waters.

The ghost of Emma Bovary hovers over Maupassant's description of his heroine's emotions regarding her future marriage: "Ils iraient, les mains dans les mains, serrés l'un contre l'autre, entendant battre leurs coeurs, sentant la chaleur de leurs épaules, mêlant leur amour à la limpidité suave des nuits d'été, tellement unis qu'ils pénétreraient aisément, par la seule puissance de leur tendresse, jusqu'à leurs plus

---

[18] *Ibid.*, II, 5.

secrètes pensées." [19] This is Flaubert without the cold scorn, for as evident as is the master's influence is that of his mother. Tolstoy praised the novel highly. And it is evident that his praise was inspired by the author's compassion, by its lack of a deterministic-positivistic objectivity that was Laure de Maupassant's contribution. Maupassant's emotional reaction to the situation in which he places his heroine is clearly resultant to his memories of life with his mother.

Jeanne's love of swimming and the sea is a manifestation of Maupassant's passion. When he describes her reveling in the presence of the sea, he is describing his own emotional response: "Elle se sentit bien dans cette eau froide, limpide et bleu qui la portait en la balançant." [20] "...Et il lui semblait que trois seules choses étaient vraiment belles dans la création: la lumière, l'espace et l'eau." [21]

It was Maupassant's opinion that idealism should not be punished by shallow laws created by stupid men. To him it was sufficiently punished by nature. But Jeanne is, nevertheless, another victim of a system which, even given the good intentions of her parents, will deny her the privilege of finding an ideal husband. Her idealism is saddening. It is saddening because we realize that Maupassant is describing a situation that was very close to him, one which he had sensed in the tragic relationship between his mother and his father. His outrage is again evident against a system which could cause a father to admonish his daughter: "...mais n'oublie point ceci, seulement ceci, que tu appartiens tout entière à ton mari." [22] There is no evidence that Laure de Maupassant ever capitulated quite so finally to her husband. There is, however, an indication that Maupassant based at least parts of his book, *Une Vie*, upon the life of his mother. His anger against all of the cowardly masculine prerogatives that enslave woman is clearly inspired by his close touch with masculine tyranny in his own home. In this novel the frail shell of woman hides a great soul.

Repeatedly Maupassant reveals his championing of the woman's cause. His philogyny is evident in the following lines where he shows such sensitive sympathy: "Et sans cesse tout le long du jour, comme

---

[19] *Ibid.*, 20.
[20] *Ibid.*, 27.
[21] *Ibid.*, 46.
[22] *Ibid.*, 82.

une pluie incessante et triste à faire pleurer, ces derniers feuilles, toutes jaunes maintenant, pareilles à de larges sous d'or, se détachaient, tournoyaient, voltigeaient et tombaient." [23] The "tristesse Verlainienne" could not more movingly portray the desolation of Jeanne's life, chained to a man who sleeps with the maid, lies to her about her own money, and with a disgusting show of selfrighteousness, condemns the maid in order to remove her and her baby, of whom he was father, so they will not disturb his tranquility. Like her creator, Jeanne's depressing condition drives her to hallucinations and to thoughts of suicide. But then there was hope: she was pregnant.

The child was a boy. She was certain he would dominate the world in which she had been enslaved. Unlike Emma Bovary, she had not turned to the wall at the sight of the child. But Flaubert was kinder to Emma: he had not stirred her hopes. Jeanne's hopes for the boy become her life. Her husband continues to disappoint her by having an affair with a Countess who had pretended to be her friend. What made it even more sorrowful for her was the fact that she admired the husband who was brave and honest and a loving husband, the exact opposite of Julien. The affair drove her to a conclusion which Maupassant himself often drew: "Tout le monde était donc perfide, menteur et faux." [24] Normandy, beloved of both the author and his heroine, where she had once been so happy, seemed to conspire to augment her cynicism as it did in Maupassant's later life. Her weeping for her illusions causes her to draw more and more within herself until her thoughts sound like Maupassant's own: "... cette sensation de vide, de mépris pour les hommes, elle la sentait grandir, l'envelopper; et chaque jour les petites nouvelles du pays lui jetaient à l'âme un dégoût plus grand, une plus haute mésestime des êtres." [25] Her description of sex now is like the author's: "sale bestialité." Jeanne is hence partly that elusive woman Maupassant never succeeded in finding in life. Her disgust with men's lack of idealism in love is just the print from the Maupassant negative. Their resignation to the fact that their idealism is inevitably doomed is strikingly similar.

Now the irony of having given her a son becomes clear. Paul is a replica of his father, not the kind to be able to take her pathetic

---

[23] *Ibid.*, 118.
[24] *Ibid.*, 222.
[25] *Ibid.*, 223.

kindness without repaying her in further suffering. She does not want to surrender him for even long enough to allow him to receive his schooling. One wonders what Laure de Maupassant thought when she read Paul's complaint: "...je n'étais pas fait pour la vie obscure, humble, et triste à mourir, à laquelle ta tendresse imprévoyante m'a condamné." [26] It is likely that at some moment or another Maupassant must have felt that way about his mother. But generally he was incapable of any but kind thoughts. Possibly because nature had equipped him with the kind of genius that made him capable of escaping whenever he chose, and so without bitterness. Not so in the case of his brother, Hervé, who may have been in the author's mind as he fashioned the character of Paul. Once away at boarding school Paul escapes, and thereafter lives a life of dissipation that leads to a series of demands for money from his mother. The totality with which he destroys the last vestiges of his mother's hope is too melodramatic to be up to Maupassant's usual standard. Irony crosses irony in an endless tangle and her old age becomes filled with hallucinations born of her great loneliness — the same kind of loneliness Maupassant knew so well in his own last days. And as if foreseeing the aggravating force loneliness was to have on his malady, the author had the peasants in the village referring to Jeanne as "la Folle." She felt pursued by an obstinate Demon who had created her solely for the pleasure of destroying her. Descriptions of her at the last are reminiscent of passages written by Maupassant during his last years describing his visions experienced in loneliness: "...elle vit, comme elle avait vu si souvent, son père et sa mère chauffant leurs pieds au feu." [27] And the sentence describing her last view of the house has a haunting similarity to François Tassart's rendering of his master's final turn to catch a glimpse of his beloved boat, "Bel-Ami": "Elle sentait en son coeur qu'elle venait de dire adieu pour toujours à sa maison." [28] The book, ironically, does not end with her death but with a scene depicting her smothering Paul's girl-baby with kisses, overjoyed that its mother had died in childbirth. His admiration for the mad woman who has taken all a cruel system has to offer and is still standing is unmistakable. Maupassant was indeed a philogynist.

---

[26] *Ibid.*, 298.
[27] *Ibid.*, 374.
[28] *Ibid.*, 375.

CHARLES FONTAINE'S IDEAS ON POETRY

W. L. WILEY
University of North Carolina

Charles Fontaine, the gay Parisian who was a member of the Renaissance school of poetry loosely attached to Clément Marot, has come down to the twentieth century as a participant in the sixteenth-century *Querelle de la Femme*, as a possible author of the *Quintil Horatian* (now assigned to Barthélemy Aneau), and as a writer of verses who did not take an uncle's advice and become a lawyer. During the last fifty years very little attention has been paid to Fontaine by scholars, either in the editing of his works or in articles about him.[1] He is much too good a poet — and was too well known in his own time — to have endured such neglect by *seiziémistes* of the present day; possibly this paper, in looking at some of Fontaine's critical ideas, may make some slight amends to his shade and drag it partway out of the River Lethe.

Fontaine wrote no formal treatise on poetry but scattered his opinions on composition throughout his writings. In the beginning of *Les Ruisseaux de Fontaine* (this "rills from the fountain" conceit was

---

[1] The standard study on Charles Fontaine was written more than half a century ago by Harvard professor R. L. Hawkins — *Maistre Charles Fontaine Parisien* (Cambridge, Massachusetts, 1916). Since then some detached editing of his works has been done and a few articles about him have appeared. There is room for a large critical edition of Fontaine. For this paper I have used a sixteenth-century collection of his poetry: *Les Ruisseaux de Fontaine: Oeuvre contenant Epitres, Elegies, Chants divers, Epigrammes, Odes & Estrenes pour cette presente annee 1555. Plus y a un traité du passetemps des amis, avec un translat d'un livre d'Ovide & de 28 Enigmes de Symposius, traduits, par ledict Fontaine.* Lyon, Thibauld, 1555. All my quotations will be taken from this volume, which will be designated simply as *Les Ruisseaux*.

considered rather puerile by Du Bellay and the Pléiade) he states in the dedicatory *Epistre au Roy* his feelings about poets:

> L'on dit tresbien, tout esprit d'autre estoffe
> Soit d'Orateur, ou soit de Philosophe
> Se fait par art, sollicitude & cure,
> Mais le Poëte est faict tel de nature.
> (*Les Ruisseaux*, p. 10)

These lines will recall immediately Thomas Sebillet's words in his *Art poétique* of a few years earlier: *le poète naît, l'orateur se fait*. The epistle of dedication to the King contains more of Sebillet's (and Plato's) notions on the poet's frenzy; Fontaine considers Bacchus the god of poetry and when his "holy nectar" takes its rise into the poet's head, the latter begins to speak "divinement." This is almost inevitable in view of the nature of poetry:

> A bien parler qu'est ce que poésie
> Fors une ardante et saincte frénésie?
> Comme bien lire en nostre Ovide on peult
> Dieu est en nous, qui nous eschaufe et meut.
> (*Les Ruisseaux*, p. 10 and *passim*)

And here Fontaine makes a blending of Platonic and Ovidian concepts, since Ovid had said at the end of the totally mundane *Ars Amatoria,* "est deus in nobis." In his second *Epistre*, which is concerned with "bonne amour," Fontaine shows allegiance to Plato in attempting to define beauty:

> Or ie ne veux la seule ombre poursuyvre,
> Et Narcissus en ce ie ne veux suyvre:
> Car comme luy en fin trompé serois,
> Quand trop en vain l'ombre i'embrasserois,
> Pour le vray corps de la beauté extreme,
> Qui est de Dieu l'image, mais Dieu mesme.
> (*Les Ruisseaux*, pp. 17-18)

In the next poem, the *Epistre à N. le Iouvre,* a continuing Neo-Platonic flavoring is found in the definition of a poet's qualities: he should have "l'esprit divinement hault, la bouche d'or, et la plume divine." (*Les Ruisseaux*, p. 31)

Poets suffer, says Fontaine, as a result of the practice of their profession; in their verses they may have said something that could irritate persons in high position and thus be forced like Ovid into exile in some bleak and barbarous clime such as the coast of the Euxine Sea. But, in the manner of Ovid, poets will continue to compose despite the miseries of their surroundings:

> Ovide escrit, & pleinement declare,
> Quand il estoit avec la gent barbare,
> Loing de sa femme, & loing de tous amis,
> Qu'en tel estat Poësie l'a mis:
> En païs froit, plein de bize & de guerre,
> Au bout du monde, & en estrange terre.
> Ostez (dit-il) Poësie & l'estude,
> Vous osterez de moy la solitude;
> Ostez mes vers vous osterez mon crime.
> Mesme en son coeur telle douleur s'imprime
> Que quelquesfoys souhaitoit pour tout seur
> N'avoir gousté des muses la douceur:
> Car luy estant ainsi banni par elle,
> Ayme son mal de trop convoiteux zele:
> Et ne se peut d'escrire contenir
> En vers, qui l'ont en exil fait venir.
>
> (*Les Ruisseaux*, pp. 33-34)

In the sixteenth century the equivalent of a poet's benishment by a Roman emperor to the inhospitable Pontic shores would have been dismissal from the *ambiance* of the court of Francis I or from that of Henry II; Charles Fontaine, fortunately for him, never endured such a severance of patronage. It is to be noted in the above lines that the poet's loneliness derives from factual conditions (Ovid had supposedly been sent away from Rome because of some gossip he had indulged in concerning Augustus' family) and geographical detachment, and not from a Romantic suffering of remembrance like that of Alfred de Musset wandering through the forest of Fontainebleau thinking about his faithless beloved, George Sand.

Fontaine returns later in his book to the sufferings that poets have traditionally endured:

> Iadis Virgile, Ovide, Homere, Horace,
> Bassius, Codrus, Claudian, Lucain, Stace,
> Par povreté ont eu maux infiniz,
> Trop enviez, haïs, les uns bannis,...
>
> (*Les Ruisseaux*, p. 274)

But despite material discomforts a poet must work and rework his verses — and here we have an echo of Horace's *labor limae* and the tenets of Du Bellay and the *Pléiade*:

> Sagement donc nous fault nos vers parer
> De longue main, polir, et reparer: ...
> (*Les Ruisseaux*, p. 34)

Thus, says Fontaine in an epistle (to his uncle) lifting poetry above the mundane profession of the law, poets who have done their work well will have immortal renown:

> Les corps, les biens, maisons, chasteaux, viellissent,
> L'or, & l'argent par la roille perissent:
> Mais les beaux vers ne vont point perissant,
> Car Apollo est touiours florissant,
> Touiours beau, ieune, & sa face en liesse
> Ne sent iamais du vieil temps la vieillesse.
> (*Les Ruisseaux*, p. 296)

Fontaine goes on in this poem to make the point very clear that he has never had any intention of becoming a lawyer, but that like Ovid (whose family had wished that he follow a legal career) he intends to stick to his verses.

As has already been suggested by the passages excerpted thus far from Fontaine's poetry, the classical writer that he admired most was undoubtedly Ovid. Their careers had many points of similarity. Ovid led a gay life in imperial Rome even as did Fontaine in the teeming metropolis of Renaissance Paris. Both refused the practice of the law, and both were clever versifiers; Fontaine, for his part, seems to have avoided the sad loneliness of Ovid's last years. Fontaine was particularly influenced by Ovid's epistles and elegies, and many critics (including Henri Chamard) have thought that Fontaine, in transferring the spirit of Ovid's limping elegiacs into his own *élégies*, made a definite contribution to Renaissance lyricism. Fontaine summed up his own attitude toward Ovid in an *épigramme*, *Charles Fontaine à D. S.*, who was evidently an admirer of Statius:

> Tu t'en vas avec ton Stace,
> Je demeure avec mon Ovide ...
> (*Les Ruisseaux*, p. 313)

A contemporary, Bonaventure du Tronchet, in an *Ode à Charles Fontaine* said that Fontaine in several ways had caused Ovid to live again — "par sa Muse son doux souci, / Et par ses beaux & divins arts."

(*Les Ruisseaux*, p. 336)

Included in *Les Ruisseaux de Fontaine* are a number of *épigrammes*, many of which are dedicated to his favored Flora — even as Ovid used his lady Corinna for inspiration. One of these short poems, *L'auteur à ses amis*, recalls Ovid's description, in the second book of the *Metamorphoses*, of the ravages of Envy:

> Ie say tresbien, ce qu'a escrit Ovide,
> Que les escrits plaisent apres la mort:
> Car faulse envie apres mort tourne bride,
> Et la chair vive elle picote, & mord: ...
> (*Les Ruisseaux*, p. 94)

In an *Epigramme, encore à sa Flora*, Fontaine speaks in very Ovidian manner of the Sun-God Phoebus and his chargers which will shortly carry Phaëthon to his death in a wild race across the heavens (all from the second book of the *Metamorphoses*):

> Le blond Phebus a prins sa robe d'or
> A ce matin, & son cler diademe,
> Bien estoffé d'un infini tresor
> De pierrerie ayant splendeur extreme:
> Ses grans coursiers qui sont bardez de mesme,
> Courent grand trot par le ciel pur, & munde:
> Les grands souffleurs laissans en paix le monde
> Ont ce iour'huy replié leurs grans ailes
> Qui parmi l'air trop se batoyent entre elles: ...
> (*Les Ruisseaux*, p. 104)

The legend of Phoebus-Apollo and his son Phaëthon was a favorite with both artists and writers in the Renaissance, and on into the seventeenth century. Fontaine also uses the death of Phaëthon in his *Elégie sur le trepas de Catherine Fontaine, soeur de l'autheur* — which is borrowed almost completely from Ovid's elegy on the death of Tibullus (*Amores*, III, 9) and is a good example of the elegy embellished by mythology:

> Si Aurora, & Tethys, grans Deesses,
> Du ciel & mer regentes, & princesses,

>   Ont tant pleuré Achilles, & Memnon,
>   Puis-je ne pleindre, & ne pleurer? ha non.
>   Et si encor du grand Souleil les filles
>   Ont eu les yeux à pleurer tant faciles
>   Dessus leur frere, abysmé sans secours,
>   Qu'en arbre humide, & qui pleure tousiours
>   Muees sont: qui me pourra deffendre
>   De ne pleurer ma soeur, ia terre, & cendre?
>
>   (*Les Ruisseaux*, p. 49 ff.)

The *élégie* was not always for Fontaine an expression of deep lamentation as is seen in these verses concerning the death of his sister; in his ninth elegy he reflects a light sorrow over his lady's loss of a dog, in the manner of Ovid's parrot elegy (*Amores*, II, 6) and Catullus' lament over the death of Lesbia's sparrow.

Like the other poets of Marot's school Fontaine was considerably interested in translating into French material from the Greek and Roman past. In this inclination he was merely following the tenets of the lawgiver of the Marot group, Thomas Sebillet, who thought that a translator made a contribution to humanity by rediscovering a treasure that had been lost — an attitude, it might be said in passing, that was not shared by Du Bellay and the *Pléiade*. In any case, Fontaine joined the group of pre-1550 translators who made renditions of classical texts and, quite expectedly, turned his attention to Ovid: he translated into French the first ten of Ovid's twenty-one *Heroides* and the "first book" of the *Remedia Amoris*.[2] Fontaine's version of some of the most popular of Ovid's epistolary exchanges between certain heroes and heroines of antiquity — in particular, the letters of Oenone to Paris, of Phaedra to Hippolytus, and of Dido to Aeneas — easily displaced the pedestrian translation of the *Heroides* done by the *rhétoriqueur*, Octavien de Saint Gelais. The Fontaine collection appeared in 1546 and was evidently quite popular with a reading public that both liked the *Heroides* and the French rendition of them:

---

[2] As was pointed out by the Abbé Goujet in the eighteenth century, the "first book" meant the first half of the *Remedia Amoris*, ending at verse 396. Goujet did not approve of any of the French sixteenth-century translations of the *Heroides* and *Amores*. Also, he thought that Fontaine could have chosen an example "plus convenable" for imitation than Ovid. For these details, see Goujet's *Bibliothèque française* (Paris, 1747), vol. VI, pp. 11-13 and vol. XI, p. 117.

the edition was exhausted in 1555 (though a reprinting was done in 1556) since at that time Fontaine was unable to obtain two copies for some of his friends.

Fontaine has given a very elaborate exposition of his theories on translation in his preliminary commentary accompanying the first part of the *Remedia Amoris* — which he has put into the standard verse form of the period, the 10-syllable couplet of alternating masculine and feminine rhyme. He contended rather amusingly that there was nothing off-color in the opening half of the *Remedia Amoris* and that his putting it into French was "pour bien et pour la vertu." As has been pointed out by Professor Hawkins, this claim was justifiable. Fontaine's gallicizing of Ovid's remedy for the ravages of love appeared first in 1555 in *Les Ruisseaux de Fontaine,* and was equipped with a lengthy preliminary discourse, *Le Translateur aux Lecteurs*; after asserting in mock-serious fashion that it is "une tresmaulvaise & tresgriéve malladie que d'amour," he gives advice on the procedures to be followed in making a good translation from one language to another:

> Je trouve donc qu'il y a trois choses que doit observer un qui veult bien traduire: La premiere, c'est qu'il retiene & rende les termes, & dictions de l'auteur, autant pres qu'il est possible: ce que lon peult appeler la robe.
>
> La secõde, qu'il rende aussi le sens par tout entier (car il ne faut tãt estre curieux des termes que de laisser le sens, ou le rẽdre obscur:) ce que lon peult appeler le corps.
>
> La tierce, c'est qu'il rende & exprime aussi, naïvement la naturelle grace, vertu, energie, la doulceur, elegance, dignité, force & vivacité de son auteur qu'il veult traduire, et des personnes introduictes parlãs ou faisans aucunes choses: ce que lon peult appeler l'ame de l'oraison: mais bien peu de ceux qui traduisent adviennent eureusement à ces trois pointz, pour la plus grant difficulté. Parquoy la plus grand part des plus sages & experts translateurs sont plus soigneux à rendre le sens & la grace que les motz: de l'advis & du nombre desquelz i'ay esté, ie suis, & vueil estre.

(*Les Ruisseaux*, pp. 348-349)

It can be seen from this excerpt — with its figured language of the *robe, corps,* and *âme de l'oraison* — that Fontaine reflects the ideas of both Sebillet and of Etienne Dolet, whose *La Manière de bien traduire* was published in Lyon in 1540.³ Fontaine wrote a second preface to his readers apropos of his version of the "first book" of the *Remedia Amoris* in which he repeats the legend that Ovid composed it as something of an atonement for the *Ars Amatoria*; it is thus a legitimate document, says Fontaine, which he has "prins peine & plaisir de traduire en vers de nostre langue Françoise, pour la bonne doctrine qui y est contenue, & deduite avec plaisir qui n'est sans fruict." Therefore, Fontaine tells his audience, read the material *hardiment, et ne craignez rien*.⁴

Fontaine, in his admiration for Ovid, uses the Roman poet as a symbol of all those who are born for the Muses and not turned away from poetry by avarice and ambition:

> Ce qui advint à Ovide, car lors
> Que de quitter les vers feit ses efforts,
> Cuidant escrire en prose, de sa plume
> Couloient les vers par nature, & coutume.
> Soymesme ainsi sans y penser se trompe:
> Adonc sentant qu'en rien ne se corrompe
> Le naturel, & que la plaiderie
> Estoit grand faix, & trop grand facherie
> Pour son esprit, né à mansuetude,
> A paix, repos, & à plus douce estude,
> Se retira, ses Muses poursuyvant,
> Et de son temps les Poetes suyvant:
> Lesquelz si bien honora en tout lieu,
> Qu'il estimoit chascun d'eux estre un dieu,
> Ainsi qu'il dit luymesme, & le confesse:
> Tant honora Poesie sans cesse: ...
> Voilà comment le naturel d'Ovide
> Ne peut iamais aux Muses tourner bride:

---

³ The scholarly Dolet's *La Manière de bien traduire* was an influential document destined to be a part of a treatise on oratory which Dolet never completed. In the first five pages of *La Manière de bien traduire* Dolet gives five rules that the translator should observe: (1) he should understand *parfaictment le sens & matiere de l'auteur;* (2) he should know the language that is to be translated; (3) he should avoid word for word, line for line renditions; (4) he should avoid giving words in the vulgar tongue an uncommon meaning; (5) he should choose words of pleasant sonority — *noms oratoires* — so that the translation will have an agreeable sound when read aloud. Dolet's little manual had a broad influence in the middle years of the sixteenth century, particularly with Marot's group.

⁴ For these last points, see *Les Ruisseaux*, p. 353.

Il n'avait pas son inclination
A l'avarice & à l'ambition.
(Les Ruisseaux, p. 298)

It is most evident that, in the midst of the homage that was lavished upon Ovid by the poets of the mid-sixteenth century in France, none was more ardent in his admiration for the author of the *Metamorphoses* than was Charles Fontaine.

But Ovid's limping elegiacs and dactyls were not the only verses from ancient Rome that were admired by Fontaine; in his twelfth ode, *A sa Flora*, when he says he will sing to his beloved in his "bas stile doux" he recalls that Horace, Propertius, and Tibullus (along with Ovid) all sang songs to their ladies:

> Ie trouve qu'il ya
> Nemesis cynthia,
> Puis aussi la Corinne,
> Puis encor Lesbia
> Dont maint poëte insigne
> A chanté maint bel hymne.
>
> Ie trouve tout ainsi
> Lalage, & Cloe aussi
> Avoir esté chantees:
> L'espoir & le souci
> Sous qui sont inventees
> Mille chansons notees.
>
> On en voit mainte bulle
> Chez Properse & Tibulle:
> Puis Ovide en douceur
> N'y a fait faute nulle,
> N'Horace le harpeur
> Ore en ris, or en pleur.
(Les Ruisseaux, p. 149)

Fontaine, in his admiration for the practitioners of verses among the Romans, was not lacking in his praise for the poets of his own age. In a series of *Epigrammes pour estreines* (*Les Ruisseaux*, p. 161 ff.) he pays his respects to almost all of the poets of his time — Melin de Saint-Galais, Ronsard, Jean-Antoine de Baïf, Du Bellay, Forcadel, Belleau, Saint Romat, and others. And in an earlier *épigramme* dedicated to the leader of his school, Clément Marot, he suggests that Marot may well have surpassed in resonance the verses of the ancients:

> Tes vers François en douce noise
> Vont surpassans le stile antique.
>
> *(Les Ruisseaux,* p. 82)

In a succeeding *épigramme, Remonstrance aux detracteurs de Poësie Françoise,* Fontaine gives additional argument for his feeling that French poetry might well be superior to that of the Romans:

> I'ay congnu des gens de savoir
> Qui estimoyent en leur langage
> Les vers rimez, c'estasavoir
> Tant que Latins, ou davantage:
> Car (sans au Latin faire outrage)
> La rime avec son harmonie
> Donne à l'oreille une infinie
> Volupté, par voix concurrente:
> Aussi nul bon esprit ne nie
> Que la rime riche, & fluente,
> (Mais de bon sens, sus tout, fournie)
> L'Oreille et le coeur ne contente.
>
> *(Les Ruisseaux,* p. 98)

It is to be observed here how much Fontaine, with his leanings toward rhyme (and even rich rhyme) as opposed to rhymeless poetry in Latin, is following the general critical pattern of his time.[5]

In concluding this summary of Charles Fontaine's ideas on poetry — wherein I have included a large amount of quoted material because of the lack of easy access to Fontaine's writings — it might be noted that he is not too divergent from the opinions either of Sebillet or of Du Bellay. Like his contemporaries he was thoroughly steeped in the mythology of classical antiquity (chiefly through Ovid's *Metamorphoses*) and participated freely in the revival of Latin poetic forms like the epistle, elegy, and epigram; and he did his part, in keeping with the suggestion of Sebillet, in translating material from the ancients. However, he also reflects the nationalistic pride seen in Du Bellay's *Défense* and, like Du Bellay, defends the poetic efforts of his own age.

---

[5] This whole question of rhyme in French poetry — as opposed to the rhymeless verses of the Greeks and Romans — has been taken up more fully in my book, *The Formal French* (Harvard University Press, 1967).

Charles Fontaine was not a great poet, but he was a clever one and very typical of the versifiers of the first half of the French Renaissance. He does not deserve the relative oblivion to which he has been consigned.

ELIPHAS LEVI AS POET

Thomas A. Williams
East Carolina University

We know Eliphas Lévi today — when we know him at all — almost solely for his three books on the esoteric tradition, *Dogme et rituel de la haute magie, Histoire de la magie,* and *La Clef des grands mystères.* In this we do an injustice both to the range of his ideas and to his energy in getting them down on paper. In addition to an impressive and impassioned pre-1848 series of books expounding his own brand of radical Christian socialism — two of which landed him in jail — he also found time to produce a six hundred page *Dictionnaire de la littérature chrétienne,* translate the poetry and commentaries of Saint John of the Cross, write short stories dealing rather fancifully with the youth of Rabelais (whom he seemed to admire above all other French writers), compose a full length verse play (*Le Mystère de Babel, ou Nemrod*) and turn out an endless stream of manifestoes and articles for newspapers as ephemeral as they were radical.[1]

Above all else, Lévi found time to write poetry. Even during his school days he translated into French verse the *Vers dorés* of Pythagoras, began his *Nemrod,* and wrote numerous short poems and songs. He continued to do so all of his life.

---

[1] Eliphas Lévi, *Dogme et rituel de la haute magie.* Paris: Germer-Baillière, 1856. *Histoire de la magie.* Paris, 1860. *La Clef des grands mystères.* Paris, 1861. The *Dictionnaire de la littérature chrétienne* (Paris, 1851) is Volume VII in the *Nouvelle Encyclopédie Théologique,* edited and published by J. P. Migne. In the *Dictionnaire* see especially the articles "allégorie," "fiction," and "mystères," which contains the entire text of Lévi's play *Le Mystère de Babel, ou Nemrod.* For details of Lévi's other early works, see the anthology by E. P. Bowman, *Eliphas Lévi, visionnaire romantique* (Paris, 1969).

What is this poetry like? Is it difficult, hermetic, obscure? Not at all. In intent at least it is simple, straightforward and clear. If Lévi's books did in fact influence the formation of the Symbolist aesthetic — as so many generally assume and so few stand ready to prove — it would seem that he was, as a poet, peculiarly without influence upon himself. Which of the Renaissance lyricists did he prefer? Marot. And in his own day his great favorite, along with Hugo, was Béranger.

Lévi's most notable single achievement as a poet came in 1845 with the publication of his collection *Les Trois Harmonies*.[2] Apart from the simple *chansons*, much of the verse in this book is written with an epic quality which reminds one today of the later Hugo. The titles alone — "Le Créateur," "La Bacchante endormie," "Chronos," "Le Rêve de Prométhée" — call to mind *La Légende des siècles*. But though the subject matter of these poems turns very often to the metaphysical, the over-all style is that of a naïve Romanticism which has not yet learned the essential Symbolist lesson: that the poetical activity itself can be an occult and mystical instrument.

Here, from *Les Trois Harmonies,* is "Le Créateur":

Le Createur

Commençons par l'amour: l'amour a tout fait naître;
Des hommes et des Dieux c'est le souverain maître.
Sa tristesse est la nuit, son sourire est le jour,
Et rien dans l'univers ne vit que par l'amour.
L'amour a tout fait naître et n'a point d'origine:
C'est le foyer brûlant de l'essence divine,
C'est le feu des esprits, et sa féconde ardeur
A du premier soleil allumé la splendeur.
Lui seul des éléments a terminé la guerre,
Quand l'air, la flamme et l'eau se disputaient la terre,
Et quand sur l'infini le chaos suspendu
Dormait d'un lourd sommeil dans l'espace étendu.
Du carquois de l'amour les flèches de lumière
Sillonnèrent d'abord la masse tout entière;
Puis au sein du chaos lui-meme il s'élança,
Sur les vagues de l'être en riant se berça,
Laissant autour de lui se soulever les ombres,
Et de l'antique nuit rouler les voiles sombres;

---

[2] Alphonse Constant de Baucour [sic], *Les Trois Harmonies*. Paris, 1845. Alphonse Constant was, of course, Eliphas Lévi's real name. In this instance, he added his mother's family name, Baucourt.

Puis d'un souffle vivant prompt à la pénétrer,
Pour créer l'univers, il n'eut qu'à respirer.
Enceinte de l'amour, le terre maternelle
Arrondit comme un oeuf son écorce fidèle
Qui dissipe les eaux par ses douces chaleurs,
Et transpire l'amour en mille jets de fleurs.
Bientôt du créateur les flammes renfermées
S'échappèrent au jour en formes animées.
Sa colère forma les lions furieux;
Ses ruses, le serpent aux plis insidieux;
Sa douceur, la brebis et la colombe pure,
Les candides amours de toute la nature.
On vit alors la vigne embrasser les ormeaux,
Et la génisse en feu chercher les fiers taureaux.
Tout vécut, tout aima, tout s'empressa de naître:
Mais au monde naissant l'amour gardait un maître.
Quand son berceau de fleurs ombragé de forêts,
Quand le ciel et la terre et les eaux furent prêts,
Lui-même corrigeant ses ébauches difformes,
En lui de l'univers il résuma les formes,
De sa retraite alors s'élança triomphant,
Et vint sourire au ciel sous les traits d'un enfant:
Puis façonnant l'argile à son heureuse image,
Du premier des humains il orna le visage,
Et donnant à sa bouche un souffle ambitieux,
Il jeta dans son sein la semence des Dieux.

The most interesting poem from this collection, and the only one that has gotten any special attention, is "Les Correspondances." It was written at least a year earlier than Baudelaire's sonnet on the same subject.

Les Correspondances

> Le sentiment des harmonies extérieures
> fait les poètes.
> L'intelligence des harmonies intérieures
> fait les prophètes.

Quand succombent nos sens débiles
Aux enchantements du sommeil,
Le pinceau des songes mobiles
Présente à l'âme un faux réveil.
Alors nos vagues fantaisies
De formes au hasard choisies
Colorent leur égarement:

Toute idée enfante une image,
Et les formes sont un language
Que nous nous parlons en dormant.

Le rêve est le miroir de l'âme;
Ses élans planent sur les airs,
Ses désirs s'allument en flamme,
Ses chagrins la chargent de fers;
La terreur dont elle est la proie
Se change en monstre qui la broie
De ses hideux embrassements;
Et ses espérances chéries
S'étendent en ombre fleuries
Sur des paysages charmants.

Par une secrète harmonie,
La terre ainsi répond aux cieux,
Et l'instinct sacré du génie
Voit leur lien mystérieux.
Notre vie est un plus long rêve,
Et ce que la mort nous enlève
Trouve au ciel sa réalité.
En dormant nous rêvons la vie,
Mais la veille, au temps asservie,
N'est qu'un rêve d'éternité.

Formé de visibles paroles,
Ce monde est le songe de Dieu;
Son verbe en choisit les symboles,
L'esprit les remplit de son feu.
C'est cette écriture vivante
D'amour, de gloire et d'épouvante,
Que pour nous Jésus retrouva;
Car toute science cachée
N'est qu'une lettre détachée
Du nom sacré de Jéhova.

C'est là que lisent les prophètes;
Et ceux dont les yeux sont ouverts
Sont d'eux-mêmes les interprètes
De l'énigme de l'univers;
Les astres, serviteurs mystiques,
Tracent en signes elliptiques
Le mot que le Seigneur écrit;
Et la terre, à sa voix naissante,
N'est qu'une cire obéissante
Sous le cachet de son esprit.

Tout signe exprime une pensée,
Et toute forme dans les cieux
Est une figure tracée
Par le penseur mystérieux,
Depuis l'herbe de la campagne
Jusqu'au cèdre de la montagne,
De l'aigle jusqu'au moucheron,
Depuis l'éléphant, masse informe,
Et la baleine, plus énorme,
Jusqu'à l'invisible ciron.

Comme les soleils dans l'espace
Indiquent leur route aux soleils,
Comme le jour qui brille et passe
Promet aux cieux des jours pareils:
Ainsi, par un calcul possible,
L'invisible est dans le visible,
Le passé prédit l'avenir;
Et, dans Ninive confondue,
La prophétie inattendue
N'est que la voix d'un souvenir.

Rien n'est muet dans la nature
Pour qui sait en suivre les lois:
Les astres ont une écriture,
Les fleurs des champs ont une voix,
Verbe éclatant dans les nuits sombres,
Mots rigoureux comme des nombres,
Voix dont tout bruit n'est qu'un écho,
Et qui fait mouvoir tous les êtres,
Comme jadis le cri des prêtes
Faisait tressaillir Jéricho.

Passez, passez, sans rien comprendre,
Vain troupeau d'aveugles penseurs!
Le néant dort pour vous attendre
Auprès des chimères ses soeurs.
Mais, dans l'éternelle pensée,
Votre route est déjà tracée,
Et tous vos systèmes obscurs
Rehaussent d'une ombre effrayante
Cette inscription flamboyante
Que les rois lisent sur les murs.

Mais que l'âme simple et fidèle,
En attendant l'agneau vainqueur,
Écoute, active sentinelle,

> Le verbe de Dieu dans son coeur:
> Car toute pensée extatique
> Est comme une onde sympathique,
> Où se reflète l'univers;
> Et l'âme, à soi-meme attentive,
> Comme le pêcheur sur la rive
> Peut contempler les cieux ouverts.

Did Lévi "influence" Baudelaire? Perhaps. Jean Pommier has turned up evidence that the two writers probably did know each other in the mid eighteen-forties, and Baudelaire may indeed have read Lévi's poem. Moreover there are specific wordings in Lévi ("Rien n'est muet dans la nature," "Les fleurs des champs ont une voix," etc.) which anticipate lines both in "Correspondances" and in "Élévation." Still, the idea of universal correspondences was in the public domain in those years. No one had to read Lévi to find out about them.

Lévi developed his ideas on the correspondences in the article "Allégorie" in his *Dictionnaire de la littérature chrétienne*. There exist, he says

> des rapports sympathiques entre les formes de la création et les dispositions de l'âme. Qui ne sait combien la pureté d'un beau ciel est en harmonie avec la tranquillité d'un coeur pur? Qui n'a ressenti plus vivement, dans les jours froids et tristes de l'automne, les atteintes de la tristesse? Pourquoi aimons-nous mieux, quand nous sommes dans la joie, les paysages animés et les sites fleuris? Pourquoi, dans la mélancolie, cherchons-nous les lieux sombres et solitaires? N'éprouvons-nous pas des sympathies particulières pour des animaux ou pour des fleurs, tandis que pour d'autres nous éprouvons une répulsion en quelque sorte instinctive? N'avons-nous pas nos préférences en fait de couleurs, de parfums et de mélodies, et ces attraits comme ces répugnances ne s'expliqueraient-ils point par certaines correspondances cachées entre nos dispositions morales et les objets qui affectent agréablement ou désagréablement notre organisation physique? Plus les sciences physiologiques feront de progrès, plus cela deviendra incontestable.
>
> Il existe donc dans la nature, entre les pensées et les formes, entre les choses visibles et les choses invisibles, entre les relations physiques et les relations morales d'abord, puis entre les choses corporelles elles-mêmes, à divers degrés de lumières et de beauté, ainsi qu'entre les choses spirituelles

prises séparément à divers degrés d'élévation vers Dieu, selon l'ordre hiérarchique, il existe, disons-nous, des harmonies réelles et des correspondances essentielles antérieurement à toute poésie, la poésie n'étant d'ailleurs que le sentiment de ces correspondances et de ces harmonies, dont la prophétie supérieure à la poésie sera la révélation.

The language of correspondences, according to Lévi, was known to the earliest Egyptians and was the source of their hieroglyphic writing. It was later lost in Egypt though it survived to some extent farther east in the land of the Chaldeans and the Jews, "cette terre natale de la poésie et des prophètes.... Là les destinées humaines se rattachent encore aux étoiles, et l'on s'écrit toujours dans la langue symbolique des fleurs." [3]

But in the long run, as surprising as it may seem, the esoteric exploitation of poetry did not interest Lévi. He gave more of his attention to his *chansons* — especially during the second half of his life — than to any of his other verse. Perhaps this is not too hard to understand on the part of a man for whom "le rire est un acte de foi" and for whom "les larmes sont la pénitence du doute ou de la fausse croyance." The good humour and laughter of Rabelais represented, for Lévi, "l'archétype de la plus parfaite intelligence de la vie." [4] When one reads beyond the books on magic one discovers in Lévi a man of considerable wisdom and humanity.

Here is a *chanson* which, in *Le Sorcier de Meudon*, is sung by the minstrel Guilain, whom Lévi represents as a friend and protégé of Rabelais: [5]

La Chanson de Guilain

Air: Des Flons-flons

En remplissant leurs verres,
Le gentil Rabelais
Disait à ses confrères
Marot et Saint-Gelais:

---

[3] *Dictionnaire*, columns 59 and 61.
[4] *Le Sorcier de Meudon*. Paris, 1861.
[5] *Ibid.*, p. 255.

Trinquons donc, la rira dondaine,
Gai, gai, gai,
La rira dondé.
Trinquons donc, la rira dondaine,
Et flon flon flon,
La rira dondon!

Malgré les balivernes,
Des cracheurs de latin,
Nous sommes des lanternes
Dont l'huile est le bon vin.

Trinquons donc, etc.

Le système du monde,
Je vais vous l'expliquer:
C'est une table ronde,
Où l'on vient pour trinquer.

Trinquons donc, etc.

De la bonne nature,
Le sein qui nous attend
Est une source pure
De nectar indulgent.

Trinquons donc, etc.

Est-il de mauvais frères
Est-il des gens aigris?
Vite emplissons leurs verres;
Puis, quand ils seront gris,

Trinquons donc, etc.

Grâce au vin charitable,
Ils vont n'y plus penser;
Et bientôt sous la table,
Ils iront s'embrasser.

Trinquons donc, etc.

L'un croit et l'autre doute,
Tous les deux ont du bon;
Le plus fin n'y voit goutte,
Le plus simple a raison.

> Trinquons donc, etc.
>
> Vous passez sur la terre,
> Jouvencelle et garçon;
> La fille avec un verre
> L'autre avec un flacon.
>
> Trinquons donc, la rira dondaine,
> Gai, gai, gai,
> La rira dondé.
> Trinquons donc, la rira dondaine,
> Et flon flon flon,
> La rira dondon!

These may indeed be the most profound lines Eliphas Lévi ever wrote.

Lévi had sent some of his songs to Béranger and was delighted with the response: "Vous êtes né chansonnier," wrote Béranger, "et mieux que cela, vous êtes poète." And he invited the younger poet to call. "Le lendemain," wrote Eliphas Lévi, "je me rendis à Passy et

> frappai à la porte que tout le monde me désignait avec amour et avec orgueil, car les bonnes gens de Passy étaient fiers de leur Béranger. Une bonne vieille vint ouvrir, pas la bonne vieille de la chanson, une autre qui lui ressemblait, mais qui n'avait jamais été Lisette. C'était une belle et douce figure de bonne maman, avec une voix sympathique et les manières les plus polies.
>
> Je demandai Monsieur Béranger, et comme on parut s'étonner de ma visite, je me hâtai de montrer ma lettre; je fus enfin annoncé, et le vénérable grand homme qui demeurait au premier, vint lui-même au devant de moi jusqu'à la moitié de l'étage. Je le vis donc non plus en portrait, mais lui-même avec sa naïve et malicieuse physionomie, son regard tellement observateur qu'il paraît triste et sa bouche tout empreinte de jolies chansons. La chambrette où il se tenait près d'un bon feu, car c'était l'hiver, était proprette et mansardée; le chansonnier a-t-il toujours vingt ans? La conversation s'engagea et se mit d'elle-même, je ne sais comment, sur les choses les plus sérieuses et les plus graves. Béranger parle de théologie mieux qu'un évêque, puis il revint à nos chansons.
>
> On croit, me dit-il, que la chanson est un genre facile, parce que tout le monde peut tourner un couplet. Mais le

bien tourner, voila la difficulté. Cependant, ajouta-t-il, je vois dans les vôtres certains tours originaux, certaines difficultés vaincues qui me font augurer qu'un jour vous le ferez tres bien. Continuez donc et je vous donne ce conseil à mes risques et périls.

Ces derniers mots furent dits en souriant avec une fine et gracieuse bonhomie. J'étais vivement ému et ne pus trouver que ces paroles:

Permettez-moi de serrer la main qui a écrit vos chansons?

Volontiers, dit Béranger en me tendant cordialement la main, car je serrerai en même temps pour ma part la main qui écrira les vôtres.[6]

Lévi often wrote *chansons* on themes from his personal life. Here is an autobiographical one in which we meet his shoemaker father:

Ma Noblesse

Je suis dauphin d'un cordonnier;
    Le ciel, mon premier père,
Sourit par le trou d'un grenier
    Au louvre de ma mère.
Qu'on soit patrice ou plébéien,
Pourvu qu'on soit bon citoyen,
    C'est bien;
Mais porter, sans baisser les yeux,
    La mandille de ses aïeux,
    C'est mieux.

Mon père ne m'apprit jamais
    Comment on fait fortune,
Il est allé dormir en paix
    Dans la fosse commune.
Des trésors du roi citoyen
A prix d'honneur grossir le sien,
    C'est bien;
Mais libre et pur vivre joyeux
Et sans souci devenir vieux,
    C'est mieux.

---

[6] Quoted in Paul Chacornac, *Eliphas Lévi, rénovateur de l'occultisme en France* (Paris, 1926), p. 91.

Un voisin venait-il chez nous
    Escorté de misère,
Mon père n'avait que deux sous
    Et partageait en frère.
Dans son ventre enterrer du bien,
Aux yeux d'un noble et grand vaurien
    C'est bien;
Mais d'un gain pauvre et vertueux
Nourrir encor le malheureux,
    C'est mieux.

Tout en rendant un juste honneur
    Au progrès des lumières,
Il crut en Dieu de tout son coeur
    Et m'apprit mes prières;
Pour nos savants ne croire à rien,
Vivre en pourceau, mourir en chien
    C'est bien;
Mais mon père, en vivant heureux,
Risqua de l'être encore aux cieux,
    C'est mieux. [7]

Lévi had given up his political activities after failing to have himself elected to the revolutionary assembly in 1848, but at least once during the 1850's he reverted to type and dashed off the following *chanson* on Napoleón III:

Caligula

Nous vivons dans un siècle juste;
C'est vraiment le règne d'Auguste.
Par notre Empereur bien aimé,
L'Art satirique est désarmé (bis).
Mais il lui reste pour domaine
La fable et l'histoire Romaine;
Et je vais dans ce genre- là,
M'exercer sur Caligula (bis).

Caligula fut un pauvre homme
De son temps Empereur de Rome;
Triste enfant d'un chef adoré
Que l'Univers avait pleuré (bis),
Du grand homme il souilla la Gloire
Mais il était fou, dit l'histoire.

---

[7] *Les Trois Harmonies*, p. 50.

Décadence et forfaits, voilà
Le règne de Caligula (bis).

Jaloux de l'honneur militaire,
Il feignit d'aller à la guerre,
Et pourchassa quelques gredins
A coup de pierre et de gourdins (bis).
Puis au Capitole et sans rire
Il disait: J'ai sauvé l'Empire!
Mensonge et lacheté, voilà
Le règne de Caligula (bis).

Démolissant avec folie,
De sa Capitale embellie,
Il croyait tarir les dégoûts
En agrandissant les égouts (bis).
Mais de sa Cour, sa fange immonde
Débordait toujours sur le monde.
Faste et servitude, voilà
Le règne de Caligula (bis).

A la bassesse, à l'insolence,
Il distribuait la puissance.
Et riant du peuple animal,
Il nommait Consul, son cheval (bis).
On eut gagné peut-être en somme
D'avoir la bête au lieu de l'homme.
Sottise et cruauté, voilà
Le règne de Caligula (bis).

Sa noblesse était la police;
Et de la horde délatrice,
Il soldait les honteux conscrits
Avec les deniers des proscrits (bis).
La vertu pauvre et vagabonde
Bientôt n'eut plus d'asile au monde.
Mais il restait à Cheréa
Un poignard pour Caligula (bis).

The Emperor was not flattered by this attention on the part of his unknown and impertinent subject. Lévi, somewhat less intransigeant than in the greener days of his radicalism and perhaps feeling his joints a bit too creaky for another stay in prison (he had been quickly tried, condemned, and jailed) dashed off a second song to exorcise the evil effects of the first one:

L'Anti-Caligula

Chanson adressée des prisons de la Préfecture à l'Empereur Napoléon III

Sire, une chanson me fait faire
Pour vous une méchante affaire.
On tourne votre majesté
En monstre de l'Antiquité (bis).
Votre génie est plus moderne;
Et le prince qui nous gouverne
De personne n'acceptera
Le surnon de Caligula (bis).

Accoupler le nom d'un sauvage,
D'un fou plein de sang et de rage,
Et celui de Napoléon,
Serait sans rime ni raison (bis).
Préservez la Magistrature
D'accepter pour vous cette injure.
Quel tribunal me prouvera
Que vous soyez Caligula (bis)?

Quoi donc! On me met à la chaîne
Pour parler d'histoire Romaine!
Pourtant l'ancien monde est fini,
Et Brutus n'est pas Orsini (bis),
Qu'à Brutus le diable pardonne,
Moi, je ne veux tuer personne.
Je ne suis pas plus Cheréa
Que vous n'êtes Caligula (bis).

Votre police est inhumaine;
Et quand je parle d'une chaîne,
Ce n'est pas, Sire, au figuré;
Comme un voleur, on m'a ferré (bis).
Serait-il vrai que sous l'Empire
La Magistrature conspire?
Vous voyez bien que ces gens-là
Vous prennent pour Caligula (bis). [8]

In addition to his songs and poems, Lévi was interested in poetic drama and wished to revive the biblical *mystère* in a new form in which "les grandes ressources de la musique" would be used to augment "l'effet et la pompe" of the drama itself. Shakespeare, says

---

[8] Chacornac, pp. 165-168.

Lévi in his article *Mystères,* prodigiously expanded the possibilities of the theatre by mixing the genres and combining ghosts, fairies and rustic songs with the profoundest poetry. In France, he continues, in spite of the revolutionary efforts of Hugo, the new drama, "la littérature du futur," still awaits its discoverer. [9]

This new literature would be dramatic, vast in scope and christian in inspiration. Perhaps such a work as Claudel's *Le Soulier de satin,* produced some hundred years later, would have convinced Lévi that, in literature at least, the new age had finally dawned. For the time being, however, he was thrown back on his own work, and to illustrate his meaning he reproduced the whole of his own *mystère* — or libretto, as he calls it in his introduction — *Nemrod.*

One does not, on reading this play, get the impression that one is working one's way into some new literary territory; but then Lévi himself was modest about it and wished it to serve other writers only as a guide and not as a model.

The action takes place during the time of the building of the tower of Babel; the protagonist is the legendary king Nemrod. In a prologue, Nemrod, in an attempt to solidify his power, offers the Hebrew prophet Enos clemency from a charge of sedition and impiety if he will agree to create a new priesthood to the god Baal:

NEMROD: Vieillard, ne force pas ton maître à te punir.
Si ton oeil dans la nuit peut chercher l'avenir,
Moi, j'ai des jours présents mieux compris le mystère;
Tu regardes le ciel et je vois sur la terce.
Le peuple, à ta parole autrefois entrainé,
Au culte des autels te croit prédestiné.
Moi, pour des Dieux nouveaux je cherche des ancêtres,
Et mes jeunes autels ont besoin de vieux prêtres,
A nous deux le pouvoir; toi l'esprit, moi les bras;
Tout ces troupeaux humains que tu m'ameneras,
Je serai leur pasteur.

ENOS: Ou leur bourreau.

NEMROD: Peut-être;
Mais tu viendras t'asseoir à la table du maître:
Car pourquoi feindre ici? J'ai tout lu dans ton oeil,

---

[9] *Dictionnaire,* column 829.

> Et tu n'es vertueux que par excès d'orgueil.
> Tu me hais par envie...et moi je te fais grâce,
> Car j'en ferais autant si j'étais à ta place,
> Et sachant que tout prêtre en son coeur se fait roi,
> Si je n'étais Nemrod...je voudrais être toi. [10]

But Nemrod, with the blindness of power and the inability to see other motivations than that of his own ambitious opportunism, has fatally misjudged Enos, who refuses the offer and curses Nemrod and all who serve him. Then, in order to keep his young children, Ada and Ariel, from falling into the tyrant's hands, Enos leaps into a river, clasping them in his arms. Nemrod's soldiers manage to drag Enos' son Ariel out of the water; Enos himself and Ada are presumed dead.

There is thunder, lightening, a storm. Nemrod, in grandiose frenzy, shouts his intention to build a great tower and challenges God himself to rival him:

NEMROD: Jusqu'à Dieu maintenant que mon orgueil s'élève
Rendons la vérité jalouse de mon rêve!
Lève enfin en Babel ton front audacieux,
Tour dont la majesté fera palir les cieux;
Multiplie en tournant tes arches colossales,
Enlace des palais dans tes vastes spirales,
Et que de l'horizon les longs voiles dormants,
N'atteignent que tes pieds de leurs sommets fumants.
Alors sous les plaisirs de Babel dédaigneuse
Que Dieu fasse éclater sa fureur orageuse;
Aussi haut que son trône, et plus haut que sa loi,
Je lui dirai: Sois Dieu, si tu peux...Je suis roi!
(Le tonnerre gronde) [11]

The prologue ends. Fifteen years have passed. Ariel has been brought up as the adopted son of Nemrod and does not know the identity of his real father. As the first act opens, Ariel learns that great things are in store for him. Nemrod, who has no male heir of his own, intends to make him Chief Priest of Baal and Prime Minister. He will in time succeed to the throne. Moreover, and to his great

---

[10] *Ibid.*, column 832.
[11] *Ibid.*, column 837.

joy, Ariel learns that he is to marry Zelpha, Nemrod's daughter, with whom he has long been in love.

Things are going, of course, entirely too well for Ariel; he discovers his true identiy when his father and sister, having miraculously escaped drowning and having recently returned to Babylon, are brought before him to stand trial on a charge of impiety toward Baal. Ariel is torn between his love for Zelpha and his duty toward his father, but he ends by taking Enos' part against the cult of Baal.

Ariel, Enos and Ada are imprisoned and sentenced to death, as is Zelpha, who follows the martyrs into their prison, where she helps Ada escape in order to rescue the "holy book" which belongs to her father and which contains the secret wisdom of the Hebrews.

Meanwhile, Enos' curse has ripened; there is chaos in the kingdom. The people rise up against Nemrod, but with a mad kind of violence (Lévi's insight into the workings of mobs is astonishing), lacking direction or purpose. Nemrod is able to prevail against the mob:

ENOS: Le sang des justes crie, il faut qu'il soit vengé.
NEMROD: Et par quel droit en est-il [le peuple] donc l'arbitre?
Que vient-il demander? que veut-il? à quel titre?
Est-ce d'avoir rampé sous moi pendant vingt ans,
Qu'il réclame l'honneur par ses cris insultants?
Si j'ai versé le sang, lui, bourreau sans colère,
Il fut de mes rigueurs l'instrument mercenaire.
Il n'est point de tyrans quand le peuple obéit,
El l'on absout les rois du jour qu'on les trahit!
Le taureau révolté peut-il juger le prêtre?
Est-ce au tigre échappé de condamner son maître?
Je laisse à mon mépris de juger vos desseins,
Je cherche un peuple ici; je vois des assassins! [12]

The mob, faced with Nemrod's scorn, loses its momentum and becomes disoriented. In the end it much prefers a comfortable slavery to a freedom it does not yet deserve.

But if Nemrod correctly estimates the impotence of the people he rules, he gravely misjudges the power of Jehova's wrath. Ariel, Ada and Enos are to die by burning, but as they praise the Lord and hold aloft the holy book, the flames are extinguished. A fierce wind leaps up and the earth trembles. Zelpha had earlier been killed by

---

[12] *Ibid.*, column 864.

her father's own hand; now her soul appears hovering over the crowd in a kind of mystical "barque" and gives voice to God's judgment on Babel:

ZELPHA: Peuple, dispersez-vous, le Seigneur vous exile;
Allez, comme Caïn, chercher un autre asile
Car vous avez trempé dans le sang innocent.
... ...
Vos langages divers, désormais confondus,
Entre les nations qui ne s'entendront plus,
Vont semer pour toujours la discorde et la guerre.
Dispersez-vous!

Zelpha gives Nemrod his chance for repentance; he refuses:

ZELPHA: Une larme! un soupir! parle, le Ciel attend;
Pour ton éternité tu n'as plus qu'un instant.
NEMROD: L'enfer aussi m'attend, c'est bien! je le mérite,
Et ton Dieu me maudit, puisque je l'ai maudite.
Je ne suis pas vaincu, non, je suis malheureux.
Il triomphe, et je meurs...parce que je le veux.
Ramasse qui voudras ma puissance abbatue,
Je souris à ses coups, et c'est moi qui me tue.[13]

The palace and the tower crumble; the city is in ruins. Ada, Ariel and Enos climb into the mystical conveyance piloted by Zelpha, and sail off, presumably for paradise:

ZELPHA: Montez dans ma nacelle, et voguez avec moi.
Je suis l'ange gardien que le Ciel vous envoie,
Et vers les régions de l'éternelle joie
Je conduirai votre âme à travers les douleurs,
Malgré les flots amers de l'océan de pleurs.
... ...
Rois, courbez votre front sur le seuil du saint lieu,
Peuples, obéissez au roi qui vient de Dieu!
(Ils montent dans la barque; tout le ciel
s'illumine; des nuages s'abaissent, et des anges
leur jettent des fleurs.)

If Lévi wanted to create a new christian drama, he failed. His plot lacks all nuance and the characterization is flat. *Le Mystère de*

---

[13] *Ibid.*, column 873.

Babel is closer to Cecil B. DeMille than to total theatre. Nevertheless, in his treatment of the ambition and the megalomania of Nemrod and of the ambivalent cowardice of the population which he enslaved, Lévi achieves some insights which are quite modern and amply repay our reading.

BIBLIOGRAPHY OF ALFRED G. ENGSTROM

ROBERT T. CARGO AND EMANUEL J. MICKEL, JR.

"The Formal Short Story in France and Its Development Before 1850," *Studies in Philology*, XLII (1945), 627-39.

"In Defence of Synaesthesia in Literature," *Philological Quarterly*, XXV (1946), 1-19.

"Flaubert's Correspondence and the Ironic and Symbolic Structure of *Madame Bovary*," *Studies in Philology*, XLVI (1949), 470-95.

"Dante, Flaubert, and *The Snows of Kilimanjaro*," *Modern Language Notes*, LXV (1950), 203-05.

Edited (with U. T. Holmes, Jr. and Sturgis E. Leavitt), *Romance Studies Presented to William Morton Dey* (Chapel Hill, 1950).

"Lucretius and *Micromégas*," in *Romance Studies Presented to William Morton Dey* (Chapel Hill, 1950), pp. 59-60.

"The 'Horus' of Gérard de Nerval," *Philological Quarterly*, XXXIII (1954), 78-80.

"Chateaubriand's *Itinéraire de Paris à Jérusalem* and Poe's *The Assignation*," *Modern Language Notes*, LXIX (1954), 506-07.

"The Symbol of the Bird in Flight," *Lectures in the Humanities, Tenth Series, 1953-54*, UNC Extension Bulletin, XXXIV, No. 2 (1954), 25-43.

"Baudelaire's Title for *Les Fleurs du Mal*," *Orbis Litterarum*, XII (1957), 193-202.

"Vergil, Ovid and the Cry of Fate in *Madame Bovary*," *Philological Quarterly*, XXXVII (1958), 123-26.

"Poe, Leconte de Lisle, and Tzara's Formula for Poetry," *Modern Language Notes*, LXXIII (1958), 434-36.

"Baudelaire and Longfellow's 'Hymn to the Night,'" *Modern Language Notes*, LXXIV (1959), 695-98.

"Paul Verlaine and Dioscorides on Poetry and the Scent of Thyme," *Romance Notes*, I (1960), 106-08.

Translation from Théophile Gautier's "Preface to *Mademoiselle de Maupin*," in O. B. Hardison, Jr. (ed.), *Modern Continental Literary Criticism* (New York, 1962), pp. 141-53.

Translations of Baudelaire's "Correspondences" and "New Notes on Edgar Allan Poe," *ibid.*, pp. 155-73.

Translation of Verlaine's "Art poétique," *ibid.*, pp. 175-76.

Translation of Charles Maurras's "Chateaubriand; or, Anarchy," *ibid.*, pp. 292-300.

"The Single Tear: A Stereotype of Literary Sensibility," *Philological Quarterly*, XLII (1963), 106-09.

"Gérard de Nerval's Lobster and the Tarot Cards," *Romance Notes*, VI (1964), 33-36.

Entries on *accord, audition colorée, décadence, drame (romantique), huitain, Iambes (les), lyrisme (romantique), poème, poète maudit, rejet, Symbolism (movement), synaesthesia, tétramètre, trimètre,* and *unanimism* for the *Encyclopedia of Poetry and Poetics,* ed. by Alex Preminger, Frank J. Warnke and O. B. Hardison, Jr. (Princeton, 1965), *passim.*

"The Voices of Plants and Flowers and the Changing Cry of the Mandrake," in *Mediaeval Studies in Honor of Urban Tigner Holmes, Jr.,* ed. by John Mahoney and John Esten Keller (Chapel Hill, 1965), pp. 43-52.

"A Few Comparisons and Contrasts in the Word-craft of Rabelais and James Joyce," in *Renaissance and Other Studies in Honor of William Leon Wiley,* ed. by George Bernard Daniel, Jr. (Chapel Hill, 1968), pp. 65-82.

"The Changing Accent in English and American Criticism of Baudelaire," *South Atlantic Bulletin,* XXXIII (1968), 1-4.

"Introduction" to Emanuel J. Mickel's *The Artificial Paradises in French Literature* (Chapel Hill, 1969), pp. 13-17.

"The Man Who Thought Himself Made of Glass, and Certain Related Images," *Studies in Philology,* LXVII (1970), 390-405.

Professor Engstrom has contributed numerous reviews to *South Atlantic Bulletin, Modern Language Journal, Comparative Literature, Yearbook of Comparative and General Literature, Modern Language Notes,* and *French Review.* Since 1965 he has been a bibliographical contributor to *English Language Notes* and *French VI Bibliography.*

TABULA GRATULATORIA

George C. S. Adams
John N. Alley
Fred J. Allred
Raymond N. Andes
Juan Bautista Avalle-Arce
Anna Baker
Spurgeon Baldwin
W. T. Bandy
Elizabeth Barineau
William H. Baskin, III
Sarah F. Bell
Mary D. Bellamy
Richmond P. Bond
Ann Boyles
M. H. Brockmann
Paul W. Brosman, Jr.
Robert T. Cargo
Paul N. Chryssikos
Calvin Claudel
Pauline Bryson Collins
Alex Corriere
Julio Cortés
Lyman A. Cotten
Mary Hunter Kennedy Daly
Elizabeth R. Daniel
George B. Daniel
Helen Daniell
Joseph R. Danos
James Herbert Davis, Jr.
Celia Fernández de la Hoz
Yves de la Quérière
Emilie Patton de Luca
Aleyda Y. Delgado
William DeSua

Janet W. Díaz
Dorothy M. DiOrio
Ruth M. Doyle
G. Francis Drake
Edward T. Draper-Savage
Frank M. Duffey
Robert Edwin Duke
Samuel D. Duncan, Jr.
Carey D. Eldridge
Robert Emory
Eugene Falk
Hugh M. Fincher, III
Monique Forkner
W. P. Friederich
Barbara E. Gaddy
Rosalyn Gardner
Federico G. Gil
Donald W. Gilman, Jr.
Marion A. Greene
John M. Grier
John Guilbeau
Georgie A. Gurney
Edward B. Hamer
Jacques Hardré
F. C. Hayes
Marie Royce Hayes
Urban T. Holmes
H. R. Huse
A. Illiano
Kenneth Wilson Jones
John E. Keller
W. L. King
Jean-Paul Koenig
George S. Lane

John H. LaPrade
Sturgis E. Leavitt
Richard H. Lebel
Philip A. Lee, Jr.
Robert G. Lewis
Jeffrey B. Loomis
A. G. LoRé
Deborah N. Losse
Augustin Maissen
G. Mallary Masters
Robert J. Mayberry
Florence McCulloch
Harold G. McCurdy
William A. McKnight
Rosa Means
Emanuel J. Mickel
E. D. Montgomery
Edward W. Najam
Charles L. Nelson
Margaret Newhard
Catherine E. Neylans
Ruth B. Paine
James S. Patty
Rosalie Ortolani Payne
Hilliard Phillips
Manuel D. Ramírez
Dana Phelps Ripley
Gino Rizzo
Simone Bassett Robbins
Mildred C. Roebuck
Charla Rusché
H. K. Russell
Maria A. Salgado
J. Dennis Sanchez

Robert Morrison Sandarg
Aldo Scaglione
Peter M. Schluter
Anne Lindsey Seay
Karl-Ludwig Selig
Lawrence A. Sharpe
Carol Sherman
Robert N. Shervill
J. Carlyle Sitterson
J. C. Sloane
Albert B. Smith
James M. Smith
Jackson G. Sparks
Ella MacRae Stagg
Sterling A. Stoudemire
Lewis F. Sutton
Cleo Baucom Tarlton
Cecil G. Taylor
James D. Tedder
Edward D. Terry
Eugene Hester Thompson, Jr.
Ann Travis
Alison M. Turner
Frederick W. Vogler
Albert H. Wallace
Siegfried Wenzel
Shirley B. Whitaker
Joseph W. Whitted
W. L. Wiley
Thomas Andrew Williams
Mrs. Joseph P. Williman
E. L. Winn, III
William S. Woods

www.ingramcontent.com/pod-product-compliance
Lightning Source LLC
Chambersburg PA
CBHW022015220426
43663CB00007B/1092